Recognizing Women's Leadership

Recognizing Women's Leadership

Strategies and Best Practices for Employing Excellence

Tiffani Lennon

Foreword by Geena Davis

 PRAEGER

AN IMPRINT OF ABC-CLIO, LLC
Santa Barbara, California • Denver, Colorado • Oxford, England

Library of Congress Cataloging-in-Publication Data

Lennon, Tiffani.
   Recognizing women's leadership : strategies and best practices for employing excellence / Tiffani Lennon ; foreword by Geena Davis.
      pages cm
   Includes bibliographical references and index.
   ISBN 978–1–4408–3116–4 (print : alk. paper) — ISBN 978–1–4408–3117–1 (e-book)
1. Leadership in women.   2. Women—Employment.   I. Title.
HQ1233.L46   2014
658.4′092082—dc23   2014002913

ISBN: 978–1–4408–3116–4
EISBN: 978–1–4408–3117–1

18 17 16 15 14   1 2 3 4 5

This book is also available on the World Wide Web as an eBook.
Visit www.abc-clio.com for details.

Praeger
An Imprint of ABC-CLIO, LLC

ABC-CLIO, LLC
130 Cremona Drive, P.O. Box 1911
Santa Barbara, California 93116-1911

This book is printed on acid-free paper (∞)

Manufactured in the United States of America

Contents

Foreword

The power of gender stereotypes is pervasive in every aspect of our lives and does not disappear once inside a Fortune 500 company, political office, or a nonprofit organization. The United States needs gender balance; the world needs gender balance. What will it take for us to realize the power of women? I believe, or perhaps hope, we are approaching a tipping point where gender stereotypes will no longer be accepted by either men or women, and where women's contributions can no longer be overlooked.

The media has played a major role in perpetuating gender bias, unhealthy portrayals of women, and legitimizing a notable absence of female characters. The repeated depictions of women and girls have seeped into our consciousness, informing how society views females and all things feminine. Most young women and men are taught that hard work is the great equalizer, and yet we come to discover that the performance standards and compensation for women and men are different even within the same position and in the same company. Is this really a surprise considering the media messages we consume and adopt, sometimes subtly, about females?

What you will learn upon reading *Recognizing Women's Leadership* is that women are outperforming men, and yet they receive less compensation and are not attaining leadership roles despite their qualification and aspiration. The book describes where women sit in leadership positions nationally across 14 sectors. Tiffani Lennon, the author, quantifies the top-performing, largest profit-generating companies, entities, and offices and breaks down the gender of those with the greatest influence, including senior executives and boards of directors. She takes another step and begins to look at industry distinctions to better understand how women's performance compares to that of their male counterparts. The results are astonishing. The tremendous benefits of gender balance in the workplace are undeniable.

Research informs and empowers. Education ensures a more balanced future. Advocacy bridges the gap between research and education. This book, and the data contained in it, informs, educates, and offers a performance-driven approach to hiring and promotion. Performance should be the great equalizer in industry, like education is to opportunity. This is a must read book for C-level executives and those looking to work for a performance-driven organization.

Recognizing Women's Leadership raises the level of conversation and helps us to direct our focus where it should be—ensuring practices and policies that employ excellence. This book debunks myths about the lack of women in the pipeline for leadership and the lack of women choosing leadership roles. Let us move beyond the circular discussions that describe women as choosing lower paying positions and careers to raise a family or balance work and personal lives. Read *Recognizing Women's Leadership* and understand the untapped power of women.

Geena Davis
Academy Award®–Winning Actor and Advocate
Founder, The Geena Davis Institute on Gender in Media

Preface

BACKGROUND

Every March marks the celebration of Women's History Month in the United States—a time to acknowledge the change agents, thought leaders, dissenters dissatisfied with the status quo, and those whose contributions were seldom recognized by history. The month of March receives this honor because on March 3, 1913, female suffragists marched on Washington, D.C., to demand voting rights, or as a female opponent proclaimed, "an endorsement of nagging as a national policy."[1]

I write this more than one hundred years after the suffragists marched on Washington. To describe feminism in waves (i.e., first, second, third, and fourth waves) is unfortunately most apropos in that it seems that the fight for parity has been occurring in surface disruptions rather than a seism rupturing the foundation of gender stereotypes and biases. Those of us with a critical view of the media, the workplace, societal and cultural institutions, and of course, ourselves because no analysis is complete without examining how we may perpetuate disparity, wonder why the discourse about gender has not changed much. Why are salaries not reflective of performance and contributions, particularly in a capitalistic society, and why are myths about women perpetuated without much reflection, if any at all? Who is to blame for the female plight: men, women, or both? This remains the consistent question presented for the last several decades, and most recently women blaming women seems to garner the most media attention. For the last three decades, the word feminism equates to Nazism, radicalism, and fundamentalism, for many including women.

My research team[2] and I did not embark on this study because we possessed a feminist agenda, although unabashed feminists we remain, for we value the contributions of women and that which is feminine. I embarked on the research project because my university asked me to. More specifically, Marie C. Wilson, cofounder and president of The White House Project, approached the dean of Colorado Women's College of the University of Denver, Dr. Lynn M. Gangone, to query whether the college would be willing to "own" and expand the scope of the *Benchmarking Women's Leadership 2009* report. The 2009 report was the first attempt to measure women leaders in multiple sectors. I had conducted numerous descriptive research studies before on topics such as law, education, economics, and voting rights. I designed the 2012 study in an effort to ensure a meaningful and replicable methodology. Three years later, after the quantification of hundreds of organizations and businesses, and thousands of leadership positions, the college released the study's initial findings in the *Benchmarking Women's Leadership 2012* report. Utilizing much of the 2012 data, I also embarked on a qualitative study to better understand the successes of some companies and institutions, the summation of which is contained in this book. It was a deeply organic and authentic process.

In short, my research team and I discovered the falsities of promulgated myths about why women do not receive equitable compensation for equitable work. Myths, such as women choose to stop work to raise families and/or to balance work and personal lives, or they choose lower paying careers, remain unsupported in the descriptive and qualitative studies completed. We discovered that the perceptions that society has about women cannot be supported by the descriptions of leaders across 14 sectors in the United States. For instances, females comprise most high school science and mathematics teachers, and most female entrepreneurs work in the technology field, not in so-called lifestyle businesses, such as therapeutic or cosmetic fields. More women than men earn national science awards. Yet, pay disparity in most fields compares similarly to the pay disparity of the 1980s. We also discovered that women do more with far less resources, including external investments and other financial support. My research team and I examined positional, executive leadership, comparing women to men in the same positions and in the same industries, and we found gender (and race) disparity.

Why does this disparity still exist in 2014? Those, regardless of gender, race, age, or socioeconomic status, with a belief that they benefit or experience privilege by accepting or advancing gender biases and stereotypes help to perpetuate the disparity. This description may include a man of any age or race who believes that proper women must act in a certain way and have certain responsibilities, thereby ensuring male hegemonic status, or a white female baby boomer seeking to preserve her socioeconomic and marital privilege. Some men and women have even internalized a loathing to anything or anyone feminine. After all, we receive messages regularly that to be feminine is ultimately negative unless one is sexy or otherwise sexually appealing, and even then, sex appeal has its limitations.

Where is "feminism" in the discourse? If the headlines of a few, prominent leaders were semiotic of the current state of feminism, most would blame women for the pay inequities (i.e., they do not ask for raises; they lack female leaders; they do not lean in to risk and responsibility). In 1913, Alice H. Wadsworth attained media attention by belittling the work of suffragists and referring to the march on Washington as national nagging. Is Wadsworth to blame? She is no more to blame than Marissa Mayer, CEO of Yahoo!, known not for financially resurrecting Yahoo! but for eliminating telecommuting and proclaiming that she is not a feminist. Facebook COO, Sheryl Sandberg, a self-proclaimed feminist, also suggests that women are their own worst enemy in not overcoming gender biases and stereotypes. *Time* magazine's March 2013 cover story entitled, "Don't Hate Her Because She's Successful" features Sandberg in a red dress, standing with legs crossed. Perhaps Sandberg's legs crossing is resurrected symbolism of the Equal Right Amendment (ERA) era when supporters would cross their fingers. Despite the fact that Sandberg seeks to resurrect feminism, the media portrayed Sandberg as "catfight material." I find this portrayal curious. Here is a woman who is reaching out to other women based on her observations and the media positions her as fending off other women in a catfight. Debora Spar, the president of Barnard College, a women's college at Columbia University, wrote a book about "finding satisfaction in second best," and how feminism taught her generation that women could embody perfection in all roles including a perfect professional, mother, wife, cook, athlete, and homemaker.[3]

There also exists media attention that highlights, albeit briefly, the subtleties of gender bias and discrimination. For example, Marc Rudov quipped that the downside to a female president is mood swings and PMS, or more seriously, having a female agenda. A female science blogger with 4.2 million followers on Facebook revealed she is female and received an onslaught of sexist comments denigrating her previously ascribed popularity and credibility. A *New York Times* op-ed offered an explanation for the explosion of gang rape in Southeast Asia, including India, by reminding readers that Southeast Asian families prefer males over females, and most families keep more males at birth. Therefore, in Southeast Asian society, a higher number of males than females exist. The author seems to suggest that the large presence of males in society caused or at least contributed to the (natural?) aggression and tendency to rape females.

Most of us can point to example after example of gender discrimination. My grandmother, born in 1904, received a fourth-grade education, and at age 16, she entered into an arranged marriage. The value, or lack thereof, her immigrant family assigned to her sealed her fate. Unlike my grand-mother, I had the ability to vote, I had the ability to attend law school, and my family did not sell me into marriage as a teenager. This is not to say, however, that gender discrimination does not exist in 2014. I prefer to acknowledge that blatant and subvert gender biases *do* exist among men and women and move on to a meaningful discourse around resolution.

The blame question is a mediocre question. It is also mediocre to claim that gender stereotypes and biases do not pervade American culture and the global community. After all, gender stereotypes and biases do not stop at the front doors of businesses, universities, or nonprofits. Instead, let us progress to the better question. The better question, although simple, is who will benefit from women's advancement? There is also a simple answer: Everyone. This book explains how, and it maps out policies and practices for ensuring business and organizational success.

Inequality exists and not because women are not as qualified or as ready as their male counterparts. Women are outperforming men, yet they do not earn the same salary and do not receive leadership promotions. In fact, higher performing women earn less than lower performing men in the same position and industry. When women are hired and promoted, the return on investment is much greater. It is in the best interests of an organization to hire, promote, and retain the high performers. To overcome biases and stereotypes women often are more prepared and work twice as hard to be half as recognized. Yet, this does not ultimately serve a com-pany. High-performing women are more likely to leave an organization when they reach a plateau, and this loss of talent should alarm all with a vested interest in success.

HOW LEADERSHIP IS DEFINED AND MEASURED

Researchers gathered the most recent data for each sector. In some cases, 2012 data existed, but for some sectors, the most recent data available were from 2010 or 2011. This descriptive research study identifies the fre-quency of women leaders among the top echelon in each industry. For example, my research team and I identified all senior executives within the top 10 organizations, corporations, and offices to determine positional leadership held by women as compared to men. Within the top 10 entities, for example, several hundred leadership positions exist. In some incidences, we were able to also identify the percentage of people of color within a company or industry. My team and I also calculated leadership performance by identifying the frequency with which women were recognized with industry distinctions, such as national awards, best sellers lists, top revenue generators, and largest investors, among other sector-specific criteria described in greater detail in each relevant chapter. Positional leadership is defined as C-level, senior, and executive positions. Industry distinctions are defined as recognition, accolades, and/or awards bestowed upon those with the most noteworthy, industry-specific accomplishments.

My research team and I identified the top organizations, corporations, institutions, and offices in the United States within each of the 14 sectors. We determined the top echelon by size, profitability, budget, and political or governmental influence. We gathered public information available on original source data, such as annual reports and proxy statements. In measuring leadership, we employed a unique set of characteristics relevant to the specific industry when raw data was unavailable. After my team and I identified the characteristics, we scanned thousands of data points to narrow down the top 10. For example, a research associate measured the influence of reporters on the evening news shows by the number of minutes each reporter appeared on screen for the year, whereas the visibility of public figures on Twitter was measured by the number of followers. In measuring Sunday morning talk shows, the number of guest experts was counted for the year to determine the most frequently interviewed guest experts to determine the presence and visibility of female experts versus male experts.

We relied on the following databases to pull and analyze data on female positional leaders and top performers:

- Bureau of Labor Statistics
- Department of Defense
- Department of Labor
- National Center for Education Statistics
- National Information Center
- National Institutes of Health
- National Science Foundation
- U.S. Census
- U.S. National Library of Medicine
- U.S. Office of Personnel Management
- U.S. Patent Office

My research team and I limited the characteristics further when unusual trends presented themselves. To illustrate, during an election cycle, the researchers noticed an increased presence of presidential candidates on Sunday morning talk shows. Including presidential candidates would have skewed the data showing a much greater presence of men; therefore, researchers chose to exclude these guests from the top 10 lists. I excluded journalist Arianna Huffington and media personality Oprah Winfrey from salary calculations because as media owners and moguls their salaries would skew the overall average earnings of journalists and media personalities. The study also contains secondary analyses of other studies where necessary to supplement and verify the findings, including studies from the *2012 Catalyst Census*, *Justice System Journal*, Pew Research Center, National Council on Research for Women, and the *Chronicle of Philanthropy*.

By narrowing the focus of the study to just the top echelon in each industry, we identified the women and men who have self-selected into a competitive, national arena. This nullifies a commonly cited explanation for lack of women in leadership based on their preferring a more balanced personal/professional life or because they are happy with others leading versus pursuing highly competitive positions. While it may true that many women *and men* do not choose to devote their lives to the attainment of positions of power and influence, this study does not focus on the average manager or staff leader who opts out of the ascent to leadership because of a lifestyle preference. Instead, we focused on women and men ascending the corporate ladder.

Our hope remains that you contemplate the data contained herein and employ the proffered strategies and best practices, wherever appropriate, in your organization or business to ensure the success and advancement of the best and brightest employees, including all women and men of color.

NOTES

1. Alice H. Wadsworth, President of the National Association Opposed to Women's Suffrage, in a letter dated March 3, 1913.

2. Special thanks and recognition to my research team: Dorey Lindemann Spotts, Marissa Mitchell, Julie Koobs, Leah Sullivan, and Alma Arredondo. Your contributions and patience were immeasurable. I would also like to recognize and thank Colorado Women's College of the University of Denver and The White House Project for the tremendous support and idea for the original study and investment in the follow-up study.

3. Kantor, Jodi. (September 15, 2013). "Finding Satisfaction in Second Best." *The New York Times*, Sunday. Accessed from http://www.nytimes.com/2013/09/15/fashion/finding-satisfaction-in-second-best.html?_r=0.

1

Introduction

The hint of a southern drawl, along with a pleasant demeanor and down-to-earth style, sounds as she begins to explain the challenges and successes that helped to determine and shape a $10 million business. In 2012, after 20 years in business, she sold her company for an undisclosed amount and said farewell to more than 10,000 clients. From a vice president of a securities trade corporation to a successful entrepreneur, Emily Spencer's approach closely resembles the best practices and strategies for success described in this book.

Spencer points to three things that drove the success of her company: (a) creating a "respectful, ethical and compassionate" corporate climate that seeks to "partner" with employees and customers alike; (b) creating a performance driven culture, with accompanying performance criteria; (c) and having a staff developmental plan that ensures alignment with performance and climate. The formula proved successful, and her industry and peers lauded her approach. She has received multiple awards, including *ColoradoBiz* Magazine naming her company as one of Colorado's top 250 private companies and top 100 women-owned businesses. *Denver Business Journal* recognized the company as one of Denver's top 25 women-owned businesses and named it as one of Denver's fastest growing private companies. She was a finalist for the Ernst & Young Entrepreneur of the Year for the Rocky Mountain Region award in 2010. In 2011, Spencer was a finalist for an Outstanding Woman in Business award from the *Denver Business Journal*.

When asked about her earlier experience as a female in the financial industry, Spencer shared that at the time she never attributed the obstacles she faced to gender. She indicated that she *did* recognize that she had to outperform everyone around her to be successful in the industry. She recalls the demography as predominantly white male, and when asked to present in a meeting, Spencer knew she could not just be good in her presentation, she had to be outstanding, and she was. She remembers "blowing everyone in the room out of the water."[1] While Spencer encountered gender biases, she focused on ways to overcome them and became more determined to contribute significantly to the financial industry.

Starting her business proved another difficult feat. Spencer invested her personal resources initially, but she struggled to attain financing, vital to the company's growth. After numerous banks rejected her loan applications, she called on her professional network to assist in securing bank financing. She found a bank that loaned her money with the requirement that her husband act as a cosignatory, which Spencer viewed innocuously because her husband's start-up required the same of her. However, once her company reached the multimillion dollar revenue mark, some banks still required her husband's signature. Spencer, familiar with the financial industry, knew that a personal cosignatory at this stage in her company's history was discrediting and disparate to how banks would treat male entrepreneurs under similar circumstances. She shopped around until she found a bank that did not require her husband as cosignatory.

Spencer trained her senior leadership team to continue the climate she worked hard to build over the years. Exemplifying a holistic approach, the corporate climate exuded customer and employee satisfaction. For example, corporate policy granted maternity and paternity leave when such a practice was highly unusual. Policies and their equitable enforcement are an important part of corporate climate, yet climate must also address employee attitudes because they could derail corporate efforts. Overhearing male employees disparaging another male colleague for taking paternity leave, Spencer immediately expressed her disapproval, making it clear that her company does not tolerate such remarks. Spencer also found that focusing on employee performance, particularly how it relates to the services delivered, leveled the playing field, giving the best and brightest the opportunity to excel. Moreover, she ensured that her employees had an opportunity to perform, equipping them with tools for success through cross-training and exposure within the company.

Spencer's experience foretells that creating an inclusive climate built on performance, while recognizing the importance of life outside of work, helped to create loyalty and respect from employees. This climate helped to ensure greater employee performance and therefore higher customer satisfaction. She recognized that for her business to be successful, *all* of her employees had to be successful, so they could, in turn, perform exceptionally. The attitude and beliefs of the corporate leader sets the tone for the corporate climate, as many studies have demonstrated over the years. Spencer ensured a "respectful, ethical and compassionate" climate that cultivates "partnerships," and describes what this book refers to as an inclusive climate. As this book also explains, and as her experience supports, an inclusive climate helps to drive employee performance. Her focus on performance, as illustrated throughout this book, gives all talented employees the opportunity to succeed and enables female leaders to occupy senior positions.

Various postulations have sought to explain the underrepresentation of women in leadership positions and pay inequities on reasons that tend to place the onus on women and/or their decisions and choices. Such theories include the circuitous climb to the top due to family responsibilities preventing women from achieving their highest goals.[2] Some have argued that women, more than men, prefer less-demanding jobs to achieve a life-work balance, and they tend to drop out of the labor force to raise children therefore losing skills and experience. To illustrate, a 2009 report stated, "all but 5–7 cents of the pay gap can be explained by factors other than outright discrimination."[3] Others guess that women choose lower paying fields compared to their male counterparts resulting in lower salaries. More recently, several have claimed that women do not take the risks necessary for leadership and do not ask for pay increases.[4] While such hypotheses may reflect the decisions and choices of some men and women, after extensive research the data contained herein debunks many of the myths surrounding women leaders.

In 2012–2013, my research team and I identified and compared senior and executive leadership positions across industries by gender. We compared percentages of leaders in the industry as a whole to the top 10 largest, most profitable companies, institutions, and organizations. We also compared female salaries to their male counterparts at peer institutions in the same industry. In narrowing the scope to the top echelon, we sought to limit the erroneous conclusions seeking to explain why women do not have a proportional representation of leadership positions and equitable salaries. These conclusions often center on the belief that women choose staff positions over leadership roles to accommodate family or lifestyle preferences, and/or select lower paying fields. Yet, this is not what we found. To illustrate, we examined the pipeline of K–12 leadership. When we compared teachers in public school, who taught the same subjects and with the same years of experience, schools were more likely to pay men higher salaries than they were females. Pay gaps and disproportionate representation of leaders were evident across sectors, where females were the majority *and* minority in the workforce.

There is no doubt that women have accomplished significant milestones in the workforce during the past 50 years. Since Congress passed the Equal Pay Act in 1963, women's earnings have increased from 58.9 percent of what men make to a historic high of 82.2 percent.[5] The challenge remains that during the last two decades, women's advancement has stagnated. Since the late 1980s, the pay disparity has remained constant at roughly 80 cents on the dollar for women leaders. The pay disparity for women in the pipeline is often wider, averaging 77 cents on the dollar. In addition, there have not been significant positional leadership advancements, with women comprising roughly 10 to 20 percent of leadership roles across sectors. Women senior leaders were also more than three times as likely to have lost their jobs due to downsizing or restructuring.[6]

The following chapters detail where women sit in positional leadership roles across major sectors, their compensation relative to their male counterparts, and their performance as distinguished by each industry. I have adopted and adapted data from a 2013 report I researched and authored, supported by my home institution, Colorado Women's College of the University of Denver: *Benchmarking Women's Leadership in the U.S.* My research team and I captured a descriptive "snapshot" of women's leadership during a particular time period that reflects trends that have been reoccurring over the last 30 years. During the editing of this book, a woman assumed the CEO position of General Motors, another the Federal Reserve Chair, and many others left leadership positions. The 30-year "dance" where women make strides, then lose ground has not changed the overall makeup of leadership in the United States. While leadership positions change often, women have remained stagnant in how the public views them as leaders and whether they are deserving of equitable pay. Moreover, the message of the book remains timeless: a gender (racial and ethnic) bias exists among both public and private entities alike. This bias adversely influences performance and an organization's bottom line.

Chapter 12 culminates trends across sectors, and identifies strategies and best practices for ensuring the best and brightest rise in leadership ranks. We investigated six top companies and agencies in the United States, and we detailed some of their experiences in creating a competitive workforce. I include companies that continually seek to eliminate gender (racial and ethnic) bias by ensuring a performance-based, inclusive climate, an instrumental step. It is erroneous to presume that inclusivity and climate are "soft" issues that may or may not directly affect an organization's bottom line. Performance is intricately interdependent on climate and inclusivity, and collectively these attributes determine who will sit in leadership, and how well an organization will do relative to its peers. Performance and inclusivity level the playing field, and together they are good for business and productivity, and in cultivating a competitive workforce.

NOTES

1. Spencer, Emily. (2013). Interview for *Recognizing Women's Leadership*, October 17.

2. Association of American Colleges and Universities (AACU). (1999). "Circuitous Routes: AAUW Study Examines Women's Paths to College." *Diversity Digest*. Accessed from http://www.diversityweb.org/digest/sm99/study.html.

3. Coy, Peter, and Elizabeth Dwoskin. (2012). "Shortchanged: Why Women Get Paid Less Than Men." *Business Week*, June 21. Accessed from http://www.businessweek.com/articles/2012-06-21/equal-pay-plaintiffs-burden-of-proof.

4. Sandberg, Sheryl. (2013). *Lean In: Women, Work, and the Will to Lead.* New York: Random House Publishing.

5. National Committee of Pay Equity (NCPE). (2012). "Pay Equity Information." *NCPE*. Accessed from http://www.pay-equity.org/info.html.

6. Catalyst. (2012f). "Women MBAs." *Catalyst Knowledge Center*. Accessed from http://www.catalyst.org/knowledge/women-mbas.

2

Business

To better understand the stagnation of women's leadership, this chapter details the percentage of female executive leaders in both publicly and privately held businesses, and finance and technology companies, and it also looks at female entrepreneurs. In examining some of the industry's most influential companies, with the largest revenue and/or profit, a company's failure to promote and retain women in executive roles ultimately affects its financial and organizational well-being. The top public companies across sectors have a higher representation of women leaders than the industry on average. Companies that have begun to close the gender-leadership and pay gaps possess commonalities. The companies possess a performance-based culture and objective performance measurements for hiring and promotion detailed in chapter 12.

PUBLICLY HELD COMPANIES

Women's overall representation in the labor force has climbed slightly from 48 percent in 2008 to 49.1 percent in 2012.[1] With a greater overall representation in the labor force during last several years, it is rational to presume that female leadership would also climb, yet the percentage of female leaders has declined since 2008.[2] During 2011–2012 women held 15.2 percent of leadership roles in Fortune 500 companies compared to 18 percent in 2008–2009.[3] The adverse economic consequences of the Great Recession may help to explain the decline in women's leadership and widening salary gaps. It is common for corporations to resort to comfortable notions of leadership when financial fears lurk or become reality.[4]

In understanding the representation of senior leaders, it is imperative to understand the overall representation of women in the workforce. Education plays a key role in women's advancement. The average number of women enrolling in MBA programs has risen from 30.6 percent to 35.5 percent in the last decade,[5] but after graduation, women "lag behind men in job level and salary starting from their first position and do not catch up."[6] Many have blamed women for this disparity, arguing women negotiate poorly or choose less demanding positions for a variety of reasons. While it may be easy to blame women, and perhaps convenient, a more nuanced examination suggests a more complex systemic set of biases embedded in hiring and promotion. Consider the following:

• Women earn on average $4,600 less in their initial jobs, even after accounting for experience, time since MBA, industry, and region.[7]
• Between 1996 and 2007, 31 percent of female MBA graduates received promotions compared to 36 percent of men.[8] This gap grows larger as the positions increase in pay and influence.

Interestingly, women made up 49.1 percent of the labor force in 2012 and held 51.4 percent of management, professional, and related positions. However, the average percentage of female executive officers drops sharply to 14.1 percent.[9] Based on these data, women experience proportional representation in mid-management and professional roles but not in senior leadership roles. The percentage of female senior and executive leaders is not representative of the labor force, nor is it representative of the number of women in management and professional roles. For a synthesized account of business leaders by U.S. regions, refer to Appendix I of this chapter.

Over the last five years, women's representation in executive positions has remained virtually unchanged.[10] There was a steady increase in CEO positions from 2008 to 2010, but these gains were quickly lost in one year. In 2011, women ran only 12 Fortune 500 companies, a loss of 3 CEO positions from 2010 when women occupied 15 positions.[11] The loss of female executives in just one year coincided with the consequences of the recession emerging strongly in 2009–2010.

When we examined race and gender, the percentage of women of color in executive positions in Fortune 500 companies has also remained virtually the same since 2009, when it was at 3.1 percent. The percentage of senior executives of color averages 3 percent, yet the percentage of CEOs in Fortune 500 companies, who also happen to be women of color, averages 10 percent.[12]

Positional Leadership and Influence

Interestingly, there are more women leaders among the top performing companies than in the industry as a whole. Women held 15 percent of Fortune 500 executive positions,[13] yet as table 2.1 shows, among the Fortune 10 companies, women's executive representation jumped to nearly 20 percent in 2012. Among the Fortune 500 companies, women CEOs comprise 4 percent, compared to 10 percent of the Fortune 10. The average percentage of female leaders, including executives and board of directors (table 2.2), is double among the Fortune 10 companies (20 percent) compared to the Fortune 500 companies (10 percent). Several studies have also suggested that it is in the economic interests of corporate America to do more to attract and retain women in leadership roles. More specifically:

- Businesses with women on their boards outperform companies with all-male boards by 26 percent.[14]
- The average return on equity (ROE) of companies with at least one woman on the board is 16 percent, which is 4 percentage points higher than the average ROE of companies with no females on the board.[15]
- Net income growth for companies with women on the board has averaged 14 percent over the past six years, whereas companies with no female representation have seen a 10 percent growth.[16]
- In one study, researchers found greater gender diversity in management to be associated with above-average ROE and stock performance in top-listed European companies.[17]
- Studies of Fortune 500 companies have found that the percentage of women among executives and on boards of directors is positively associated with an organization's financial performance.[18]

In capturing leadership positions that influence and chart the direction of public companies, we included board of directors in addition to executive roles. In 2011, women constituted 16.1 percent of board director positions among all Fortune 500 companies. This was a slight increase from 2010, when women held 15.7 percent of these positions. Among board chairs, females comprised 2.6 percent in 2011, the same percentage as in 2010.[19] Women of color comprised 3 percent of director positions, compared to white women who made up 13.1 percent.[20] Among women of color, African American women accounted for 1.9 percent of director positions. Hispanic women accounted for 0.7 percent and Asian/Pacific Islander women accounted for 0.3 percent of Fortune 500 board directors.[21] In comparing the percentage

Table 2.1   Executive Positions in Fortune 10 Companies, 2012

Company (Fortune 10 Ranking)	# Executive Positions	# Females in Executive Positions	% Females in Executive Positions
Exxon Mobil (1)	5	0	0%
Wal-Mart Stores (2)	32	7	22%
Chevron (3)	18	3	17%
ConocoPhillips (4)	9	3	33%
General Motors (5)	17	4	24%
General Electric (6)	40	7	18%
Berkshire Hathaway (7)	20	4	20%
Fannie Mae (8)	15	5	33%
Ford Motor (9)	34	2	6%
Hewlett-Packard (10)	12	3	25%
Total/Average	**202**	**38**	**19.8%**

Source: Compiled from *Forbes Magazine* 2012 and each company's proxy/Web site 2012.

Table 2.2   Board Positions in Fortune 10 Companies, 2012

Company (Fortune 10 Ranking)	# Board Positions	# Women in Board Positions	% Women in Board Positions
Exxon Mobil (1)	12	2	16.67%
Wal-Mart Stores (2)	17	4	23.53%
Chevron (3)	12	2	16.67%
ConocoPhillips (4)	10	1	10.00%
General Motors (5)	14	4	28.57%
General Electric (6)	18	4	22.22%
Berkshire Hathaway (7)	12	2	16.67%
Fannie Mae (8)	10	2	20.00%
Ford Motor (9)	17	2	11.76%
Hewlett-Packard (10)	11	3	27.27%
Total/Average	**133**	**26**	**19.55%**

Source: Compiled from *Forbes Magazine* 2012 and each company's proxy/Web site 2012.

of females on Fortune 10 boards of directors to Fortune 500 boards in 2011, the percentage of women on Fortune 10 boards (20 percent) was higher than the percentage of women on Fortune 500 boards (16 percent).

The two-fold challenge for women includes the advancement from management to senior leadership and executive roles and that women begin their careers with a disadvantage in both position and pay. According to the Committee for Economic Development 2012, the failure of U.S. companies to take a more active role in promoting women has caused "us to fall behind international competitors that are getting the most out of an expanding pool of talented women."[22] Countries, such as Norway and France, have mandated the percentage of female representation in boardrooms. The United States has not taken the same measures to even the playing field in executive positions nor has it done so in boardrooms.[23] As this book will illustrate, leveling the playing field is less about quotas and more about ensuring a performance-based and inclusive climate. Performance and inclusivity ensure that all women have an opportunity to receive equitable salaries and positions of leadership. Quotas become necessary when companies resist changes necessary to ensure that the best and brightest have an opportunity to succeed. There exists a greater likelihood that public companies will lead the change required to ensure a performance-based, inclusive climate. Private companies, as you will see, receive less public scrutiny and reflect a closed, white male–dominated group.

PRIVATELY HELD COMPANIES

While much attention focuses on the Fortune 500 companies, private companies in the United States have a poorer track record for promoting women to senior roles. The business sector includes, in large part, privately held companies. In understanding women's leadership in the business sector, it is important to include private companies to acquire a comprehensive overview. One study from Georgetown University's McDonough School of Business found 4.5 percent of women in executive positions at companies with $1 to $7 billion in capital.[24] Among the top 10 private companies, approximately 7 percent of women comprise the executive and board of director positions (executives, 5.8%—table 2.3). Because privately held companies are not required to provide financial and other types of information, some data were unavailable for comparison purposes. Table 2.4 shows the percentage of female board of director positions for the top 10 private U.S. companies is 7.58 percent—also significantly lower than the Fortune 10 public companies. In addition, at least 6 of the 10 companies have zero board seats held by women.

Despite the fact that there are significantly fewer female leaders in private companies compared to public companies, a similarity exists between them. Top performing private *and* public companies are much more likely to have a higher percentage of female executives and board leaders.

Table 2.3   Executive Positions in Top 10 Private U.S. Companies, 2011

U.S. Company	# Executive Positions	# Female Executives	% Female Executives
Cargill	31	4	13%
Koch Industries	5	0	0%
Mars	11	1	9%
Pricewaterhouse Coopers	21	1	5%
Bechtel	37	3	8%
Publix Super Markets	*	*	N/A
Love's Travel Stops and Country Stores	5	0	0%
Ernst and Young	21	5	23%
C&S Wholesale Grocers	6	0	0%
US Foods	5	0	0%
Total			**5.8%**

Source: Compiled from *Forbes Magazine* 2012 and each company's Web site 2012.

Table 2.4   Board of Directors Positions in Top 10 Private U.S. Companies, 2011

U.S. Company	# Board Seats	# Board Seats Held by Women	% Board Seats Held by Women
Cargill	5	0	0.0%
Koch Industries	5	0	0.0%
Mars	N/A	N/A	N/A
Pricewaterhouse Coopers	8	1	12.5%
Bechtel	15	0	0.0%
Publix Super Markets	9	3	33.3%
Love's Travel Stops and Country Stores	1	0	0.0%
Ernst and Young	30	9	30.0%
C&S Wholesale Grocers	3	0	0.0%
US Foods	11	0	0.0%
Totals	**87**	**13**	**7.58%**

Source: Compiled from *Forbes Magazine* 2012 and each company's Web site 2012.

FINANCE AND BANKING

Women comprise nearly 60 percent of the total labor force in commercial banking and 17.6 percent of executive positions in 2012.[25] Stated differently, men comprise 40 percent of the labor force in commercial

Table 2.5 Executive and Board Positions in Commercial Banking, 2012

U.S. Banks	# Executive Positions	# Female Executives	% Female Executives	# Board Positions	# Female Board Members	% Female Board Members
HSNB North America	19	2	10.5%	8	3	37.5%
The Bank of New York	16	3	18.8%	12	2	16.7%
U.S. Bancorp	13	2	15.4%	14	3	21.4%
Morgan Stanley	11	1	9.1%	14	2	14.3%
Metlife, Inc.	11	2	18.2%	12	4	33.3%
The Goldman Sachs Group	11	1	9.1%	10	2	20.0%
Wells Fargo and Company	13	3	23.1%	15	5	33.3%
Citigroup Inc.	25	1	4.0%	12	3	25.0%
Bank of America	11	4	36.4%	16	4	25.0%
JPMorgan Chase & CO.	65	11	16.9%	11	2	18.2%
Total	**195**	**30**	**15.4%**	**124**	**30**	**24.2%**

Source: Compiled from each company's Web site 2012.

banking and 82.4 percent of the senior positions. Presumably, women should have attained a higher percentage of leadership roles in a field where more women exist in the pipeline for top positions. When examining a select sample of the top 10 largest commercial banks (table 2.5), women hold a slightly higher average (19.8 percent) of executive and board positions than in the industry as a whole. This higher percentage among the top 10 is like the findings in publically and privately held companies, and this is a common theme found in most other sectors as well.

Performance and Compensation

Nothing raises eyebrows quite like the statement "women are outperforming their male counterparts." After presenting the data dozens of times throughout the United States, this statement has received the most varied, and sometimes alarming responses, including from national journalists. There is value in repeating that the performance indicators identified in each sector do not reflect the only measurements, and neither do they reflect the best determination of performance. Instead, they represent one set of industry-specific indicators. Despite the fact that women are underrepresented in leadership, their performance is quite noteworthy. Consider the following: There exist more female executives among the top 10 companies than there exist in the industry. Additionally, in examining the performance of hedge funds managers, women are performing at much higher proportional rates than men are.

- A 2011 study found that women manage only about 3.3 percent of 9,000 hedge funds;[26] however, performance, defined as "absolute returns and risk-adjusted returns," is substantially stronger for women- and minority-owned hedge funds than for male-owned hedge funds.[27]
- During economic downturns, women- and minority-owned funds are more stable and continue to outperform non-diverse funds. In 2010, non-diverse funds declined 29.4 percent while women- and minority-owned funds declined only 19.4 percent.[28]
- From 2000 to 2009, women-owned funds delivered an average annual return of 9.06 percent compared with only 5.82 percent among male-dominated hedge funds.[29]

Determining compensation in a uniform way across sectors would prove difficult if my team and I calculated non position-related income. To ensure consistency and replication across sectors, we included position-related compensation only. This approach is challenging for some critics because

Table 2.6 Fortune 10 CEO Salary Compensation, 2012

Company in 2012 (Fortune 10 Ranking)	CEO	Gender	Total Male Compensation ($Millions)	Total Female Compensation ($Millions)
Exxon Mobil (1)	Rex Tillerson	M	$21.5	
Wal-Mart Stores (2)	Mike Duke	M	$18.2	
Chevron (3)	John S. Watson	M	$18.1	
ConocoPhillips (4)	Ryan Lance	M	$17.9	
General Motors (5)	Daniel F. Akerson	M	$2.5	
General Electric (6)	Jeffrey R. Immelt	M	$11.3	
Berkshire Hathaway (7)	Warren Buffett	M	$0.5	
Fannie Mae (8)	Timothy J. Mayopoulos	M	$5.3	
Ford Motor (9)	Alan R. Mulally	M	$29.5	
Hewlett-Packard (10)	Meg Whitman	F		$16.5
Total Salary Dollars in 2012			**$124.8**	**$16.5**
Male/Female Comparison of CEO Compensation			**88.3%**	**11.7%**

Source: Compiled from *Forbes Magazine* 2012.

non position-related income remains a significant aspect of compensation in many sectors and particularly business. For critics to argue that women may have negotiated lower compensation packages for other sources of income, albeit possible, appears embroidered. The fact remains that salary and compensation disparity in the same industry and for the same position looms large.

As table 2.6 illustrates, in 2012, the range of Fortune 10 CEO salary compensation fell within $11.3 to $29.5 million, and the majority hovered between $16.5 to $21.5 million. The sole female CEO, Meg Whitman, earned $16.5 million, which was on the lower end of the salary scale. Aside from Warren Buffett, rebuker of CEO salary, take note that the two CEOs earning below $11.3 million represent companies at the center of the federal government's bailout program: Fannie Mae and General Motors. The government attempted to limit CEO compensation as a condition for receiving public dollars, which explains the significantly lower compensation packages received.

Compensation for female CEOs among the top 10 commercial banks is grossly disproportionate. Whereas only one female sits in a CEO position, she earns just 60 percent of the total compensation awarded to her male counterparts.[30] In other words, the female commercial banker earns .60 cents on the male $1. This pay differential predates the 1960's Equal Pay Act.

Additionally, the number of women serving as Chief Financial Officers (CFOs) in the Fortune companies is significant at 30 percent, yet table 2.7 shows their salaries make up only 24 percent of the total salaries paid to all CFOs in the Fortune 10 companies. Male CFOs in the Fortune 10 companies are paid approximately $270,000 more per year on average than females.

Conclusions

- Expect more from American companies and their leaders, and ask them to report the number of women they currently have in executive roles, as well as their plan to increase this number yearly.

- Investors should seek out the diversity of corporate boards before investing and question corporations about their succession plans, and how women are incorporated into those plans.

- Companies should encourage, or under certain circumstances, require a sponsorship program in which senior leaders not only mentor but also sponsor up and coming women. When women, in particular, are in positions of leadership, the "pull effect" is strong—meaning that successful

Table 2.7   CFO Salaries of Fortune 10 Companies, 2012

Company	Chief Financial Officer	Salary	Male/Female	Total Male Salary	Total Female Salary
Exxon Mobil	Donald D. Humphreys	$1,170,000	Male	$1,170,000	
Wal-Mart Stores	Charles M. Holley	$731,600	Male	$731,600	
Chevron	Patricia Yerrington	$842,500	Female		$842,500
ConocoPhillips	Jeffrey Wayne Sheets	$619,500	Male	$619,500	
General Motors	Daniel Ammann	$687,500	Male	$687,500	
General Electric	Keith S. Sherin	$1,765,000	Male	$1,765,000	
Berkshire Hathaway	Marc D. Hamburg	$962,500	Male	$962,500	
Fannie Mae	Susan R. McFarland	$600,000	Female		$600,000
Ford Motor	Lewis W.K. Booth	$1,250,000	Male	$1,250,000	
Hewlett-Packard	Catherine A. Lesjak	$825,000	Female		$825,000
Total		**$9,453,600**		**$7,186,100**	**$2,267,500**
Percentage Comparison				**76.0%**	**24.0%**

Source: Compiled from each company's 2012 Annual Report and Web site.

women will pull other women up to their level by offering a support system.[31] Additionally, young women should learn to anticipate potential roadblocks and successfully navigate the obstacles.

- For companies unable to make the necessary internal shifts in creating a performance-based, inclusive climate, policymakers should consider the lead of other countries that mandate by law the percentage of women required to be in executive positions as a way to force change at a quicker pace.

Entrepreneurship

The recent economic downturn has illustrated that entrepreneurs and small businesses play a vital role in creating jobs and stimulating growth. Not only does the small business sector directly generate many jobs, it also creates many of the innovations that stimulate overall economic growth. Studies have demonstrated that companies with fewer than 500 employees are more innovative and operate with greater efficacy than companies with more than 500 employees.[32] Small and new enterprises tend to create more local ownership, resulting in greater stability of employment, more jobs feeding local residents, and more profits reinvested in the community.[33]

Often, new fast-growth businesses generate new jobs. Approximately 11 percent of *opportunity* entrepreneurs—those attempting to create high-potential, high-growth businesses—expect to create 20 percent more jobs within five years when compared to the 2 percent expected by *necessity* entrepreneurs, who are starting new businesses for self-employment.[34] If future wealth creation depends on growth-oriented entrepreneurs, assessing whether, and at what rate, female entrepreneurs succeed should be a collective concern. Women entrepreneurs, and in particular, women of color are the fastest growing demographic of new business owners.

The valuable contributions that women make to stimulating economic progress, providing innovative solutions to existing problems, and capitalizing on new opportunities need to be recognized while myths surrounding women entrepreneurs need to be debunked. In collecting and analyzing available information on entrepreneurs, researchers of this report have generated baseline data sets from which to monitor the success of women-owned businesses. This section spans several decades of research to better understand the entrepreneurial landscape, and it also identifies several primary barriers for women through qualitative interviews, surveys, and census data.

While both men- and women-owned businesses struggle in highly competitive markets, on average men have much greater access to capital, training, and mentorship, which are important factors in growing and sustaining businesses. As a result, only 3 percent of women-owned businesses break through the million-dollar annual revenue benchmark compared to an average of 6 percent of businesses owned by men.[35] Women are often portrayed as favoring lifestyle businesses, where they can balance work and family, or as seeking opportunities to supplement household income for reasons why they do not break the million-dollar revenue mark. This assumption that women choose to remain small contradicts existing data. Research does show that women-owned businesses are smaller on average than those owned by men, both in terms of sales revenues and the number of employees. While I recognize that business growth can be a choice, and many entrepreneurs choose not to grow, there is increasing evidence that women aspire to build high-growth businesses. For example, data show that more than 3,000 women applied to participate in Springboard Enterprises in 2008, a program connecting women-led businesses with equity financiers. It is estimated that there were more than 110,000 women-owned firms, with more than a million dollars in sales, and almost 8,500 women-owned firms, with more than 100 employees and average revenues of $66 million.[36] Moreover, the types of businesses most women choose are predominately high growth, not lifestyle businesses.

Thus if women are not choosing to remain small, why are they disproportionately so? One myth that permeates most sectors (and entrepreneurship is no exception) is that women are not performing at the same levels as their male counterparts. Another myth is that there are insufficient numbers of women in the pipeline, suggesting that there are fewer women entrepreneurs. There are, in fact, women in the pipeline, and they are performing well with fewer resources, fewer outside investors, and greater reliance on support from self, family, and friends. Women overwhelmingly rely on personal assets and much less outside investment. Finally, this section seeks to explain why women-owned firms are not growing at the same rates of most male-owned firms by drawing correlations between outside funding received and those recognized by the entrepreneurial community as exceptional.

In addition to data collected and synthesized for this section, findings from a regional study funded by the Department of Commerce's Economic Development Administration (EDA) to better understand the current state of women entrepreneurs were utilized. The EDA funded interviews and focus groups to determine barriers faced by women entrepreneurs in the Denver metro area of Colorado. These findings can be universally applied to understand and explain the challenges and barriers, in particular for growth among women entrepreneurs. The EDA study confirmed two primary barriers, which have also emerged in other national studies: lack of investment capital and lack of sponsorship to assist with training and technical assistance. These findings have greatly informed the conclusions.

According to the U.S. Census, in 2007 there were 24,294,860 privately held businesses. Privately held businesses grossed $10,949,461,875 and employed 56,626,555 paid workers. Women, by comparison, owned 7,792,115 businesses, employed 2,281,878 paid.workers, and grossed $1,196,608,004. Private businesses spent $1,940,572,945 on annual payrolls. Women-owned businesses contributed $214,673,400 to annual salaries, while men contributed $1,510,450,810 to annual salaries. People of color owned 5,759,209 businesses, grossed $1,024,801,958, employed 860,492,119 paid workers, and contributed $5,816,114 annually to salaries.

Entrepreneurial Activity between 1997 and 2008

1. The number of women-owned firms increased by 43 percent from 1997 to 2007 in the United States.[37] Women-owned businesses are defined as 50 percent or more of owners are female.

2. Between 1997 and 2002, women-owned firms grew by 19.8 percent, which is more than twice the rate of all U.S. firms.[38]

3. In 2002, women-owned businesses generated $16.4 billion in revenue.[39]

4. In 2007, women businesses employed 7,520,121 people out of 56,626,555, or 13 percent of the total number of paid employees in privately owned businesses.[40]

5. In 2008, approximately 7.2 million firms in the United States were owned by women, a decrease from 7.8 million in 2007.[41]

6. Women-owned firms accounted for 40 percent of all privately held firms in the United States in 2008.[42]

7. In 2008, women-owned businesses generated $1.9 trillion in sales and employed 13 million people nationally.[43]

8. Of these businesses in 2008, 1.9 million firms were owned by women of color, and they employed 1.2 million people.

9. Women of color generated $165 billion in revenue annually in 2008.[44]

10. Access to credit is more problematic for women and women of color. In 1998, 60 percent of white women business owners had access to credit, compared to 50 percent of Hispanic, 45 percent of Asian, 42 percent of Native American, and 38 percent of African American women business owners.[45]

11. As of 2008, one in five firms with revenue of $1 million or more was woman owned; however, only 3 percent of women-owned firms had revenues of $1 million or more, compared with 6 percent of men-owned firms.[46]

12. According to the U.S. Census, women of color comprise approximately 40 percent of all female-owned companies and grossed approximately 20 percent of total sales. Men of color owned 30 percent of all male-owned business firms, grossed 10 percent of sales, employed 11 percent of paid workers, and contributed approximately 8.5 percent to annual salaries.

In 2009, an average of 0.34 percent of the adult population (340 out of 100,000 adults) created a new business each month, representing approximately 558,000 new businesses per month. This entrepreneurial activity rate was a slight increase over the 2008 rate of 0.32 percent.[47] Women comprised 39 percent of all entrepreneurial activity in 2009.[48] White non-Hispanic women represented approximately 80 percent of all women business owners.

Since 2008 women of color have remained steady with 1.9 million firms owned.[49] Latina, Asian, and African-American women each represent another 4 percent respectively.[50] Latina entrepreneurs are a growing population of female business owners. Women of color tend to operate in a wide variety of industries and own a business for an average of 12 years.[51] Female entrepreneurs of color are typically older, less educated, less likely to be married, and more likely to start a business with a partner.[52]

Entrepreneurial Activity among Women between 2009 and 2012

Women received just 11 percent of the capital investment and yet comprised 20 percent of the top entrepreneurs of 2011. Conversely, male entrepreneurs received 89 percent of the capital investment and comprised 80 percent of the top entrepreneurs of 2011. Lack of funding continues to be the biggest growth problem for all entrepreneurs, but particularly women.

Inc. Magazine identified the top entrepreneurs of 2011; as shown in table 2.8, my team and I narrowed the list of entrepreneurs to the highest grossing top 10 for-profit companies. We found that among the entrepreneurs identified, women comprised 20 percent of the top 10. Women-owned firms account for 40 percent of all privately held businesses, and while they contribute more than a trillion dollars in revenue, they remain small. The primary factor in business growth is capital investment. Capital investment refers to funds not derived from personal assets, family, and/or friends but through venture companies and angel investors. New and existing businesses compete for capital investment, which enables the business to grow—usually at a much faster pace.

Securing financial resources generally creates the greatest barrier for high-growth entrepreneurs. Access to investment pools is difficult under the best of circumstances, but for women entrepreneurs it is highly unlikely. Venture capital investment in U.S. women-led businesses is a small percentage of overall investments. In 1998, women-led firms received only 4.1 percent of all venture capital investments (figure 2.1). This percentage has increased modestly over the last decade despite the rapid increase

Table 2.8   Top Entrepreneurs of 2011

	Projected Revenue (Millions)	Women-Owned?
99 Designs	$35	No
Dropbox	$7.2	No
Instagram	$7	No
Onswipe	$6	No
Grasshopper Group	$6	No
Foodspotting	**$3**	**Yes**
Solben	$3	No
Birchbox	**$1.4**	**Yes**
Ad Parlor	Not Released	No
Freshii	Not Released	No

Source: Inc. Magazine 2011.

Figure 2.1   Venture Capital Received by Women by Year

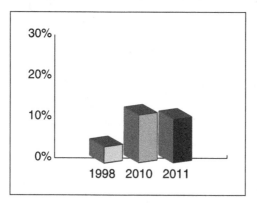

Source: Schonfeld 2011.

of female-owned businesses.[53] A disconnect appears between the value placed on female-owned businesses, and their actual and proportionate performance.

In 2012, according to Dow Jones VentureSource, only 11 percent of venture capital firms funded female entrepreneurs.[54] The findings of our national study confirmed a similar percentage. One explanation may be that the venture capital industry is male dominated, small, and geographically concentrated. A study conducted by the Diana Project mapped the U.S. venture capital industry by gender composition for the years 1995 and 2000. The Diana Project found that women lack representation in the industry and, to date, fail to make significant strides in increasing those numbers. To illustrate, among the top 10 investors of 2007 and 2008, women were unrepresented. Among the top venture capital firms, women comprised 21 percent of the leadership in 2007. In 2011, there was a slight decrease in the top women leaders in venture capital firms from 21 percent to 18.75 percent. Note that Facebook dominated the attention of tech investors in 2012. The anticipated initial public offering of Facebook could have skewed the top 10 most invested companies; however, an analysis omitting Facebook revealed no difference among the genders.

Can the gender of venture capitalists really determine the fate of women entrepreneurs? Maybe. Venture capitalists and angel investors have tremendous influence in this sector. In many ways, investors serve as lobbyists supporting specific candidates in exchange for a quantifiable return. Because there are so few women who are top investors (0 percent) or who lead venture capital firms (18.75 percent), it is difficult to determine the impact women leaders would have on funding female entrepreneurs. One snapshot captured the top female venture capitalists and suggests weakly that women may be more inclined to recognize capable entrepreneurs who also happen to be women. Female investors were more likely to support female entrepreneurs.[55] However, women are just as susceptible to gender stereotypes and biases as men; so until stereotypes and biases are recognized in society, it is unlikely that women will hold a proportional amount of leadership positions, or receive more capital investment.

The amount of initial capital used to start a business is positively related to future capital assets, number of employees, and ultimately profit. Awareness regarding lack of female venture capitalists is growing and some have sought to address the problem. For example, the Kauffman Institute for Venture Education is an institute that specializes in educating venture capitalists. Of the 61 venture capital fellows that the Kauffman program had trained, 25 percent were women. By increasing the number of women in the decision-making positions in the venture capital industry, the odds that women entrepreneurs will connect with venture capitalists and benefit from high potential deals is enhanced.

Presence of Female Entrepreneurs in Growth Industries

Women and men have a similar breakdown of businesses across industries, despite the misconception that women own a majority of personal service businesses. One myth that continues to surface in the entrepreneurial sector is that women choose small, lifestyle businesses, or service industries, such as retail, massage therapy, and so on. Yet, women are represented in construction, production, and technology-based industries, and they continue to move into those fields as quickly as those fields are growing.[56] According to two sources, women-owned businesses were concentrated in the following industries:

1. 20.9%   Professional, scientific, and technical services
2. 14.4%   Other
3. 13.4%   Retail, wholesale
4. 11%   Business services
5. 11%   Administrative, support, and waste remediation services
6. 8.5%   Health care and social assistance
7. 7.7%   Communication, media
8. 7%   Personal services
9. 6.2%   Financial, real estate, and insurance[57]

Men and women equally owned 4.6 million nonfarm U.S. businesses (17 percent of all nonfarm businesses). These firms employed 8.1 million persons (6.9 percent of total employment) and generated $1.3 trillion in receipts (4.2 percent of all receipts).[58] Women owned 7.8 million nonfarm U.S. businesses (28.7 percent of all nonfarm businesses) operating in the 50 states and the District of Columbia in 2007, an increase of 20.1 percent from 2002. These women-owned firms accounted for 28.7 percent of all nonfarm businesses in the United States. Women-owned firms employed 7.6 million persons (6.4 percent of total employment) and generated $1.2 trillion in receipts (3.9 percent of all receipts).[59] Unfortunately, data within the last 5 years were unavailable before the publication of this book.

Conclusions

Thousands of entrepreneurs launch businesses each year, and many do not succeed.[60] Women are far less likely to receive venture capital investments, lead venture capital firms, or be among the top investors. Ways to encourage investors to seek out and consider investment in women-led ventures must be found. Similarly, programs are needed that can systematically increase women's expertise in the investment community. Investors' knowledge about what women entrepreneurs have actually accomplished rather than what investors perceive to be accomplished needs to be facilitated as well.

TECHNOLOGY

Technology is a dynamic and fast-paced industry, and there exist many opportunities for growth and advancement—an ideal environment for women hoping to advance and attain leadership roles. Promises of compensation also exist in the technology field. Computer and mathematic occupations had one of the highest mean wages in 2011 at just under $95,000 annually.[61] Yet, technology is a male-dominated field, with women comprising 25 percent of computer and mathematical occupations and 13.6 percent of architecture and engineering occupations.[62] While women's overall leadership participation in technology is less than 20 percent, this is not representative of the contributions of women in the industry. For example, the number of technology patents awarded to women has experienced a 25-fold increase since the 1980s, while the sector experienced only a 9-fold increase.[63]

According to a 2011 Forbes study, which used data gathered from the U.S. Department of Labor, 9 out of 10 of the fastest-growing jobs require math or science training.[64] The same study indicated that 3 of the top 10 best-paying jobs for women are in the technology field and have some of the narrowest wage gaps among all professions.[65] For all these reasons and more, it is important to understand women's contributions to and participation in the technology field. Women over the age of 25 hold a mere 2 percent of all bachelor's degrees in engineering and 1.5 percent of all computer and information science bachelor's degrees.[66]

Some studies indicate that the number of women working in high-tech fields has actually been stagnant or decreasing since the 1990s, even while the number of high-tech jobs has steadily increased, and more women have graduated with high-tech degrees in the last decade.[67] One explanation is that women leave high-tech corporations after only a few years into their careers to start their own businesses due to corporate barriers, otherwise known as the glass ceiling.[68] To illustrate, a 2011 study from the U.S. Department of Commerce noted that women with degrees in science, technology, engineering, or math (STEM) are less likely to end up working in a STEM career than men with the same degree.[69] Among men and women with a STEM degree, about 40 percent of men work in a STEM field as opposed to 26 percent of women.[70] Moreover, one in three women with a STEM degree leaves the industry workforce within the first two years, and "slightly more than half of all women in the industry leave mid-career."[71] Other studies suggest that women leave high-tech industries for a variety of different reasons, including a lack of role models after they enter the technology workforce, a sense of isolation when working in a male-dominated field, and a real or perceived inability to advance their careers.[72] This presents a particular concern for women of color because there are even fewer women of color in STEM careers.

The percent of women earning degrees in science and engineering has increased among all ethnic groups except for African Americans and whites. The number of African American and white women receiving science and engineering degrees fell by 0.3 percent and 1.9 percent, respectively, between 2005 and 2010. The Anita Borg Institute released a report in 2011 that detailed the lack of opportunities for women of color in technology:

• Among those earning computer science bachelor's degrees, African American women receive less than 5 percent of degrees, Latinas receive less than 2 percent, and Native American women receive less than 1 percent.
• African American women in the technology field make up 4.6 percent of entry-level jobs but only 1.6 percent of high-level jobs.[73]
• Latinas in the technology field make up 4.1 percent of entry-level jobs but are virtually absent from high-level jobs.[74] Interestingly, according to the Borg Institute, there are more Latinas in the technology field than there are Latinas with degrees in technology.

An analysis suggests that when an environment is unfriendly to non-hegemonic racial and ethnic groups, it will not welcome women either. Therefore, women of color have a heightened non-hegemonic experience.

Table 2.9 Females in Leadership at Top 10 Tech Companies, 2012

Company	CEO	# Executive Positions	# Females in Exec Positions	% Females in Exec Positions	% Females in Exec Positions for Companies with a Female CEO
Hewlett-Packard (11)	**Meg Whitman**	12	3	25.0%	25%
International Business Machines (18)	**Virginia Rometty**	16	5	31.3%	31.0%
Apple (35)	Timothy D. Cook	12	0	0.0%	
Microsoft (38)	Steve Ballmer	16	1	6.3%	
Dell (41)	Michael S. Dell	11	1	9.1%	
Intel (56)	Paul S. Otellini	40	6	15.0%	
Cisco Systems (62)	John T. Chambers	13	3	23.1%	
Google (92)	Larry Page	6	0	0.0%	
Oracle (96)	Lawrence J. Ellison	26	6	23.1%	
Xerox (121)	**Ursula Burns**	33	11	33.3%	33.3%
Average				**16.6%**	**30%**

Source: Compiled from each company's Web site 2012.

The point is not to position white women versus women (or men) of color; in fact, doing so creates perhaps the most profound disservice. The point does suggest that a climate, whether inclusive or exclusive, has a great deal of influence over women's representation in leadership and the opportunities therein.

When we examined the most influential companies in technology, a much different story emerges. Among the Fortune 10 companies, as seen in table 2.9, women comprise 3 positions or 30 percent of chief executive officers, and one identifies as a female of color, 9 percent chief information officers, 17 percent executive officers, and 22 percent of board of directors. As a reminder, even though my team and I examined the top 10 tech companies, there exist hundreds of positions within those companies. Female leaders are present in the most influential technology companies, even though a small number of women earn degrees in technology-related fields.

One of the more important observations is that women CEOs are more likely to attract and hire female leaders. When a male holds the CEO position, women compose approximately 19 percent of the board positions. Yet, when there is a female CEO, women occupy approximately 30 percent of board positions. Additionally, companies with a female CEO have more women in executive leadership by an average rate of 30 percent. In comparison, companies with a male CEO have a female leadership rate of 8.9 percent.

On average, women comprise 19.5 percent of all leadership roles in the technology sector among the 10 most profitable technology companies. Note that the number of women in chief information officer (CIO) positions at Fortune 500 companies has been incrementally decreasing since 2010. In 2012, only 9 percent of CIOs were female, down from 11 percent in 2011 and 12 percent in 2010.[75]

Performance and Compensation

Despite the higher number of women in executive roles in the top technology companies, women's salaries are often significantly less than those of their male counterparts. The average CEO salary for females in this industry's top 10 companies is $5.90 million; the average male compensation for the same role is $8 million.

In measuring performance, there are a couple of ways to determine how women are doing relative to men. Looking at the profitability and revenue of a company is one way, as my team and I did throughout this book. Invariably, we have found more women among the top 10 companies across sectors than in the industry as a whole, and the technology industry was no different. Like most underrepresented groups, women must be outstanding to receive recognition, and as a result, they are more likely to over perform. This is likely why women are performing better with fewer resources and opportunities.

Another way to determine performance specific to the technology field is by comparing the percentage of patents received by men and women. Patents are an important component of the technology sector. Successful patents serve as a strategy in growing and expanding tech companies.[76] Evaluating women's success in obtaining patents is important in understanding women's leadership in the technology sector. The National Center for Women in Information Technology has been tracking the number of patents awarded to women since the 1980s. Women-invented patents are less than 10 percent of all patents, yet the number has significantly increased over the last 30 years. Figure 2.2 reflects the percentage of patents awarded to women where women are either the entire patent team or serve as the majority on the team.

Additionally, the number of technology patents developed by women has increased significantly since 1980 (25-fold increase), surpassing the overall growth rate of tech patents during the same time period (7.5-fold increase).[77] Women's participation and success in the technology field is resulting in an increased number of patented inventions. The number of women involved in patents continues to steadily increase, as reflected in figure 2.2.[78] Additionally, there is no difference between female patent applicants' success to male applicants.[79] Both women and men obtain successful patents at the same rate.

Figure 2.2   Tech Patents, 1980–2010

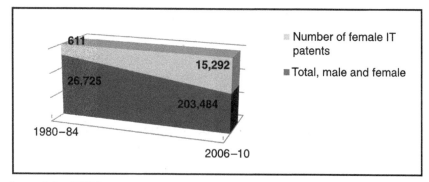

Source: Ashcraft 2012.

One possible explanation for the increasing number of patents can be attributed to women's increased entrepreneurial activity. Women are starting their own businesses to counteract a lack of career advancement opportunities in large technology companies.[80] Three of the top four fastest growing female-awarded patents are in the high-tech fields of data processing, electrical computers, and digital processing systems.[81]

While certain highly successful tech companies like IBM have a higher than average percentage of women at the top, this does not reflect the industry trend. In one study conducted by the Harvey Nash Group, 30 percent of those polled from 450 U.S. technology companies report that their own IT departments have zero women in management—yet only half of the same respondents believe that women are underrepresented in their IT department.[82] Therefore, the fact that several studies reveal that women in leadership and executive roles have shown to positively impact a company's financial performance[83] would have little impact on an industry where many believe that women—although absent—are not underrepresented.

In conclusion, the technology industry is dynamic, offering numerous opportunities for entrepreneurs to prosper even in the midst of an economic downturn. Research points to a recent downward trend, where women are stagnant or losing ground in the field. Further research should be conducted to determine the reasons for the declining trends among women in high-tech workforce and therefore their executive participation within the industry.

Conclusions

Technology leaders and, where appropriate, policymakers should:

- Promote education in the science and engineering fields to girls at a younger age, develop programs geared towards girls and women who demonstrate an interest and talent in science and technology, and offer greater opportunities for equal pay.
- Encourage inclusivity and diversity in the workplace. Women and particularly women of color are struggling to find their niche within the technology workforce. When there is a lack of diversity, women tend to feel isolated and look for other jobs, sometimes outside of their area of education. This contributes to the declining number of women in the technology field.

- Develop mentoring and sponsorship programs to promote women into leadership roles. Using Xerox, HP, and IBM as examples, research shows that having women in the CEO position increases the number of women in other executive positions. In short, it matters who heads a company because that leader has an impact on the rest of the leadership demography.
- Include women in company patent groups, and be sure that talented women are represented and that their contributions are recognized.

In summary, the compensation and leadership gap in the business sector has remained for several decades. As a result, my team and I sought to better understand factors contributing to compensation and promotion. To this end, we selected four publically held companies for case studies. The companies represent retail, financial services, and technology. Walmart, a Fortune 10 company with 22 percent female executives, while underrepresented, neither lags behind nor stands out compared to the other Fortune 9 companies. We also selected TIAA-CREF, a representative of the financial services industry and a Fortune 100 company. TIAA-CREF boasts 36 percent female executives, one of the highest across all sectors. Google and Xerox present drastically different leadership demography. In 2012, Google had no female executives, an aberration among the top technology companies. Xerox, made up of 33 percent of female executives, possesses the highest percentage of female leaders among the top technology companies during the same year. Together the four corporations, along with two federal agencies, present compelling evidence for the role of performance and climate in hiring and promotion, discussed in detail in chapter 12. A more nuanced look at the selected companies reveals more compelling evidence that recognizing women leaders serves the company and other unrepresented groups well, and vice versa.

APPENDIX I

As seen in table 2.10, when we break down the number of women in executive roles by region, we find only slight fluctuations. Some regions have a large number of Fortune 500 companies but only a small percentage of women in executive roles in those companies. For example, the NYC metro area, California, and Texas have the greatest number of Fortune 500 companies (167 combined) but have an average female executive participation rate of only 15 percent.[84]

Table 2.10   U.S. Women in Business by Region

Region	% Women Directors	% Women Executive Officers
Midwest	17.6%	15.6%
Northeast	17.4%	14.5%
West	15.7%	14.5%
South	14.0%	12.1%

Source: Catalyst 2011b.

NOTES

1. Catalyst. (2012b). "US Women in Business." *Catalyst Knowledge Center.* Accessed from http://www.catalyst.org/publication/132/us-women-in-business.

2. Catalyst. (2012a). "Statistical Overview of Women in the Workplace." *Catalyst Knowledge Center.* Accessed from http://www.catalyst.org/publication/219/statistical-overview-of-women-in-the-workplace; Catalyst. (2011). "Women's Representation by NAICS Industry." *Catalyst Knowledge Center.* Accessed from http://www.catalyst.org/etc/Census_app/11US/2011_Fortune_500_Census_Appendix_7.pdf.

3. Catalyst. (2011c). "2011 Catalyst Census: Fortune 500 Women Board Directors." *Catalyst Knowledge Center.* Accessed from http://www.catalyst.org/knowledge/us-women-business-0; Catalyst. "Women CEOs of the Fortune 1000." *Catalyst Knowledge Center.* (2012c). Accessed from http://catalyst.org/publication/271/women-ceos-of-the-fortune-1000.

4. McKinley, William, Scott Latham, and Michael Braun. (January 2014). "Organizational Decline and Innovation: Turnarounds and Downward Spirals." *Academy of Management Review* 39:1, 88–110.

5. Ibid.

6. Ibid.

7. Ibid.

8. Ibid.

9. Catalyst. (2012e). "African-American Women in the United States." *Catalyst Knowledge Center.* Accessed from http://www.catalyst.org/publication/222/african-american-women

10. Catalyst. (2011a). "Women's Representation by NAICS Industry." *Catalyst Knowledge Center.* Accessed from http://www.catalyst.org/etc/Census_app/11US/2011_Fortune_500_Census_Appendix_7.pdf; Catalyst. (2012a). "Statistical Overview of Women in the Workplace." *Catalyst Knowledge Center.* Accessed from http://www.catalyst.org/publication/219/statistical-overview-of-women-in-the-workplace.

11. CNNMoney. (2011). "Fortune 500: Women CEOs 2011." *CNNMoney.* Accessed   from   http://money.cnn.com/magazines/fortune/fortune500/2011/

womenceos/. In October 2013, another Fortune 500 company hired a female CEO, Jacque Hinman, to lead CHM2 Hill.

12. Catalyst. (2012c). "Women CEOs of the Fortune 1000." *Catalyst Knowledge Center.* Accessed from http://catalyst.org/publication/271/women-ceos-of-the-fortune-1000

13. Ibid.

14. Credit Suisse. (August 2012). "Gender Diversity and Corporate Performance." *Credit Suisse Research Institute.* Accessed from https://www.credit-suisse.com/newsletter/doc/gender_diversity.pdf

15. Ibid.

16. Ibid.

17. Pine, Karen. (2011). "Sheconomics: Why More Women on Boards Boosts Company Performance." *Significance*, 8:80–81.

18. Eagly, Alice, and Linda Carli. (September 2009). Navigating the Labyrinth. *School Administrator* 66(8):10–16.

19. Catalyst. (2011c). "2011 Catalyst Census: Fortune 500 Women Board Directors." *Catalyst Knowledge Center.* Accessed from http://www.catalyst.org/file/533/2011_fortune_500_census_wbd.pdf.

20. Ibid.

21. Ibid.

22. Committee for Economic Development (CED). (2012). "Fulfilling the Promise: How More Women on Corporate Boards Would Make America and American Companies More Competitive." *Committee for Economic Development Washington, D.C.*, p. 5. Accessed from http://www.fwa.org/pdf/CED_Women AdvancementonCorporateBoards.pdf .

23. Nevedomski Berdan, Stacie, and Anna Catalano. (2012). "Why Corporate Boards Should Be Looking for a Few Good Women" *Huffington Post*, August 9. Accessed from http://www.huffingtonpost.com/stacie-nevadomski-berdan/why-corporate-boards-shou_b_1751320.html.

24. Heavey, Susan. (2012). "In Heart of Corporate America, Women Struggle to Break into Top Jobs." *Reuters*, March 21. Accessed from http://www.reuters.com/article/2012/03/21/uk-usa-women-business-idUSLNE82K01720120321.

25. Catalyst. (2014). "Women in Financial Services." *Catalyst Knowledge Center.* Accessed from http://www.catalyst.org/knowledge/women-financial-services.

26. Managed Funds Association (MFA). (2011). "Hedge Fund Pulse: Affirmative Investing: Women and Minority Owned Hedge Funds." *Barclays Capital.* Accessed from http://www.managedfunds.org/wp-content/uploads/2011/08/HF-Pulse-Affirmative-Investing-June-2011-Letter.pdf.

27. MFA. (2011). "Hedge Fund Pulse: Affirmative Investing: Women and Minority Owned Hedge Funds." *Barclays Capital.* Accessed from http://www.managedfunds.org/wp-content/uploads/2011/08/HF-Pulse-Affirmative-Investing-June-2011-Letter.pdf.

28. MFA. (2011), p. 13. "Hedge Fund Pulse: Affirmative Investing: Women and Minority Owned Hedge Funds." *Barclays Capital.* Accessed from

http://www.managedfunds.org/wp-content/uploads/2011/08/HF-Pulse-Affirma-tive-Investing-June-2011-Letter.pdf.

29. Aylmer, Philippa. (2010). "50 Leading Women in Hedge Funds" *The Hedge Fund Journal* Accessed from http://www.thehedgefundjournal.com/maga-zine/201002/research/thfj-50-women-in-hedge-funds.pdf.

30. DeCarlo, Scott (2012). "America's Highest Paid CEOs." *Forbes Maga-zine.* Accessed from http://www.forbes.com/sites/scottdecarlo/2012/04/04/americas-highest-paid-ceos/.

31. CED. (2012). "Fulfilling the Promise: How More Women on Corporate Boards Would Make America and American Companies More Competitive." *Committee for Economic Development Washington, D.C*, p. 14. Accessed from http://www.fwa.org/pdf/CED_WomenAdvancementonCorporateBoards.pdf.

32. Organisation for Economic Co-operation and Development (OECD). (2000). "Enterprising Women: Local Initiatives for Job Creation." *OECD Publishing.*

33. Ibid.

34. Carter, Nancy M., Colette Henry, Barra O. Cinneide, and Kate Johnston, eds. (2007). *Female Entrepreneurship: Implications for Education, Training and Policy.* New York: Routledge.

35. Center for Women's Business Research. (2012). "Key Facts about Women-Owned Businesses." *CWBR.* Accessed from http://www.womensbusi-nessresearchcenter.org/research/keyfacts/.

36. Carter, Nancy M., Colette Henry, Barra O. Cinneide, and Kate Johnston, eds. (2007). *Female Entrepreneurship: Implications for Education, Training and Policy.* New York: Routledge.

37. "Expanding Opportunities for Women Entrepreneurs: The Future of Women's Small Business Programs." (2007). *Hearing before the Democratic Policy Committee* (DPC). 110th Congress.

38. U.S. Census. (2002). "SCORE: Survey of Business Owners." *U.S. Census Bureau.* Accessed from http://www.census.gov/econ/sbo/historical.html; Carter, Nancy M., Colette Henry, Barra O. Cinneide, and Kate Johnston, eds. (2007). *Female Entrepreneurship: Implications for Education, Training and Policy.* New York: Routledge.

39. Center for Women's Business Research. (2012). "Key Facts about Women-Owned Businesses." *CWBR.* Accessed from http://www.womens businessresearchcenter.org/research/keyfacts/.

40. U.S. Census. (2007). "Statistics for All U.S. Firms by Industry, Gender, Ethnicity, and Race for the U.S., States, Metro Areas, Counties, and Places: 2007." *2007 Survey of Business Owners, US Census.* Accessed from http://factfinder2.census.gov/faces/tableservices/jsf/pages/productview.xhtml?pid=SBO_2007_00CSA01&prodType=table.

41. Ibid.

42. Center for Women's Business Research. (2012). "Key Facts about Women-Owned Businesses." *CWBR.* Accessed from http://www.womensbusi-nessresearchcenter.org/research/keyfacts/.

43. Ibid.

44. Ibid.

45. Smith-Hunter, Andrea. (2006). *Women Entrepreneurs across Racial Lines*. Northampton, MA: Edward Elgar Publishing.

46. Center for Women's Business Research. (2012). "Key Facts about Women-Owned Businesses." *CWBR*. Accessed from http://www.womensbusinessresearchcenter.org/research/keyfacts/.

47. Fairlie, Robert W. (2009). "Kauffman Index of Entrepreneurial Activity." *Kauffman Foundation*. Accessed from http://www.kauffman.org/what-we-do/research/kauffman-index-of-entrepreneurial-activity.

48. Ibid.

49. Center for Women's Business Research. (2012). "Key Facts about Women-Owned Businesses." *CWBR* Accessed from http://www.womensbusinessresearchcenter.org/research/keyfacts/.

50. Smith-Hunter, Andrea. (2006). *Women Entrepreneurs across Racial Lines*. Northampton, MA: Edward Elgar Publishing.

51. Ibid.

52. Ibid.

53. National Council for Research on Women (NCRW). (2009). "Women in Fund Management: A Road Map for Achieving Critical Mass—and Why It Matters." *NCRW*, p. 200. Accessed from http://www.ncrw.org/reports-publications/women-fund-management-road-map-achieving-critical-mass-%E2%80%94-and-why-it-matters.

54. Fisher, Anne. (2012). "Leaping the Venture-Capital Gender Gap." *Crain's New York Business.com*, June 22. Accessed from http://mycrains.crainsnewyork.com/blogs/executive-inbox/2012/06/leaping-the-venture-capital-gender-gap/.

55. Casserly, Meghan. (2012). "Five most powerful female venture capitalists." *Forbes Magazine*, May 2. Accessed at http://www.forbes.com/sites/meghancasserly/2012/05/02/midas-list-five-most-powerful-female-venture-capitalists/.

56. Carter, Nancy M., Colette Henry, Barra O. Cinneide, and Kate Johnston, eds. (2007). *Female Entrepreneurship: Implications for Education, Training and Policy*, p. 12. New York: Routledge.

57. U.S. Census. (2007). "Statistics for All U.S. Firms by Industry, Gender, Ethnicity, and Race for the U.S., States, Metro Areas, Counties, and Places: 2007." *2007 Survey of Business Owners, US Census*. Accessed from http://factfinder2.census.gov/faces/tableservices/jsf/pages/productview.xhtml?pid=SBO_2007_00CSA01&prodType=table; Center for Women's Business Research. (2012). "Key Facts about Women-Owned Businesses." *CWBR*. Accessed from http://www.womensbusinessresearchcenter.org/research/keyfacts/.

58. Ibid.

59. Ibid.

60. Bhide, Amar. (1996). "The Questions Every Entrepreneur Must Answer." *Harvard Business Review*, November. Accessed from http://hbr.org/1996/11/the-questions-every-entrepreneur-must-answer/ar/1.

61. Bureau of Labor Statistics (BLS). "Median Weekly Earnings of Full-time Wage and Salary Workers by Detailed Occupation and Sex." *US Department of Labor. US Bureau of Labor Statistics.* Accessed from http://www.bls.gov/cps/cpsaat39.pdf.

62. Catalyst. "Statistical Overview of Women in the Workplace." *Catalyst Knowledge Center.* Accessed from http://www.catalyst.org/knowledge/statistical-overview-women-workplace.

63. Ashcraft, Catherine, and Anthony Breitzman. (2012). "Who Invents IT?" *National Center for Women and Information Technology.* Accessed from http://www.ncwit.org/sites/default/files/resources/2012whoinventsit_web_0.pdf.

64. Forbes. (2011). "America's Largest Private Companies." *Forbes.* Accessed from http://www.forbes.com/lists/2011/21/private-companies-11_rank.html.

65. Goudreau, Jenna. (February 2011). "Forbes Woman of the Year: Women in Tech." *Forbes.* Accessed from http://www.forbes.com/sites/jennagoudreau/2011/12/26/forbes-woman-of-the-year-women-in-tech/.

66. Catalyst. (2012). "Statistical Overview of Women in the Workplace." *Catalyst Knowledge Center.* Accessed from http://www.catalyst.org/knowledge/statistical-overview-women-workplace.

67. Stock, Kyle. (April 2011). "Women Unplug from the Tech Industry." *Fins Technology.* Accessed from http://it-jobs.fins.com/Articles/SB130080246443096737/Women-Unplug-From-the-Tech-Industry.

68. Ibid.

69. Beede, David, Tiffany Julian, David Langdon, George McKittrick, Beethika Khan, and Mark Doms. (August 2011). "Women in STEM: A Gender Gap to Innovation." *Economics and Statistics Administration. U.S. Department of Commerce.* Accessed from http://www.esa.doc.gov/Reports/women-stem-gender-gap-innovation.

70. Ibid.

71. Stock, Kyle. (April 2011). "Women Unplug from the Tech Industry." *Fins Technology.* Accessed from http://it-jobs.fins.com/Articles/SB130080246443096737/Women-Unplug-From-the-Tech-Industry.

72. Ibid.

73. Simard, Caroline. (2009). "Obstacles and Solutions for Underrepresented Minorities in Technology." *Anita Borg Institute for Women and Technology*, pp. 7–8. Accessed from http://anitaborginstitute.org/files/obstacles-and-solutions-for-under-represented-minorities-in-technology.pdf.

74. Ibid.

75. Zieminski, Nick. (2012). "Fewer Women in Top U.S. Tech Jobs since 2010 Survey." *Reuters*, May. Accessed from http://www.reuters.com/article/2012/05/14/harveynash-women-technology-idUSL1E8G93KX20120514.

76. Ernst, H. Olmand. (2003). "Patent Information for Strategic Technology Management." *World Patent Information* 25, 233–242. Accessed from http://aspheramedia.com/v2/wp-content/uploads/2011/02/Patent-information-for-strategic-technology-management.pdf.

77. Ashcraft, Catherine, and Anthony Breitzman. (2012). "Who Invents IT?" *National Center for Women and Information Technology*. Accessed from http://www.ncwit.org/sites/default/files/resources/2012whoinventsit_web_0.pdf.

78. NCRW. (2009). "Women in Fund Management: A Road Map for Achieving Critical Mass—and Why It Matters." *NCRW*, pp. 27–31. Accessed from http://www.ncrw.org/reports-publications/women-fund-management-road-map-achieving-critical-mass-%E2%80%94-and-why-it-matters

79. Ibid., p. 27.

80. Decker, Susan. (2012). "Women Inventors Double Their Share of Patents." *Businessweek*, March. Accessed from http://www.businessweek.com/articles/2012-03-01/women-inventors-double-their-share-of-patents.

81. National Women's Business Council (NWBC). (2012). "Intellectual Property and Women Entrepreneurs: Quantitative Analysis." *NWBC*, February. Accessed from http://nwbc.gov/sites/default/files/IP%20&%20Women%20Entrepreneurs.pdf.

82. Zieminski, Nick. (2012). "Fewer Women in Top U.S. Tech Jobs since 2010 Survey." *Reuters*, May. Accessed from http://www.reuters.com/article/2012/05/14/harveynash-women-technology-idUSL1E8G93KX20120514.

83. Pine, Karen. (2011). "Sheconomics: Why More Women on Boards Boosts Company Performance." *Significance* 8: 80–81.

84. Catalyst. (2011). "Women's Representation by Region." *Catalyst Knowledge Center.* Accessed from http://www.catalyst.org/etc/Census_app/11US/2011_Fortune_500_Census_Appendix_6.pdf.

3

Journalism and Media

Those who determine the content and delivery of the news have an enormous and powerful influence on the American public. From producers and publishers to the highly visible hosts of cable news programs, the decision makers in journalism and media shape both the messages we receive and the opinions we form. While media spurs public debate and often affects our culture, journalism informs the public on current news topics and influences politics and policy directly. Moreover, how this sector shapes and informs our society is changing very rapidly in every aspect from print to mobile devices to social media.

The line between journalism and media grows blurrier every day and is, at times, indistinguishable. The role of journalists is more clearly defined than that of media professionals. Journalists report on topics, such as crime, business, international relations, and politics. The public expects journalists to accurately report news and/or information, holding them to a higher standard than those in the media. Media professionals may indirectly or directly report on influential topics, but often have competing purposes, such as entertainment or shock jockeying, which can make accuracy less of a program priority. In both arenas, the concern exists that the public may perceive stereotypes, biases, and opinions as fact. These stereotypes and biases often influence social perception of gender, and this perception becomes reconstructed in the workplace and family, as many scholars have pointed out for decades. In fact, *who* reports the news has as much impact as *what* he or she reports.

Historically, the public universally regarded journalism professionals as greater authorities and experts than media personalities, and this line, too, has become more blurred. For example, in 2009, *Forbes* magazine rated top influential women in media. Three of the top five—Oprah Winfrey, Ellen DeGeneres, and Tyra Banks—reached noteworthy levels of influence through syndicated television programs designed to entertain and, at times, raise awareness about various topics, such as the humane treatment of animals, weight loss, and strategies for relationship and parental success. While the star or celebrity power of the top influential women is noteworthy, it is unclear how much influence media celebrities have on American discourse, particularly on topics such as business, diplomacy, public policy, and politics.

Readers should not underestimate the importance of this chapter; public consumption of journalism and media is widespread and greatly influences public opinion. To this end, it is essential to distinguish between journalism and media to ensure an accurate depiction and appropriate points of comparisons. To illustrate, within the various industries of this sector, women's positional leadership varies greatly from the lowest at 7.5 percent in radio to the highest at 55 percent in social media. Conclusions suggest that women have greater representation in media and social media than in journalism, and they have more opportunities to influence through social media, currently. The data suggest that broadcast networks are less accepting of female journalists. Nonetheless, women's voices are crucial in both arenas.

BROADCAST JOURNALISM

To determine the visibility and influence of women in journalism and media, we focused primarily on anchors and reporters because their names and faces are the most visible. Although we cannot fully assess the extent of their influence for the purposes of this book, it is possible to determine which reporters receive the most airtime and, therefore, the most opportunity to influence viewers. When determining their visibility, we focused primarily on evening and Sunday morning news shows. Daily morning news programs cannot be classified solely as journalism because they tend to blend journalism, media, and entertainment, yet they—and their female hosts—are influential.

While behind-the-scenes decision makers hold enormous sway, the power of visibility cannot be overemphasized. Presumably, when women achieve greater acceptance as visible figures of authority and expertise in society, they will also attain more leadership roles across all sectors. The very few female, primetime news network anchors, such as Katie Couric and Diane Sawyer, and cable news anchors, such as Christiane Amanpour, will help to pave the way for greater visibility for women as vested experts, but more visibility will be necessary.

Positional Leadership and Influence

Among the top five most influential women, *Forbes* magazine included two journalists: Diane Sawyer and Barbara Walters. The familiarity of these names to the average American and their collective influence and success might suggest that the field is remarkably open to women. Yet, despite the visibility of these two, and the fact that most college journalism majors since 1977 have been female, women overall are underrepresented in leadership positions in journalism.

This poor representation extends into the highly visible and executive positions. The top media and journalism companies of 2012 reflect female chief executive officers and board leaders in approximately 13 percent of the positions. As seen in table 3.1, the Walt Disney Company maintains the highest

Table 3.1   Females as CEOs and Board Members at the Top 10 Journalism and Media Companies

Company	CEO's Gender	# Board Members	Board Chair's Gender	# Female Board Members	% Female
Time Warner Inc.	Male	11	Male	2	18%
Walt Disney Company	Male	10*	Male	4	40%
Viacom Inc.	Male	11	Male	2	18%
News Corporation	Male	16	Male	2	13%
CBS Corporation	Male	14	Male	2	14%
Cox Enterprises	Male	10	Male	2	20%
NBC Universal	Male	4	Male	0	0
Gannett Company, Inc.	**Female**	**10***	**Female**	**3**	**30%**
Clear Channel Communications, Inc.	Male	12	Male	0	0
Advance Publications, Inc.	Male	2	Male	0	0
Average Percent of Women					**15.3%**

*These companies appear to have the most diverse boards among the top media companies.
Source: Mondo Times 2012.

percentage of women board members and has the most diverse board of any of the top media companies, along with Gannett Company, Inc. However, a number of boards have lost females in recent years, including the New York Times Company, Hearst Corporation, McGraw Hill, and Cox Enterprises.

As each industry is detailed, it will become clear that women make up a significant percentage of the workforce and experience an underrepresentation in executive leadership roles. During the last decade in particular, there have been virtually no advancements on the whole. The adage "for every two steps forward there is one step back" applies, yet it seems at times that women have taken one step forward and two back. This explains why women have remained stagnant for some time, as this chapter, and the remaining chapters will illustrate.

NEWSPAPER JOURNALISM

In 2011–2012, women comprised an estimated 19.2 percent of leadership positions in newspaper journalism. More specifically, women comprised 23.3 percent of top-level management positions, which include publisher, CEO, director general (DG), and CFO.[1] Of the 25 largest daily newspapers in the United States, only one female publisher is listed (4 percent): Katharine Weymouth of the *Washington Post*.[2]

There are four female editors-in-chief (16 percent): Jill Abramson of *The New York Times*; Debbie Henley of *Newsday*; Nancy Barnes of *The Star Tribune*, and Debra Adams Simmons of *The Cleveland Plain Dealer*.[3] Among the 100 largest newspapers, there is a greater representation of women, particularly among the editorial page editors, of whom 30 are female (30 percent).[4] Among the 10 most visited news Web sites, women own 10 percent.[5]

No woman owns any of the most visited news and media Web sites, although Yahoo! hired a female CEO in 2012, Marissa Mayer, who has acquired the highest portion of the market. Ironically, Ms. Mayer found herself in the middle of a media firestorm because of her decision to prohibit telecommuting beginning April 2013. Many claim this adversely affects the women of Yahoo! primarily. Because Ms. Mayer is female, her decision has garnered much media attention, perhaps unduly so, portraying her as a combative figure against the interests of other women.

TELEVISION JOURNALISM

Women lost significant ground in television news programming in 2011–2012. Despite the fact that women filled approximately 60 percent of the newsroom, they comprised 23.9 percent of all executive leadership positions.[6] More specifically, women accounted for 28 percent of all news directors[7] and made up "16.5 percent of general managers at network affiliates and independent stations."[8] This means that males comprised 40 percent of the newsroom staff and 76.1 percent of executive teams.

The percentage of women varies slightly by market size. This variation is unexplained in the current literature. In a 2010 survey, the smallest markets had 3 percent more women than the biggest markets. In 2011, that grew to 5.6 percent. The representation of gender was not contingent upon network affiliation.[9] All networks decreased their percentage of women, except for the Cable News Network (CNN). Conversely, women of color experienced a representational increase in many networks, except for ABC, CBS, and CNN. Overall, women made up 21.3 percent of all behind-the-scenes leadership in 2011.[10] In 2012, minority women comprised 5.6 percent of the total leaders of color.[11] Women of color were not as well represented when compared to men of color in 2011–2012.

Table 3.2 shows that in 2012, only one woman, Nancy Cordes, was in the top 10 reporters (10 percent), a 20-percent decrease from 2009 when there were three women: Andrea Mitchell, Betsey Bazell, and Nancy Cordes. In the top 20 reporters, five (25 percent) were women. No women of color were present, and there were two men of color among the top 20 in 2012.[12] Top news anchors remained relatively consistent over the last five years. In 2010, Candy Crowley succeeded CNN's *State of the Union* host John King, but CNN executives cut the program from four hours to one. Christiane Amanpour hosted *This Week* from

Table 3.2   Top 10 Most Visible Reporters on the Evening News in 2012 (Anchors Excluded)

Reporter	Minutes	Assignment	Network
1. David Muir	343	Domestic	ABC
2. Jake Tappe	283	White House	ABC
3. Richard Engel	246	Foreign	NBC
4. Nancy Cordes	**226**	**White House**	**NBC**
5. Chuck Todd	226	Capitol Hill	CBS
6. Jim Avila	211	Domestic	ABC
7. Jonathan Karl	205	Capitol Hill/Campaign	ABC
8. Tom Costello	201	D.C. Bureau	NBC
9. Anthony Mason	198	Economy	CBS
10. David Martin	193	Pentagon	CBS

Source: ASNE 2012b.

Table 3.3   Top 10 Most Frequent Guests on Sunday Morning Talk Shows in 2011*

Rank	# Appearances	Name	Gender	Position
1	53	Mitch McConnell	M	Senator (R-KY)
2	52	David Axelrod	M	Political Consultant
3	49	John McCain	M	Senator (R-AZ)
4	49	Lindsey Graham	M	Senator (R-SC)
5	36	Dick Durbin	M	Senator (D-IL)
6	34	Jon Kyl	M	Senator (R-AZ)
7	30	Chuck Schumer	M	Senator (D-NY)
8	**30**	**Hillary Clinton**	**F**	**Secretary of State**
9	26	Paul Ryan	M	Representative (R-WI)
10	24	Robert Gibbs	M	Former White House Press Secretary
Total			**10%**	

*Excluding presidential candidates.

Source: Compiled from the archives of each network.

August 2010 to December 2011, when she was replaced by former host George Stephanopoulos.

Sunday morning news programs are among the top-rated and most-watched weekly programming. They often provide exposure for politicians, cover domestic and international affairs, and review the top news stories of the week. To determine the visibility of women on these programs, my research team and I collected the names and frequency of nationally syndicated expert guests and journalists to determine how often women appeared when compared to men. Such programs consisted of 4,510 guests, 1,049 of whom were women, or 23 percent. Among the 1,049 female guests, networks hosted the 3 female journalists a minimum of 18 times and no more than 36 times. Networks hosted the most frequently appearing male journalist 139 times.

Among the 10 most frequently appearing guests in 2012, only one woman appeared on Sunday morning talk shows: Secretary of State Hillary Clinton (table 3.3). As shown in table 3.4, women were better represented as roundtable guests (30 percent), where several men also appeared, than as singularly represented experts.[13] When *all expert guests*, excluding 2012 presidential candidates, were compared, 4 of the top 25 guests were women, or 16 percent. If we included presidential candidates, the representation of women would have been far less.

Table 3.4   Top 10 Most Frequent Guests on Roundtables

Rank	# Appearances	Name	Gender	Position
1	139	George Will	M	Journalist
2	130	Bill Kristol	M	Journalist
3	127	Juan Williams	M	Author/Journalist
4	**94**	**Mara Liasson**	**F**	**Journalist/ political pundit**
5	72	Brit Hume	M	Political commentator/ journalist
6	**49**	**Donna Shalala**	**F**	**Former Secretary of Health and Human Services**
7	40	David Brooks	M	Political and cultural commentator
8	**36**	**Cokie Roberts**	**F**	**Journalist/ Author**
9	34	Matthew Dowd	M	Political consultant
10	31	Ed Gillespie	M	Political strategist, senior advisor to Mitt Romney
Total % Women			**30%**	

Source: Compiled from the archives of each network.

Performance and Compensation

Evaluating Pulitzer Prize winners is one way to measure top journalists in the industry. Overall, women comprise 42 percent of all Pulitzer Prize winners.[14] Only 5 percent of winners consisted of groups comprised of all males. Among the 10 highest paid journalists, just two were women.[15] Among the two highest earners, Dr. Arianna Huffington, media mogul, is somewhat of an enigma—the "Oprah Winfrey" of journalism—and should not be compared to other journalists who do not own media and journalism companies.

RADIO MEDIA

Women continue to lose ground in radio media, comprising just 7.5 percent of national leadership roles in 2011.[16] This percentage included top radio hosts and behind-the-scenes leadership, and it was significantly disproportionate to the overall workforce. Women comprised 25 percent of the workforce in both national and local broadcasts, down from 30 percent in

2007–2008.[17] A similar decline exists in television. Across local small, medium, and major markets, women's representation varies. In major market stations, women make up 36.6 percent of the workforce; however, in the medium and small markets, women make up only 11.2 percent and 11.7 percent of the workforce, respectively.[18]

Positional Leadership and Influence

In 2011, national broadcasting, women accounted for an average of 14.4 percent of behind-the-scenes leadership roles. Since 2005, the percentage of men of color has increased slightly, the percentage of women of color has remained stagnant, and white women's leadership has decreased.[19] Female general managers have maintained their 2009 representation and continue to account for 18.1 percent in radio.[20] Women news directors in radio are now at 10.7 percent—the lowest percentage in 17 years.[21]

In comparing pipeline to leadership positions, 64 percent of white males make up all radio staff, and they hold nearly 90 percent of leadership roles. There has virtually been no positive or negative change in white male leadership over the last decade, and in particular, since 2008. People of color, particularly men, have experienced incremental increases in both staff and leadership roles over the last decade.

Performance and Compensation

Only one woman, Laura Ingraham, has a top percentage of weekly listeners and sat among the top 10 media personalities in 2011.[22] Dr. Laura Ingraham was represented as among the highest paid hosts. The relationship between the performance of the female host and her compensation correlates, unlike what my team and I found in other industries, such as film and television entertainment.

MAGAZINES: MEDIA AND JOURNALISM COMBINED

In 2008, editorial staffs included women in large numbers, averaging over 40 percent. One reason for this strong presence is the existence of the so-called "seven sister" magazines—mass-market publications developed more than 50 years ago for the women's market. Despite women's magazines having the highest circulation, the pay and leadership gaps between men and women persist. This section examines that pay gap by analyzing the most trusted magazines, the national magazine awards, and the magazines with the highest circulation.

Table 3.5   Top Leadership Positions in 10 Largest Circulated Magazines

Magazine	Editor-in-Chief	Creative Editor / Director	Managing Editor / Deputy Editor
AARP Magazine	Female	Female	Male
AARP Bulletin	Male	Female	Male
Costco Connections	Male	N/A	Female
Better Homes and Gardens	Female	Female	Female
Game Informer	Male	Male	Male
Reader's Digest	Female	Male	Female
National Geographic	Male	Male	Female
Good Housekeeping	Female	Female	Female
Women's Day	Female	Female	Female
Family Circle	Female	Female	Female
Percentage of Women in Leadership	60%	60%	70%

Source: Pew 2011.

A strong female presence in the magazine industry continued in 2011–2012. Women leaders in the top magazine industry averaged 63.33 percent. This percentage included the top leaders of the 10 largest magazines by circulation. Table 3.5 shows that in the industry distinction of being named a most trusted media, female editors-in-chief claim 7 of the top 10 spots, or 70 percent.[23] The most trusted title impacts a magazine's circulation, reputation, quality, and revenue. In 2011, 16 of the top 25 magazines by circulation boasted female CEOs or editors-in-chief (64 percent).[24] When examining the largest top 10 magazines by circulation, women comprised 63.33 percent of the top leadership.

Compensation and Performance

Twenty females (23 percent) and 67 males (77 percent) won national magazine awards in 2012.[25] When researchers of this report examined each award category individually, they uncovered two inherent biases in the selection process. Men's magazines are not recognized as a distinct category, yet women's magazines are. For example, two of the five nominees for magazine of the year specifically targeted a male audience, and all five nominees for the "active category" targeted a male audience.[26]

The pay gap between men and women averages approximately $12,350 per year or 17 percent in each of the leadership roles.[27] The highest gap in pay exists in the editor and executive editor positions, where women earn 25.2 percent less than men earn.[28] Despite female leaders outnumbering males in behind-the-scenes roles, they still lag in pay.

BLOGGING AND SOCIAL MEDIA

Any discussion of media must include blogging and social media. Though success is difficult to track and quantify with any certainty, women have found success in these unrestricted social media outlets and in blogging. The fast-changing world of media Web sites, blogs, YouTube, and Twitter makes it particularly difficult to evaluate consistent measurements. Yet, it is clear that just as the Internet is transforming print and radio journalism, social media is radically reshaping the role of women in the media.

Blogging requires an inclination, audience, and an Internet connection. In its early days, bloggers were overwhelmingly white and male. Now, women in social media comprise 55 percent of the most popular and/or followed blog sites. Women do not enjoy this level of representation in any other sector, including print and radio.

Perhaps most noteworthy in social media is the lack of any establishment that guards content or visibility, which could alleviate more common stereotypes or biases that block women's progression elsewhere. To illustrate, according to *Forbes* magazine, three out of the top 10 social media influencers are women, or 30 percent.[29] *Forbes* ranked the social media influencers by the number of "social pulls" gathered by each blogger, a similar method employed by other sources.

On Twitter, celebrities would naturally elicit the most followers because of name recognition and multimedia exposure. Yet even among the top 10 most followed accounts (all celebrities), women comprised 80 percent.[30] When women (who are not celebrities with multimedia exposure) blog, they attract an audience almost double that of men.

Conclusions

- There exists a lack of a correlation between performance and compensation. Women are performing at high levels across the sector as a whole, and yet their positions and compensation do not match their performance.
- Inherent gender biases abound in journalism and in magazine publishing. Networks are four times more likely to highlight men as experts. Displaying men as experts perpetuates and fuels gender stereotypes both subtly and overtly.

- Women occupy more behind-the-scenes positions—a common finding of this study. The journalism and media sector, like most other sectors, grows more uncomfortable when women are the face of the network or newsroom. As the visibility of the positions grows, the presence of women shrinks. Society should stop making excuses as to why this is the case because it reflects a classic inherent bias.

- The ubiquitous male normative in the magazine industry creates a structural bias. The industry classifies magazines targeting a male population (*GQ*, *Men's Health*, etc.) as general interest while those targeting a female population as special interest. Despite the penchant towards men's magazines, women's magazines still perform better.

NOTES

1. American Society of News Editors (ASNE). (2012). "Numbers and Percentages of Men and Women by Job Category." *American Society of News Editors*. Accessed June 2012, from http://asne.org/content.asp?pl=140&sl=144&contentid=144.

2. Lulofs, Neal. (2012). "The Top U.S. Newspapers for March 2012." *Audit Bureau of Circulations*. Accessed June 2012 from http://www.editorandpublisher.com/PrintArticle/ABC--Newspaper-Circulation-Increased-in-Last-Six-Months--5--on-Sundays.

3. Ibid.

4. Easy Media Lists. (2012). "Top 100 US Newspaper Opinion Editors." *Easy Media Lists*. Accessed June 2012 from http://www.easymedialist.com/usa/top100opinion.html.

5. Ibid.

6. ASNE. (2012). "Numbers and Percentage of Whites and Minorities by Job Category." *American Society of News Editors*. Accessed June 2012 from http://asne.org/content.asp?pl=140&sl=144&contentid=144.

7. Papper, Bob. (2011). "RTDNA/Hofstra Survey Finds Mixed News for Women & Minorities in TV, Radio News." *RTDNA*, p. 6. Accessed June 2012 from http://www.rtdna.org/media/RTDNA_Hofstra_v8.pdf.

8. Catalyst. (March 2012). "Women in Media." *Catalyst Knowledge Center*, p. 3.

9. Papper, Bob. (2011). "RTDNA/Hofstra Survey Finds Mixed News for Women & Minorities in TV, Radio News." *RTDNA*, p. 6. Accessed June 2012 from http://www.rtdna.org/media/RTDNA_Hofstra_v8.pdf.

10. ASNE. (2012). "Numbers and Percentage of Whites and Minorities by Job Category." *American Society of News Editors*. Accessed June 2012 from http://asne.org/content.asp?pl=140&sl=144&contentid=144.

11. Ibid.

12. Ibid.

13. American University's Women & Politics Institute. 2012. "Industry Statistics: Women's Portrayal in the News." Accessed from http://www.mediareport-towomen.com/statistics.htm.

14. Lennon, Tiffani. (2012). "Benchmarking Women's Leadership in the United States." *Colorado Women's College.* Accessed from http://womenscollege.du.edu/media/documents/BenchmarkingWomensLeadershipintheUS.pdf.

15. Ibid.

16. During the research stages of publication, the 2012 data were unavailable; therefore, we relied on 2011 data.

17. Papper, Bob. (2011). "RTDNA/Hofstra Survey Finds Mixed News for Women & Minorities in TV, Radio News." *RTDNA*, p. 7. Accessed June 2012 from http://www.rtdna.org/media/RTDNA_Hofstra_v8.pdf.

18. Ibid.

19. ASNE. (2012). "Numbers and Percentage of Whites and Minorities by Job Category." *American Society of News Editors*, p. 7. Accessed June 2012 from http://asne.org/content.asp?pl=140&sl=144&contentid=144.

20. Papper, Bob. (2011). "RTDNA/Hofstra Survey Finds Mixed News for Women & Minorities in TV, Radio News." *RTDNA*. Accessed June 2012 from http://www.rtdna.org/media/RTDNA_Hofstra_v8.pdf.

21. Ibid.

22. Talkers. (2011). "The Top Talk Radio Audiences." *Talkers.* Accessed June 2012 from http://www.talkers.com/top-talk-radio-audiences/.

23. Simmons Marketing. (2009). "Experian Simmons Multi-Media Engagement Study." *Experian.* Accessed June 2012 from http://www.experian.com/assets/simmons-research/white-papers/multi-media-engagement-study.pdf.

24. Pew Research Center. (2011). "State of the Media: Top Circulated Magazines." *Pew Research Center.* Accessed June 2012 from http://stateofthemedia.org/2011/magazines-essay/data-page-4/.

25. ASME. (2012). "The National Magazine Awards." *ASME*, May 3. Accessed June 2012 from http://www.magazine.org/events-training/conferences/past-conferences/amc-2012-conference-highlights.

26. Ibid.

27. Ibid.

28. Ibid.

29. Shaughnessy, Haydn. (2012). "Who Are the Top 50 Social Media Power Influencers?" *Forbes*, January 25. Accessed June 2012 from http://www.forbes.com/sites/haydnshaughnessy/2012/01/25/who-are-the-top-50-social-media-power-influencers/.

30. Twitaholic. (2012). "The Twitaholic.com Top 100 Twitterholics Based on Followers." *Twitaholic.* Accessed June 25, 2012, from http://twitaholic.com/top100/followers/.

4

Law

My research mentor, the late Professor Ann C. Scales, claimed a spot among the original legal feminist scholars and cofounded Celebration 25 in 1975,[1] which later became the *Harvard Journal of Law and Gender*. Her work and contributions are immeasurable. This chapter is dedicated to her. Celebration 25 honored the first female law school student admitted to Harvard (in 1950), and in 2013, as I write this chapter, my colleague Professor Dolores Atencio, along with a group of Colorado Women's College students, has located and honored the first Latina lawyers in the United States. I am struck by how the United States is just now learning the accomplishments of Latina lawyers. These renowned feminist lawyers bookend women's leadership in law. Recognizing the contributions of all women is essential in understanding positional leverage and influence in law. We cannot fully understand the direction we head, if we do not know where we began, or where we sit presently.

Many women and men, like the ones I acknowledge above, have accomplished a great deal toward equity and parity in the law field. As this chapter will reveal, however, much more needs to be done to ensure that the best and brightest talent rises to positional leadership roles. In the early 2000s, I was a law student serving on the board of a law review journal. Charged with selecting the new review board, fellow editors openly expressed doubt about a colleague's ability to be an editor because she was an expectant mother. During this same time, a male superior advised me to wear a skirt to court to leave a better impression on the judge. On a job interview, a hiring male (civil rights) attorney, well known and respected, remarked about his necessity to have attractive females around him. More than 50 years after Harvard admitted its first female law student is it a surprise that women still face such micro-aggressions? While these anecdotal examples happen to reference male attorneys, this is not to suggest that females do not contribute to an aggressive, unwelcoming climate. They do, and collectively as a society, we do.

In 2012, the percentage of female law students decreased to 46.7 percent, continuing a decline from 50.4 percent in 1993, 49 percent in 2003, 48 percent in 2009, and 47.3 percent in 2010.[2] As a result, the percentage of female law graduates dropped slightly as well. This trend suggests that female law students may continue to decrease in 2013–2014. Likely, this decline will also contribute to a decrease in women's positional leadership.

In 2011, women comprised 47.4 percent of summer associates and 45.4 percent of associates.[3] In other words, males were 52.6 percent of summer associates and 54.6 percent of associates. Summer associates refer to the training and practice law students receive during their studies at firms and agencies, and associates refer to the initial foray into the practice of law as officers of the court. In an attempt to explain the disparities between men and women, many point to women choosing to start families, which is why many who have labored in law school (pun intended) do not choose to practice law or find that the practice of law prohibits a life-work balance.

Concededly, this may be the choice of some, but due to the rampant decline in numbers of women from education to entry in many traditional, highly structurally institutionalized fields, such as medicine, science, journalism, engineering and law, it is unlikely that such a conclusion explains the consistent decline across sectors. The highly institutionalized sectors where male norming is rampant the gender gap is wider. Further, technology and social media, for example, are noninstitutionalized, nontraditional fields with the opposite phenomenon. There is a greater presence of women in those fields than a pipeline would predict. Such a conclusion referencing women's choices in raising their families rather than working also suggests that women have a choice to work or not, which is an erroneous hegemonic, heterosexual female presumption.

In understanding where women sit in law, this chapter details the breakdown of women in public and private firms, leading law schools, and within the American Bar Association. Judgeships, both federal and state, will be included in the chapter on politics and government.

POSITIONAL LEADERSHIP AND INFLUENCE

Women have lacked a representational proportion of leadership roles since the late 1980s. In the 1980s, women comprised nearly half of all professionals, and they hold a similar percentage of professional jobs today. Yet, women represent less than 20 percent of leaders in law. This lack of proportional representation is particularly true of roles that have influence and impact. In fact, women have remained relatively stagnate and/or have declined in some influential areas. There is not a significant difference between the trends of women of color and white women. Both groups of women face a similar proportionally disparate trajectory in law when compared to men.

Public and Private Firms

Positional leadership in law consists of general counsels, partners, managing partners, and equity partners. Female general counsels inched up by one percentage point from 19 percent in 2011 to 20 percent in 2013, or 101 women, to claim this top legal position in Fortune 500 companies.[4] This is the highest percentage of women ever to hold the position of general counsel, according to the Minority Corporate Counsel Association. In fact, there exist more women general counsels in Fortune 500 companies than in Fortune 501–1000 companies. On average, women hold just 16.40 percent of these jobs at Fortune 501–1000 companies.[5]

When we disaggregated the data by race, the trends among women persisted. The overall representation among general counsels who are also women of color in Fortune 500 companies have also increased: from 2 percent in 2005, to 3 percent in 2011, and then to 17 percent in 2013.[6] A higher percentage of women of color exist in Fortune 500 companies than in Fortune 1000 companies. Women of color comprised just 8 percent of general counsels among Fortune 501–1000 companies in 2013.[7] A similar trend is found among white women.

A review of law firm partners reveals a staggering disproportionality. Although women make up 45 percent of all associates, and have for decades, less than 20 percent of partners are women. Stated differently, of the 55 percent of male associates, roughly 80 percent or more become partners.[8] The percentage of female partners has hovered between 15 and 20 percent for decades. Therefore, the percentage of women in the pipeline has done little to inform the percentage of female leaders in law.

Likewise, the percentage of female lawyers of color has remained virtually unchanged since 2009, accounting for approximately 6 percent of all lawyers[9] but 12.8 percent at the largest firms—those with more than 700 lawyers. Among associate lawyers, women of color accounted for 8.25 percent at firms with 100 lawyers or fewer.[10] In leadership, the largest and smallest firms, those with over 700 lawyers and those with 100 lawyers or fewer, accounted for similar representation of women of color as partners, 2.47 percent and 2.25 percent, respectively. At firms with 101–250 lawyers, that percent drops to 1.33 percent of partners.[11]

Larger firms, in general, have more women leaders. When examining the data as a whole, size is not the only factor that drives a greater representation of women. Firms with a greater number of women also have greater revenue, profits, industry reputation, and recognition. Table 4.1 shows that in 2012, women held 17 percent of the leadership positions among the top 10 law firms. Note that the top 10 law firms have more than two thousand partners, a significant sample. Within the top 10 firms, only one firm had a female managing partner—Goodwin Procter LLP. This firm

Table 4.1   Top 10 Private Law Firms

	Gender of Chair/ Managing Partner	# Partners	# Women Partners	% Women Partners
Bingham McCutchen LLP	M	115	27	23%
Davis Polk & Wardwell LLP	M	158	27	17%
Dechert LLP	M	20	3	15%
Gibson, Dunn & Crutcher LLP	M	NA	NA	NA
Goodwin Procter LLP	**F**	**329**	**63**	**19%**
Ropes & Gray LLP	M	313	54	17%
Sidely Austin LLP	M	520	106	20%
Skadden, Arps, Slate, Meagher & Flom LLP	M	415	72	17%
Willkie Farr & Gallagher LLP	M	155	27	17%
Cooley LLP	M	26	3	11%
Total/Average	**1**	**2,051**	**382**	**17%**

Source: U.S. News 2012.

also had a slightly higher percentage (19 percent) of women than the overall average (17 percent). Larger firms tended to have a higher percentage of female partners.

This trend addresses two issues. First, firms seem to hire and promote women to partners once they reach a minimum of 20–25 attorneys. It seems that when firms have fewer than 20 partners, they do not address, or perhaps notice, the lack of female leadership. There is a roughly 20:3 (male to female) ratio among law partners. Second, firms that have a larger reach, influence, and profits, promote more women. This fact bodes well for women. One of two or both scenarios is present, either the most successful firms want more women lawyers, or females help to make the firm more successful.

According to the National Association of Women Lawyers (NAWL), equity partnerships, which have more economic and political consequences than any other type of partnership, have been historically low among women. In 2012, the percentage of women equity partners declined slightly to 15 percent.[12] Because equity partners are the most influential of all law partnerships, this decrease is particularly concerning.

Additionally, women comprise just 5 percent of managing partners, another area where women have remained stagnate.[13] Yet, this type of position has tremendous influence within a firm, including recruiting and retention, benefits, management issues, and the strategic visioning of the firm. Another influential role that lacks significant representation among women is governing committees of law firms. In 2011, 35 percent of all law firms had only one woman represented, 54 percent had two or more women, and 11 percent had no women represented.[14]

Academia

Women's career progress as academicians and administrators at law schools declines as the status and prestige of the positions rise. However, women have gained ground overall since 2008. In 2012, women made up approximately 47 percent of the students, 40 percent of the faculty, and 26.4 percent of law school deans.[15] Among the top 10 law schools in the United States, women headed two of them, or 20 percent. There was just one male of color at Berkeley, who was on a leave of absence.

Not surprisingly, women are overrepresented among the mid-level positions of associate and assistant deans. On average, women hold 60 percent of associate and assistant deans.[16] This overrepresentation suggests that women are performing at high rates and are somewhat recognized for their leadership, yet a barrier still exists for the highest levels of leadership. This overrepresentation of women in middle-level leadership roles is present throughout most sectors.

There exists a positive trend showing a gain among women deans. In three years, the percentage of female deans rose 6 percent,[17] These percentages align with a robust period for law schools. More recently, law schools have experienced enrollment declines, and typically, such industry declines follow a decrease in women's leadership.

When disaggregated, the data reflect that the percentage of men of color holding the highest leadership positions at law schools is approximately double that of women of color. All men are underrepresented in middle-level leadership positions, such as in associate and assistant dean positions.

American Bar Association

As in any regulated profession, law has a governing body that establishes standards—the American Bar Association (ABA)—and understanding women's leadership in law requires analyzing the composition of that governing body. Women average approximately 26 percent of the leadership roles within the ABA (table 4.2). The ABA elected its first two female members in 1918,[18] before most universities would admit women into law school. It is common to find a higher percentage of women in leadership within organizations like the ABA, although substantiated explanations for this are unknown. The ABA influences academic curricula and accreditation, legislation, the practice of law, and the conduct of legal professionals. The ABA serves an important, albeit less conspicuous role.

Table 4.2   ABA Leadership, 2012–2013

Leadership Position	Total # Leaders	# Women	% Women
Presidents	3	1	33%
Board of Governors	38	11	28%
House Delegate Chairs	16	3	18%
ABA Officers	7	2	28%
Total/Average	**64**	**17**	**26%**

Source: ABA 2012b.

Figure 4.1   Women's Weekly Salary as a Percentage of Men's

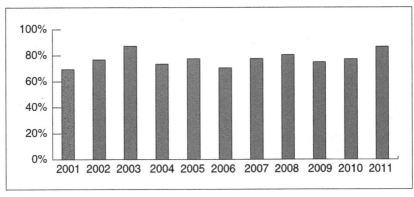

Source: BLS 2001; BLS 2011.

PERFORMANCE AND COMPENSATION

Like most professions, if not all, pay often reflects the value, or lack thereof, of lawyers. When examining the pay differentials between women and men, in addition to leadership stagnation, it becomes clear that women are not as valued as their male counterparts. When examining similar leadership roles among similar firms, the data demonstrates that, despite their performance and contributions, women receive disparate compensation.

Women experienced a significant salary decrease in recent years, coinciding with the economic recession. The economic recession did not affect men and women similarly. Female earnings, in general and across most sectors, declined much more than male earnings. In 2011, women attorneys earned 87 percent of male salaries,[19] down from 93.5 percent on average in 2010.[20] While female associates have begun to close the pay gap, since 2001 the gap has widened among female partners. Women equity partners earn 86 percent of what men earn (figure 4.1), or $70,000 less. In addition to salaries, one study found that women associates also receive smaller bonuses than their male counterparts in all practice areas.[21] The value firms place on women leaders reflects their (lack of) compensation.

CONCLUSIONS

• The climate of the legal profession requires a thorough examination. Having so few women in influential positions at firms while nearly half of law students and associate lawyers exist for several decades demonstrates that a systemic issue exists.

- With so few female partners, particularly in influential roles, such as equity and managing partnerships,[22] firms may need to take extra steps to achieve parity. One way to achieve parity is for firms to evaluate how managing and equity partners view and engage women both formally and informally within the profession.[23] Firms should improve women's access to networks and opportunities for sponsorships.[24]

- Firms should also integrate performance-based criteria in blind application processes, where the gender, race, and age of the applicant are unknown.

- Managing partners should set concrete goals in retaining and promoting women and track the progress of the firm. For models, it may be helpful to look at the annual report provided by the American Bar Association that tracks women in leadership within their organization.

NOTES

1. In 1975, the group celebrated the 25th anniversary of Harvard's first female law school admit.

2. Catalyst. (2012). Women in Law. Accessed at http://www.catalyst.org/knowledge/women-law-us.

3. Ibid.

4. Minority Corporate Counsel Association (MCCA). (Oct. 2011). MCCA Survey: Women Serving as General Counsel at Fortune Companies Reaches New High. Accessed at http://www.mcca.com/index.cfm?fuseaction=Feature.showFeature&featureID=276.

5. American Bar Association (ABA). (Feb. 2013). Commission on the Women in the Profession. Accessed at http://www.americanbar.org/content/dam/aba/marketing/women/current_glance_statistics_feb2013.authcheckdam.pdf.

6. National Association for Law Placement (NALP). (2011). "Law Firm Diversity Wobbles: Minority Numbers Bounce Back While Women Associates Extend Two-Year Decline." *NALP.* Accessed at www.nalp.org/uploads/PressReleases/2011WomenandMinoritiesPressRelease.pdf

7. ABA. (Feb. 2013). Commission on the Women in the Profession. Accessed at http://www.americanbar.org/content/dam/aba/marketing/women/current_glance_statistics_feb2013.authcheckdam.pdf.

8. Ibid.

9. NALP. (2011). "Law Firm Diversity Wobbles: Minority Numbers Bounce Back While Women Associates Extend Two-Year Decline." *NALP.* Accessed at www.nalp.org/uploads/PressReleases/2011WomenandMinoritiesPressRelease.pdf

10. Ibid.

11. Ibid.

12. National Association of Women Lawyers (NAWL). (2011). NAWL Report of the Sixth Annual National Survey on Retention and Promotion of Women in Law Firms. Accessed at http://www.nawlfoundation.org/pav/docs/surveys/NAWL-Survey2011.pdf

13. NAWL. (2011). NAWL Report of the Sixth Annual National Survey on Retention and Promotion of Women in Law Firms, p. 3. Accessed at http://www.nawlfoundation.org/pav/docs/surveys/NAWL-Survey2011.pdf.

14. NAWL. (2011). NAWL Report of the Sixth Annual National Survey on Retention and Promotion of Women in Law Firms, p. 15. Accessed at http://www.nawlfoundation.org/pav/docs/surveys/NAWL-Survey2011.pdf.

15. ABA. (2012). First Year and Total J.D. Enrollment by Gender 1947–2011. Accessed at http://www.americanbar.org/content/dam/aba/administrative/legal_education_and_admissions_to_the_bar/statistics/jd_enrollment_1yr_total_gender.authcheckdam.pdf.

16. ABA. (2012). Law School Staff by Gender and Ethnicity. Accessed at www.americanbar.org/content/dam/aba/administrative/legal_education_and_admissions_to_the_bar/statistics/ls_staff_gender_ethn.authcheckdam.pdf.

17. Ibid.

18. ABA (2013). "ABA Timeline." Accessed at http://www.americanbar.org/about_the_aba/timeline.html.

19. Bureau of Labor Statistics (BLS). (2012). Annual Averages: Median weekly earnings of full-time wage and salary workers by detailed occupation and sex. Accessed at http://www.bls.gov/cps/cpsaat39.pdf.

20. NAWL. (2011). NAWL Report of the Sixth Annual National Survey on Retention and Promotion of Women in Law Firms, p. 18–19. Accessed at http://www.nawlfoundation.org/pav/docs/surveys/NAWL-Survey2011.pdf.

21. NAWL. (2011). NAWL Report of the Sixth Annual National Survey on Retention and Promotion of Women in Law Firms, p. 9. Accessed at http://www.nawlfoundation.org/pav/docs/surveys/NAWL-Survey2011.pdf

22. Bagati, Deepali. (2008). Women of Color in U.S. Law Firms. *Catalyst*. Retrieved from http://www.catalyst.org/knowledge/women-color-us-law-firms%E2%80%94women-color-professional-services-series

23. Ibid.

24. Ibid.

5

Medicine

More than 160 years after the first woman received her doctor of medicine degree, female medical students near parity with males. The presence of female physicians has more than doubled in the last thirty years. Despite this increase of females in the medical field and their noteworthy achievements, women are still underrepresented in leadership and receive disparate salaries. In examining the industry as a whole, women comprise 18 percent of hospital CEOs and 4 percent of CEOs in medical services companies.[1] Women dominate in managerial positions, holding 71.4 percent of all medical and health service managers in 2011.[2] When we examined just the 10 top-grossing for-profit hospitals in the United States, the percentage of female CEOs jumped to 30 percent, nearly double the industry average. In fact, on average, 25.5 percent of women occupy the leadership positions among the top medical school faculty, the regulatory agencies, and public and private hospitals, including CEOs, executive positions, and board members. Yet, women receive less than 60 percent of the salaries earned by their male counterparts. This sector claims one of the largest pay gaps among the 14 sectors analyzed for this book.

In studying medicine, my team and I examined medical school students to understand how many women enter the field and the demography of faculty, private and public hospitals, and state medical boards in order to explore and better understand the composition of the medical field and its leadership. Regarding the pipeline of women, females comprised almost half of the medical students and new physicians in the United States, comprising 47 percent of all first year students in 2010–2011[3] and 45 percent of all residents and fellows.[4] This is a considerable increase since 1980 when women comprised just 21.5 percent of all residents.[5]

While females comprise nearly half of all medical students, the gender gap surfaces once women enter the medical profession as practicing physicians or academicians. In 2012, only 32 percent of physicians and surgeons were female, a decrease from 33.8 percent in 2011.[6] Among the 32 percent of doctors who were female, women of color represented 38.5 percent of women physicians.[7] Another interesting point worth mentioning is that among the 33.8 percent of physicians who were women in 2011, 80.5 percent were in patient care compared to 74.6 percent of male physicians.[8]

POSITIONAL LEADERSHIP AND IMPACT

In understanding positional leadership and impact, this chapter examines medical schools, for-profit and nonprofit hospitals, state medical boards, and the federation of state medical boards to capture a snapshot of where women leaders sit in influential positions in medicine.

Academia

In 2009–2010, among the 129,929 members on full and part-time medical school faculties,[9] 46,155 were tenured or on the tenure track. Among those 46,155 faculty members, women comprised approximately 28 percent of tenured or tenure track faculty (48,428 versus 17,340).[10] Women are less likely to attain promotion and tenure than their male counterparts, and they are overrepresented in junior faculty roles. One study examined female promotion and rank after 11 years on a medical school faculty. Researchers found that 59 percent of the tenure track female professors achieved the rank of associate or full professor compared to 83 percent of men.[11] Perhaps most alarming, just 5 percent of women on medical school faculties had achieved full professor status compared to 23 percent of men.[12] In other words, 72 percent of all tenure track professors and 95 percent of full professors—the most influential and impactful faculty leadership positions—are male. On average, women comprise 13 percent of deans and chancellors among the top 10 academic institutions in the United States. Table 5.1 shows that in 2012, 20 percent of deans and 22 percent of chancellors in the top 10 institutions were women.

Hospitals

Where women sit in positional leadership among U.S. hospitals informs the business side of medicine. Women comprise 18 percent of all

Table 5.1   Gender of Top Medical School Leaders, 2012

Institution	Dean	Chancellor /CEO of Health System
Harvard University	M	Affiliates Only
Johns Hopkins University	M	M
University of Pennsylvania	M	M
Stanford University	M	M
University of California, San Francisco	M	M
Washington University	M	M
Yale University	M	F
Columbia University	M	M
Duke University	F	M
University of Chicago	M	F
Total % of Women	**20%**	**22%**

Source: U.S. News 2012; individual Web sites.

hospital CEOs.[13] Measuring all hospitals depicts one aspect but one can argue that each of the hospitals represent a different kind of institution. Narrowing the types of hospitals allows a more succinct, descriptive picture of female leadership, and arguably performance. In better understanding female leadership, the top-grossing, for-profit hospitals in the United States were examined. While women comprise 18 percent of all hospital CEOs, when just the top-grossing hospitals in the United States were studied, female CEOs and presidents jump to 30 percent among the for-profits (table 5.2). Note that information on for-profit boards of directors was not always available, and we were, therefore, unable to report on those data.

Examining the top revenue-generating institutions is just one way to understand leadership, yet it is an important aspect of medicine even among nonprofit hospitals. As shown in table 5.3, among the 10 highest-grossing nonprofit hospitals, women made up 20 percent of CEOs, 25.12 percent of board of directors, and 35 percent of executive positions, or a total average of 28.33 percent of the highest grossing nonprofit hospitals. This is significant because women average only 18 percent of all hospital CEOs in the United States. Additionally, when a female CEO exists there is a higher percentage of females on the board of directors. This trend—in which women are better represented in the top echelon than in the industry as a whole—was found consistently among most if not all sectors included in this book.

Table 5.2   CEOs of Top-Grossing For-Profit Hospitals, 2012

Hospitals	2012 Revenue ($ billions)	Gender of CEO
1. Methodist Hospital (San Antonio)	$4.22	F
2. Hahnemann University Hospital	$3.03	M
3. CJW Medical Center (Chippenham Campus)	$2.76	M
4. Sunrise Hospital & Medical Center	$2.73	F
5. Brookwood Medical Center	$2.73	M
6. Doctors Medical Center of Modesto	$2.68	M
7. Medical City Hospital	$2.38	M
8. Oklahoma University Medical Center	$2.30	M
9. Las Palmas Medical Center	$2.30	M
10. JFK Medical Center	$2.24	F
Percent women CEOs		**30%**

Source: Becker 2012.

Table 5.3   Leadership of the 10 Top-Grossing Nonprofit Hospitals, 2012

Hospital	CEO	# Board Positions	# Females on Board	% Females on Board
University of Pittsburgh Medical Center	Jeffrey Romoff	33	9	27.3%
Cleveland Clinic	Delos Cosgrove	22	4	18.2%
New York-Presbyterian Hospital	Herbert Pardes			Unavailable
Florida Hospital Orlando	Lars Houmann	18	6	33.3%
Cedars-Sinai Medical Center Los Angeles	Thomas Priselac	35	7	20.0%
Stanford Hospital and Clinics	Martha Marsh	25	3	12.0%
Montefiore Medical Center, Bronx NY	Steven Safyer	47	14	29.8%
Hospital of the University of Pennsylvania	Garry Scheib			Unavailable
Temple University, University Hospital, Philadelphia	John N. Kastanis			Unavailable
Orlando Regional Medical Center	Sherrie Sitarik	17	6	35.3%
Total	**20%**			**25.12%**

Source: Stanford 2012; Herman 2012.

Regulatory Agencies

When the positional leadership of state and federal regulatory bodies was examined, women averaged a slightly higher representation in leadership positions compared to academic and hospital leadership. Female executives held 32 percent of the leadership roles in state and federal regulatory agencies. Tables 5.4 and 5.5 show that women were better represented among state medical boards (51 percent) than on the federation of state medical boards (22.5 percent). The federation of state medical boards has national scope and visibility, unlike the state medical boards, which focus on state regulatory compliance and professional conduct. A similar finding emerged in the law field, where female leadership among the regulatory bodies was higher than in firms or in academia. The selection process of each individual state medical board may inform why women are overrepresented among state regulatory agencies and underrepresented elsewhere. Of the 45 percent of medical residents that are female, only 32 percent go on to become physicians and surgeons. Therefore, only 32 percent of regulatory agencies' positions should presumably be held by females. Yet, among state agencies, women sit on 51 percent of state medical boards, an overrepresentation.

Typical explanations have often centered on the fact that women choose such positions, such as regulatory agency positions, because of lifestyle or internal motivational reasons to do good or help. However, when looking at the entire picture of positional leadership, this conclusion does not consider all the correlative factors. On the one hand, women are less likely than men to obtain residency positions, do not earn as much as their male counterparts, are less likely to obtain physician positions, and are far less likely to attain positional leadership roles. On the other hand, women comprise 32 percent of physicians in the United States, and yet when looking at the top-performing hospitals in the United States, women average a proportional representation of the for-profit hospital leadership and within the regulatory agencies. The argument that women make lifestyle decisions

Table 5.4   Females on Federation of State Medical Boards Leadership, 2012

CEO	# Executive Positions	# Females in Executive Positions	% Females in Executive Positions	# Board Positions	# Females in Board Positions	% Females in Board Positions
Humayun J. Chaudhry	5	1	20%	16	4	25%

Source: FSMB 2012b.

Table 5.5   Leadership of State Medical Boards, 2012

State	Director of State Board	State	Director of State Board
Alabama	M	Montana	M
Alaska	F	Nebraska	F
Arizona	F	Nevada	M
Arkansas	F	New Hampshire	F
California	F	New Jersey	M
Colorado	M	New Mexico	F
Connecticut	M	New York	M
Delaware	F	North Carolina	M
District of Columbia	F	North Dakota	M
Florida	F	Ohio	F
Georgia	F	Oklahoma	M
Hawaii	F	Oregon	F
Idaho	F	Pennsylvania	F
Illinois	M	Rhode Island	M
Indiana	F	South Carolina	M
Iowa	M	South Dakota	F
Kansas	F	Tennessee	F
Kentucky	M	Texas	F
Louisiana	M	Utah	F
Maine	M	Vermont	M
Maryland	F	Virginia	M
Massachusetts	M	Washington	F
Michigan	F	West Virginia	M
Minnesota	M	Wisconsin	M
Mississippi	M	Wyoming	M
Missouri	F		

Males 49% and Females 51%

Source: FSMB 2012a.

must extend to their choices to also run the top hospitals and regulatory agencies. After all, a representational composition is reflected among the state and national leaders. Rarely does society view women as choosing to run the top organizations, and yet, they do. I contend that the difference is that most of the top performers in the United States evaluate and select candidates differently than mediocre or average institutions.

COMPENSATION AND PERFORMANCE

Women leaders contribute positively to a company's bottom line. Yet, women still fall behind in earnings. Research from Duke University and

Michigan Health System found that women who receive a "highly competitive early career research grant" will earn approximately $12,194 less than her male counterparts, even when all factors remained the same. Over a 30-year career, this equates to over $360,000 in pay difference.[14]

Some have claimed that this pay discrepancy is due to women gravitating towards careers in lower-paying medical fields, such as pediatrics and obstetrics/genecology.[15] However, that is false for three reasons: First, obstetrics/genecology consistently ranks fourth among the highest paid medical professions in the United States.[16] Second, women make up emergency-room physicians and general surgeons at high rates, which are the top two highest paid medical positions.[17] And, third, in 2010, there were 10 specialties with the highest concentration of women: internal medicine, pediatrics, general/family medicine, obstetrics/gynecology, psychiatry, anesthesiology, emergency medicine, pathology, general surgery, and diagnostic radiology.[18] Interestingly, urology, focused on male reproductive systems, is considered a high demand, competitive medical field, and therefore, high paying. Gynecology, focused on female reproductive systems, offers lower salaries than urology. The lack of irony that accompanies this observation hopefully is obvious to the reader.

Only data on CEO compensation among the top-grossing nonprofit hospitals was available, providing only a snapshot of the pay discrepancy between men and women. Based on the information available and shown in table 5.6, male CEO salaries average $3,418,429, while female salaries average $1,920,000. This means that female CEOs earn 57 percent of what male CEOs earn, at least within the top-grossing nonprofits. This paltry percentage reflects gross gender disparities, which cannot be minimized by arguing that women choose low-paying careers or disciplines or work at or for less prestigious positions and organizations. Many sought to explain the disparity of earnings by citing maternity and child rearing; however, research has demonstrated that motherhood is *not* a factor in wage disparity.[19] Additionally, women earn less than males who occupy the same type of position.

U.S. News and World Report identifies the top hospitals in the field through its Honor Roll listing. Table 5.7 shows that among the top 10 honorees, women average 10 percent of the CEOs, 22 percent of the board members, and 34 percent of the executive leadership. Women are not as well represented in industry distinctions as they are in the top-grossing hospitals. In other sectors, women were better or comparably represented among the top 10 entities *and* in industry distinctions than in the industry as a whole. This trend does not emerge in the field of medicine. Instead, women are either comparably represented among the industry's distinctions or below their overall representation.

Table 5.6   CEO Compensation among Top-Grossing Nonprofit Hospitals, 2011

Hospital	CEO	Total Earnings	Female Earnings
University of Pittsburgh Medical Center	Jeffrey Romoff	$5,970,000	
Cleveland Clinic	Delos Cosgrove	$2,310,000	
New York- Presbyterian Hospital*	Herbert Pardes	$4,350,000	
Florida Hospital Orlando	Lars Houmann	$2,929,000	
Cedars-Sinai Medical Center, Los Angeles	Thomas Priselac	$2,770,000	
Stanford Hospital and Clinics**	Martha Marsh	$1,920,000	$1,920,000
Montefiore Medical Center, Bronx NY	Steven Safyer	$4,070,000	
Hospital of the University of Pennsylvania	Garry Scheib	$1,530,000	
Temple University, University Hospital, Philadelphia	John N. Kastanis	Unavailable	
Orlando Regional Medical Center	Sherrie Sitarik	Unavailable	Unavailable
Total	**20%**	**$25,849,000**	**$1,920,000**

*Steven Corwin became the CEO of New York-Presbyterian Hospital in June 2012.

** Amir Dan Rubin became the CEO of Stanford Hospitals and Clinics in January 2011.

Source: Stanford 2012; Herman 2012.

In assessing industry distinctions, we did not rely on *U.S. News and World Report* in all sectors, but we did in K–12 education, academia, and medicine for these sectors often utilize and reference the publication. To earn a place on *U.S. News* Honor Roll in medicine, a hospital had to earn at least one point in each of the six specialties. A hospital earned two points if it ranked among the top 10 hospitals in America in any of the 12 specialties including survival rates and patient safety. Other points were earned for doctor opinions and hospital reputation among physicians.[20] *U.S. News* uses similar point systems for other sectors.

Additionally, every year, the American Medical Association (AMA) recognizes outstanding physicians who have made a significant contribution to the field. Thirty-six percent of award recipients were women in

Table 5.7 Women in Leadership in the Top 10 Hospitals on *U.S. News* Honor Roll, 2012–2013

	CEO/ President	# Women on Board	Total # Board Positions	% Women on Board	# Women in Executive Positions	# Executive Positions	% Women in Executive Positions
Massachusetts General Hospital, Boston	David Torchiana, MD	5	16	31.2%	3	6	50%
Johns Hopkins Hospital, Baltimore	Ronald R. Peterson	2	14	14.2%	8	15	53.3%
Mayo Clinic, Rochester MN	John H. Noseworthy, M.D.	8	31	25.8%	3	17	17.6%
Cleveland Clinic	Delos Cosgrove, M.D.	4	22	18.2%	3	23	13.0%
Ronald Reagan UCLA Medical Center, Los Angeles	David T. Feinberg, M.D., M.B.A.				1	4	25.0%
Barnes-Jewish Hospital/ Washington University, St. Louis	Richard J. Liekweg	4	24	16.7%	3	11	27.2%
New York-Presbyterian University Hospital of Columbia and Cornell, NY	Steven J. Corwin, MD	18	94	19.1%	39	82	47.6%
Duke University Medical Center, Durham, NC	Victor J. Dzau, MD	5	20	25.0%	7	29	24.1%
Brigham and Women's Hospital, Boston	Elizabeth G. Nabel, MD	6	19	31.6%	6	11	54.6%
UPMC-University of Pittsburgh Medical Center	Jeffrey A. Romoff	9	33	27.3%	3	14	24.4%
Percent Women	**CEO 10%**			**Board 22.3%**			**Executive 33.8%**

Source: U.S. News and World Report 2012–2013.

2012–2013, which is slightly higher than the percentage of women in the field of medicine, post-residency. Among Nobel Prize winners, however, women are underrepresented at just 11 percent.

CONCLUSIONS

- One of the areas that needs immediate address is the loss of 13 percent of female doctors early in their careers. Women composed 45 percent of residents and fellows and just 32 percent of new physicians in 2012. Men made up 55 percent of residents and fellows, but 68 percent of all new physicians. Understanding why female doctors are more likely to leave the profession is vital in remedying the problem. Critics have assumed that women leave the profession to have children and raise families; however, they fail to account for professional stressors and extraordinary pressures unique to female physicians.[21]

- The pay gap, which exists in all sectors, needs to be addressed. The myth-based explanations around why women earn $360,000 less than men over their careers should be revealed as such. To address this pay gap, medical facilities and organizations should voluntarily take action before the government compels it, which will likely occur if discrimination persists.

- The nation's hospitals should hold themselves to the same transparent standards seen in other professional sectors, thereby disclosing gender composition and salaries of board of trustees and executive leadership in addition to hospital revenues.

- The complexity and conglomeration of hospitals and the business of practicing medicine creates challenges in collecting data on the c-level executive teams and boards of directors or trustees. Parent corporations usually own multiple medical centers and hospitals, particularly those mentioned in this chapter. Policy aimed at parent corporations should be considered. More specifically, the scope of the parent company's authority and active decision-making role with subsidiaries should be examined.

- Little data is available on salaries earned by senior executives in the field of medicine. However, what data was available revealed a 57-percent pay gap—one of the highest pay gaps found in all sectors. More comprehensive data is needed among the nation's top hospitals. Several studies have been conducted regionally, but there lacks a comprehensive knowledge of executive compensation. It is not surprising that when an industry lacks transparency, females tend to experience gross pay inequities.

NOTES

1. Gamble, M. (July 27, 2012). Women Make Up 73% of Healthcare Managers but Only 18% of Hospital CEOs. Becker's Hospital Review. Accessed at http://www.beckershospitalreview.com/hospital-management-administration/women-make-up-73-of-healthcare-managers-but-only-18-of-hospital-ceos.html

2. Catalyst. (2012). Women in Medicine. Accessed at http://www.catalyst.org/publication/208/women-in-medicine

3. Ibid.

4. Ibid.

5. Ibid.

6. Rock Health. (2012). Women in Healthcare. Retrieved from http://www.slideshare.net/RockHealth/rock-report-iii-women-in-healthcare)

7. Catalyst. (2012). Women in Medicine. Accessed at http://www.catalyst.org/publication/208/women-in-medicine

8. Ibid.

9. Ibid.

10. American Association of Medical Colleges [AAMC] (2011). "Table 19: Distribution of U.S. Medical School Faculty by Gender, Race." Accessed at https://www.aamc.org/44826/search.html,s=rel,q=tenure+and+tenure+track,p=2,fc=100

11. Selhat, L. (Winter 2011). The Goal Is Transformation. Accessed at http://www.med.upenn.edu/focus/user_documents/PennMedicine-2011-01-winter-issue_GoalisTransformation.pdf

12. Ibid.

13. Gamble, M. (July 27, 2012). Women Make Up 73% of Healthcare Managers but Only 18% of Hospital CEOs. Becker's Hospital Review. Accessed at http://www.beckershospitalreview.com/hospital-management-administration/women-make-up-73-of-healthcare-managers-but-only-18-of-hospital-ceos.html

14. Duke University Medical Center, Durham, NC. (2012). Accessed at http://www.dukemedicine.org/Leadership/Administration/

15. Ibid.

16. Merritt Hawkin. (2012). 2012 Review of Physician Recruiting Incentives. Merritt. Accessed at http://www.merritthawkins.com/uploadedfiles/merritthawkins/pdf/mha2012survpreview.pdf

17. Smith, J. (2013). "The 10 Best Paying Jobs for Doctors." *Forbes Magazine.* Accessed at http://www.forbes.com/sites/jacquelynsmith/2013/07/18/the-best-paying-jobs-for-doctors/

18. Catalyst (2012). Women in Medicine. Accessed at http://www.catalyst.org/publication/208/women-in-medicine

19. Taylor, K. (June 13, 2012). "Even Women Doctors Can't Escape the Pay Gap." *Forbes.* Accessed at http://www.forbes.com/sites/katetaylor/2012/06/13/even-women-doctors-cant-escape-the-pay-gap/

20. Comarow, A. (2012, July 16). "U.S. News Best Hospitals 2012–13: the Honor Roll." *U.S. News and World Report.* Accessed at http://health. usnews.com/health-news/best-hospitals/articles/2012/07/16/best-hospitals-2012-13-the-honor-roll

21. Shannon, Diane (October 1, 2013). "Why I Left Medicine: A Brunt-Out Doctor's Decision to Quit." NPR. Accessed at http://commonhealth.wbur. org/2013/10/why-i-left-medicine-a-burnt-out-doctors-decision-to-quit

6

Politics and Government

In examining the leadership of the United States government, both elected and appointed positions have great influence over the direction and agenda of the nation. Where women sit in leadership determines their influence, or lack thereof, and how poised they are to guide the country. To this end, chapter 6 details the percentages of women leaders in state and federal appointments, state and federal judgeships, and major state and federal elected offices. Some interesting trends emerged, forming the thesis of this book. For instance, when a woman or man of color heads a federal agency, a higher percentage of female senior leaders existed, except for two agencies: Social Security Administration and the Department of the Treasury. These exceptions triggered a more nuanced, deeper inquiry detailed later in the book about performance-driven promotional and hiring practices and how those practices inform leadership positions. While administrative and appointed positions can disclose a great deal about women's leadership, elected office draws much attention. Mayoral, gubernatorial, and legislative offices tend to draw the most attention nationally. Few have examined political campaign contributions from a gendered perspective. When examining party, political action committee (PAC), and lobbyist dollars, women receive 15 percent of contributions. Democratic Party dollars significantly aided the 2012–2013 historic election when the largest percentage of women, particularly Democratic women, won seats in Congress.

Despite the historic 2012–2013 election of female Senators, women have remained relatively stagnant in elected office over the last two to three decades. On the one hand, such as the recent Senate election, women have made progress, composing 20 percent of the Senate and 17.7 percent of the House of Representatives (58 female Democrats and 19 female Republicans). Women of color also celebrated gains, with 36 percent of seats among all female representatives, with 5 percent in the Senate, and with 6 percent in the House. On the other hand, Congress has an under-representation of white women and women of color with just 18 percent and 5.5 percent of the seats, respectively.

Running for elected office presents specific challenges for women. Women seeking elected office face an interdependent, three-fold problem. They often contend with media questions and criticisms that have less or nothing to do with political issues and positions and much to do with personal and/or family concerns and gender stereotyping. Additionally, major companies and law firms will more often recruit and support male candidates over females, creating more structural advantages for men.[1] Women also receive less in terms of campaign contributions. As a result, women are less inclined to run for office, meaning fewer women can win elected office. Some studies have claimed that despite barriers, women in Congress, on average, introduce more bills, attract more cosponsors, and bring more money to their home districts than their male counterparts[2]:

- "Within districts over time, roughly 9 percent more federal spending is brought home when there is a woman representing the district in Congress than when the same district is represented by a man."[3]
- "Congresswomen cosponsor about 26 more bills per congress than congressmen."[4]
- "[W]omen score significantly higher on their measure of legislative effectiveness than men do. In short, women's bills make it further in the 'legislative process' and are more likely to be considered 'important,' as measured by the public and media coverage."[5]

Other studies have suggested a correlation between the presence and visibility of women candidates and an increase in female political and societal participation. Beginning in 1980, women have voted at higher rates than men in every presidential election, and the gender gap in civic participation has grown slightly larger with each successive election. In the 2004 elections, 8.8 million more women than men turned out to vote.[6] According to the Census Bureau, in the 2008 elections, 10 million more women voted than men did, and in 2012, the gender gap widened to the largest in history.[7]

POSITIONAL LEADERSHIP AND INFLUENCE

On average, women comprise 22.8 percent of all political and governmental leadership roles. If the overall leadership calculations eliminated federal appointments, women would comprise less than 17 percent of elected office. Cabinet appointments and federal administrative agencies have bumped the overall percentage of women in government up in 2012. Smaller metropolitan cities elect more women than larger ones. In most other sectors, women seem to fare better in larger markets; for example, in journalism and media and within school districts, women leaders were more likely to occupy leadership positions in larger markets and districts. The amount of media coverage may affect elected office in that candidate outreach to constituents may rely on a grassroots, canvassing efforts in smaller markets rather than a mass media approach in larger markets. Future research in this area may uncover a better understanding of the disparate representation among different market sizes.

City Elected Offices

Women have lost ground in mayoral offices from 2009–2012. As of January 2012, women held 17.4 percent of mayoral offices in cities with populations over 30,000 (217 of 1,248).[8] The percentage of women decreases significantly in the 100 largest cities, where women comprise just 9 percent (9 out of 100), and two are women of color.[9] As mentioned, this is somewhat unusual among sectors in this study, in that women were generally more likely to have a higher representation among larger markets and audiences, such as in radio and school districts.

However, this unusual trend in elected office is similar to the trend among nonprofits, where female representation in leadership shrinks as the size and budget grows. It is highly unlikely that this trend is due to a preference to lead smaller cities, particularly since more women dwell in larger cities; therefore, there is a greater likelihood that there would be more females interested in running for a mayoral seat. More likely, large city mayoral elections require different exposure, nomination tactics, and campaign strategies that women do not have the same access to as men. Uncovering the differences in exposure and strategies will reveal more about gender disparity.

Statewide Offices and Appointments

State Legislatures   In state legislatures across the United States, women have made little progress in the last decade. As of June 2009, women held

24 percent of the seats in state legislatures, only two percentage points more than a decade earlier. As of December 2012, approximately 1,750 women served in the 50 state legislatures out of the 7,382 total seats. Women comprised 23.7 percent of all state legislators.[10] At the state level, women of color made up less than 5 percent of the 7,382 state legislators, and they were only 2 percent of the 314 statewide elected executives. Women of color constituted 4.8 percent of the total 7,382 state legislators and 3.5 percent of the total 317 statewide elective executives in Congress. The number of elected officials of color has risen only slightly over the last decade.

Female legislators have the largest presence in western, northern Midwest, New England, and some southwestern states, and they are less visible in southern Midwest and southern states. Colorado with 40 percent and Vermont with 38.9 percent have the largest percentages of female legislators in the country.[11] The cultural differences within these regions may help to further explain the gender gap.

State Judicial Branch   Some state judgeships are elected, others are appointed, or some combination therein. Women's overall representation in state appellate judgeships has increased since 2005, when 26.61 percent of all female judges sat on state appellate courts. In 2012, 32 percent of state appellate court judges are women.[12] In seven years, women gained five percentage points on state appellate courts. What is unclear is whether the gains achieved reflected elected or appointed offices. In either case, the gains do reflect a greater awareness of the contributions and importance of female judges.

State Executive Positions   Women have lost ground in the last decade as statewide executive officials, including governors and lieutenant governors. The gender gap that exists in gubernatorial offices occurs in the same previously mentioned regions where there is a gender gap in legislative offices, with some exceptions, such as in Colorado. This regional difference suggests that the gender gap is not coincidentally prominent in certain regions but is attributable to cultural nuisances that are unfavorable to women.

- In 2009, women made up 23.6 percent of state executive officials.[13]
- In 2010:
  - 36 states held gubernatorial elections

- 26 women filed to run for governor, 10 women ran as candidates, and 3 won office.
- 40 women filed to run for lieutenant governor, 23 were candidates, and 8 won office.
- In 2012:
  - 11 states held gubernatorial elections
  - 4 women filed to run for governor, and 1 won office.
  - 11 women filed to run for lieutenant governor, and 7 won office.[14]
- As of December 2012, 75 women held statewide elective executive offices across the country, which is 23.4 percent of the 320 available positions.[15]
- As of January 2013, there are 5 female governors, and of the 43 states that elect a lieutenant governor, 12 of them are women.
- In general, at the state and local level, women comprise 12 percent of governors, 9 percent of large city mayors, 23 percent of the state legislatures, and 22 percent of state executive offices.
- Twenty-four states have never elected a female governor:
  - Arkansas
  - California
  - Colorado
  - Florida
  - Georgia
  - Idaho
  - Illinois
  - Indiana
  - Iowa
  - Maine
  - Maryland
  - Minnesota
  - Mississippi
  - Missouri
  - Nevada
  - New York
  - North Dakota
  - Pennsylvania
  - Rhode Island
  - South Dakota
  - Tennessee
  - Virginia

Federal Elected Offices

The United States continues to fall behind other countries, with one of the largest gender gaps in the world in elected offices, particularly in national legislatures. From 2005 to 2012, the United States fell from 71st to 79th among 189 countries with a proportional percentage of women in national legislatures. Pakistan, Iraq, Sudan, most Western European countries, and much of Latin America have a far greater percentage of women in their national legislatures.[16] Women continue to hover around 18 percent in Congress. In June 2009, women constituted less than 17 percent of the U.S. House of Representatives, up only four percentage points from 2000. In 2012, women held 16.8 percent of the seats in the House of Representatives. In 2013, women held 20 percent of the seats in the Senate and 17.7 percent of the House—a gain of three percentage points and one percentage point, respectively, from the previous year.

In 2012, of the women who filed to run for national legislative seats, more than 50 percent won the election. Stated differently:

- 36 women filed to run for U.S. Senate, and 18 won office, and
- 299 women filed to run for the House, and 166 won office.

Women of color comprise less than five percent of the House, and hold one seat in the Senate. Women of color constitute 5 percent of the total 535 members of Congress.[17] From 1993 to 1999, the Senate had one woman of color: Carol Mosley-Braun. Voters did not elect another woman of color to the Senate until more than a decade later, when in 2013, Hawaii elected Mazie Horono.

A brief historical account of congressional wins by women of color provides context for their constant underrepresentation. In total, 44 women of color have served in the U.S. Congress.

- Representative Patsy Mink of Hawaii won election to the U.S. House of Representatives in 1964; four other Asian-Pacific-American women have since followed her.
- The first African American female elected to Congress in 1968 was Shirley Chisholm (D-NY), who was also the first woman to run for the Democratic presidential nomination.
- Since Senator Chisholm, 30 African American women have followed her
- The first Latina American elected to Congress, Representative Ileana Ros-Lehtinen (R-FL), entered the house in 1989; six other Latina Americans have since followed her.

The chairpersons of the Senate and House committees have tremendous power in determining which bills will move for a full vote and in establishing legislative priorities. These powers are particularly true in a divided Congress. In 2012, among the 20 standing Senate committees, four have women chairs and four have female ranking members, an increase from 2009. In 2002, Nancy Pelosi (D-CA) became the first female House minority leader, and from 2007 to 2011, she was the first female Speaker of the House. In 2012, the Democrats lost a majority in the House and Representative Pelosi returned as the minority leader. Since 2009, however, the House experienced a decline in ranking committee chairs held by women. Only one woman chairs a House of Representatives committee (5 percent), with three other House committees having a ranking female on them (15 percent).

Certain chair and committee positions wield greater leverage and influence than others. For example, no women have served in leadership roles on the five most powerful committees in the House: Appropriations, Ways and Means, Rules, Budget, and Energy and Commerce in either body. Nor have women served on the five most powerful committees in the Senate. Chairs and ranking members for 2012 are shown in tables 6.1 and 6.2.

Table 6.1   2012 Women Committee Chairs in Congress

Chairperson	Committee
Senator Debbie Stabenow	Agriculture, Nutrition, and Forestry
Senator Barbara Boxer	Environment and Public Works
Senator Mary Landrieu	Small Business and Entrepreneurship
Senator Patty Murray	Veterans' Affairs
Representative Ileana Ros-Lehtinen	Foreign Affairs

Source: Derived from www.house.gov/committees/; www.senate.gov/pagelayout/committees/d_three_sections_with_teasers/committees_home.htm.

Table 6.2   2012 Congressional Committees with Ranking Women

Senate Committees	House Committees
Energy & Natural Resources	Rules
Commerce, Science & Transportation	Science, Space & Technology
Homeland Security & Government Affairs	Small Business
Small Business & Entrepreneurship	

Source: Derived from www.house.gov/committees/; www.senate.gov/pagelayout/committees/d_three_sections_with_teasers/committees_home.htm.

On average, women Representatives and Senators comprise 15 percent of the ranking members and chairs of the U.S. Congress.

Federal Appointments

Presidential appointments vary from federal judges to the leadership of the executive branch. While the president may appoint nominees, Congress must confirm them. On a rare occasion, Congress rejects a nominee or a nominee withdraws due to public and congressional pressure. A close examination reveals congressional rejections delineate along gender lines. Of the approximate 500 executive and 125 Supreme Court appointments before Congress in its history, eight (less than 2 percent) have either been rejected or withdrawn, primarily due to mounting criticism. Three of the eight have been women (38 percent), which is a high percentage, considering the few female appointees. These women include President Clinton's appointee Zoe Baird and President George W. Bush's appointees Linda Chavez and Harriet Miers.[18]

Judicial Appointments   Three of the nine Supreme Court Justices are currently women, or approximately one third of the bench. The 2013 court has the greatest representation of gender and ethnic diversity in its history. Throughout history, only 4 of the 119 Supreme Court Justices have been women. Of the 32 federal judges awaiting congressional confirmation, 9 are women. There are currently 341 women judges in the federal judiciary and 314 people of color.[19] In 2012, approximately 26 percent of women occupied federal judgeships.

Federal Cabinet Appointments   Since Franklin D. Roosevelt appointed the first female, Frances Perkins, to his cabinet in 1933, a total of 40 women have been named to these prestigious and highly visible positions. In 2012, there existed 16 cabinet appointments, including the Office of the Vice President, and seven cabinet-level appointees, including the President's Chief of Staff, for a total of 23 cabinet and cabinet-level appointments.[20] Prior to 2008, 22 cabinet and cabinet-level positions existed, when President Obama elevated the Ambassador to the United Nations to a cabinet-level position, making the seventh female appointment possible.

President Barack Obama appointed 4 of the 16-member cabinet positions to women during his first term in office—approximately 25 percent. He had also appointed three of the seven cabinet-level positions to women, or 42 percent. President Obama appointed eight women to active appointments, with one, Dr. Christina Romer, who was chairwoman of the Council of Economic Advisers, resigning within three months after speculated economic policy disagreements.[21] Seven women remained as cabinet and cabinet-level appointees. Acting Secretary of Commerce, Dr. Rebecca M. Blank, was not reflected in the total cabinet and cabinet-level positions because of her interim role in 2012. In total, President Obama had 30 percent of his cabinet as female during his first term. Women of color comprised 13.6 percent of President Obama's cabinet (one of the 16 cabinet members and one of the 6 cabinet-level positions.[22] To date, a woman has yet to hold three leadership positions: the Department of Defense, Department of Treasury, and the Department of Veterans Affairs.

During his second term, President Obama has appointed Administrator Gina McCarthy, to lead the Environmental Protection Agency, and Penny Pritzker, to lead the Department of Commerce. As a result, his cabinet includes three women in 2013, or 18 percent, and three cabinet-level officials, or 42 percent. President Obama has appointed only one woman of color in a cabinet-level position, and none in the cabinet. Acting Social Security Administrator Commissioner Carolyn Colvin is not reflected in the total 2013 figures because of her interim role.

Federal Agency Appointments   The public often pays little attention to agency appointments, and yet these appointments directly affect all Americans rather immediately. The various federal agencies set agendas and create, enforce, and adjudicate policies. Tremendous power lives with the agency head and within the agency. The following chart breaks down the demographic profile of senior agency leaders. Women constituted 26 percent of senior leadership roles on average across all governmental agencies in 2012.[23]

None of the major federal agencies had a representational number of women or women of color in senior leadership roles. The agencies with the poorest representation of both white women and women of color have had only one person of color or only one female agency head over the last 12 years. The six agencies with an average of 30 percent or more representation have had at least two persons of color and/or one or more females in the top agency position over the last 12 years, except two: Treasury and Social Security Administration (SSA).

The Department of the Treasury has had more than 31 percent female in senior leadership positions, and yet never had a female or person of color as the agency head. In seeking to understand why, we compared how employees of the Treasury and those in the SSA viewed their workplace. SSA was selected, because the agency has a large percentage of women employed but a small percentage of women in leadership roles.

The Office of Personnel Management conducted an employee satisfaction survey in May 2011, otherwise referred to as the Federal Employee Viewpoint Survey of the Social Security Administration, as mandated by federal regulations with all government agencies. SSA employees evaluated the organization very favorably overall. SSA demographic information showed the SSA was 68 percent female, 32 percent male, and 45 percent of employees identified as people of color. More than 55 percent of SSA employees completed the survey. Of the survey respondents, 66 percent were females, and 87 percent were in nonsupervisory roles. Approximately 45 percent were non-white or identified as people of color. OPM determined that questions with a positive response rate of 65 percent or higher indicated employees were very satisfied with their individual accomplishments and personal commitment to the agency. Responses that received a positive response rate of 35 percent or lower indicated that respondents were dissatisfied with promotions, hiring, and merit increases.

In examining the employee responses, my research team and I delineated a positive response rate of 50 percent or higher as positive, which is more generous than the delineation made by the government. We also delineated a negative response rate of 49 percent or lower. This delineation was made because of the statistical and representational significance of the survey respondents. In other words, if less than half of the respondents were dissatisfied, their responses are not as significant as those for whom dissatisfaction was found among the majority of respondents. We were hoping to explain the lack of women leaders in the SSA. SSA respondents reported:

- My work unit is able to recruit employees with the right skills. Negative-Neutral (44.8 percent)
- Promotions in my work unit are based on merit. Negative (37.3 percent)
- Pay raises depend on how well employees perform their jobs. Very Negative (21.5 percent)
- How satisfied are you with the opportunity of getting a better job in your organization? Negative-Neutral (45.5 percent)
- How satisfied are you with life-work programs (Life-Child Care/Life-Elderly programs and telecommuting/flexible work schedules) in your organization? Very Negative (22 percent)

Table 6.3   Federal Agency Appointments, 2006[24]

	Total # Senior Women	Total # Senior Men	Senior People of Color*	Total % Senior Women	2000 Agency Head a Woman?	2006 Agency Head a Woman?	2012 Agency Head a Woman?
Agriculture	126	353	83	25.7%	No	Yes	No
Commerce	138	536	75	25.7%	No***	No**	No
Education	64	97	27	39.8%	No/No**	Yes	No
Energy	114	483	86	19.1%	No**	No	No
EPA	114	221	49	34.1%	No	Yes	Yes**
Health & Human Services	705	1,657	420	29.8%	Yes	No	Yes
Housing & Urban Dev.	91	165	75	35.5%	No**	No**	No
Interior	99	264	81	27.3%	No	Yes	No**
Justice	1,245	2,915	651	30%	Yes	No**	No**
Labor	74	164	38	31.1%	Yes*	Yes	Yes**
NASA	106	457	89	18.8%	No	No	No**
Social Security	258	1091	186	19.1%	No	Yes	No
State	65	155	16	29.5%	Yes	Yes**	Yes
Transportation	126	320	73	28.2%	No*	Yes	No
Treasury	169	367	92	31.6%	No	No	No
Total Agency Representation	4,961	13,955	2,798	26.2%			

*Blacks, Asians or Pacific Islanders, Hispanic, American Indian or Alaskan Native.

**The department head also identified as a person of color.

*** Secretary Norman Mineta served as the Commerce's head for six months beginning July 2000–January 2001.

Source: Derived from www.opm.gov/feddata/html/2009/September/table26.asp; www.opm.gov/feddata/html/2009/September/table11.asp; www.opm.gov/feddata/html/2009/September/charts.asp; www.opm.gov/feddata/demograp/table2w.pdf; www.opm.gov/feddata/html/2009/September/table26.asp; www.opm.gov/feddata/demograp/table2w.pdf.

It is important to note that an average of 22 percent of survey respondents indicated that they were satisfied with life-work programs, and yet only 2 percent of survey respondents actually participated in such programs. This is significant because many claim that life-work programs are particularly important for women's advancement.

According to table 6.3, in a ranking of the top government agencies to work for, the Department of the Treasury ranked ninth while the SSA ranked higher in fourth place. Whereas SSA employees reported much higher levels of satisfaction with the type of work and their individual contributions, Treasury employees reported higher levels of satisfaction with promotion and merit increases. On average, Treasury employees reported 5 to 22.2 percent higher levels of satisfaction in areas related to promotions and hiring practices, and in particular, life-work programs such as alternative work schedules and telecommuting. These programs may have the greatest impact on female employees due to family responsibilities.[25] In addition, the Department of Treasury identifies a diverse workplace, opportunities for career advancement, and flexible schedules as key reasons to work for the agency. See Appendix II for specific Treasury language.

The distinction to be made in examining these administrative agencies is two-fold. On the one hand, women's leadership has been shown to increase when a female or at least two men of color headed the agency during the last 12 years. On the other hand, the SSA was the only agency with a female head during the last 12 years, yet it still had a low percentage of women leaders. Conversely, the Department of Treasury has never had a female or a man of color as its head, yet it has a high percentage of female senior executives. Employees directly reported differences in how their agency hires and promotes. Treasury employees indicated that performance drove promotion and hiring practices, whereas the SSA employees indicated that personal relationships drove such practices. Determining the role of hiring and promotions in women's leadership is an important area of future research, and it is examined in chapter 12.

COMPENSATION

Salaries for government employees are established by law and do not vary with the gender. But because women are still concentrated on the lower rungs of politics, on average, they will earn less over the span of their careers than men. For example, only 32 women in the history of the United States have been elected governor, and only one woman was among the 10 highest-paid governors, whose salaries ranged from $70,000 to $179,000 in 2010.[26]

POLITICAL DONORS AND LOBBYISTS

Americans have become very familiar with the high cost of running for office and the fundraising machine that surrounds top political campaigns. The machine usually refers to the origin of campaign contributions, which can often become rather convoluted and complex, particularly with the influx of PACs and lobbyists in political campaigns. Contributions and influence from PACs and lobbyists have a growing presence in U.S. politics.

To exclude this analysis would leave a gap in understanding the gender disparity in politics and government created by the lack of outside funding for women. Outside funding reflects campaign contributions given on behalf of and/or in support of a candidate and are provided in addition to a candidate's direct campaign fundraising. Data were compiled on three major areas of outside funding: PACs, parties, and lobbyists. On average, women receive 15.3 percent of campaign dollars.

More specifically, among the top 10 House candidates who received the most PAC dollars, no woman was represented.[27] Among the top 10 Senatorial candidates, two were women. In total, women received 11 percent of the top 10 PAC contributions in 2012.[28]

Among the 10 top U.S. Senate candidates who received the most PAC dollars, two women out of six Democrats received PAC dollars and zero women out of four Republicans. The dollars received by female candidates for Senate may explain the increase in elected female Senators.

Three of the top 10 candidates who received the most party dollars from both the House and the Senate were women receiving 15 percent total.[29] Since September 2012, the Democratic Party has contributed more to female congressional candidates than the Republican Party. In fact, Democrats distributed dollars almost evenly between male and female candidates, although they gave to fewer women than men. It is unclear why the Republican Party contribution was disproportionately low for female candidates. Historically speaking, more women officeholders have been Republican.

In expanding the criteria to the top 20 funded candidates, three were Democratic females, nine were Democratic men, and eight were Republican males.[30] In comparing all congressional candidates, only one female Republican, out of 17 total candidates, received party contributions for

House races. For the Senate, one woman received funds out of eight Republican candidates. In sum, 23 male Republican congressional candidates received party contributions, compared to two female candidates.[31] More Democratic lobbyists and their family members have supported female candidates than Republican lobbyists. Among the top 10 Democratic candidates, two were women (20 percent).[32] There was no Republican woman represented in the top ten. Among the 100 political candidates who received lobbyists, 52 were Democrats and 48 were Republican.[33] This data, based on 100 candidates, should be tracked and evaluated over the course of several years to better understand the correlative factors present, if any.

CONCLUSIONS

Women's underrepresentation in top political and governmental positions at the city, state, and federal levels creates an intellectual power gap in the United States, and ultimately is a detriment to the American people. Women's representation in politics and government can improve in some obvious ways:

• Challenge pundits, newspaper editors, and even family members and neighbors who suggest women make poor or emotional decisions and/ or are not equipped to hold political leadership roles.

• Hold media outlets and journalists accountable for their coverage of women leaders and candidates.

• Form networks and communities to support women in their bid for office.

• If you are a woman, run for political office. Expect unfair criticisms, but do not allow those criticisms to deride your campaign.

• Donate to and volunteer for women candidates that reflect your political views.

• A consolidated effort needs to be made to elect or appoint women to head offices never held by a woman before: Offices of the President and Vice President, Department of Treasury, Department of Veterans Affairs, and Department of Defense.

• A public awareness campaign should be launched bringing attention to the fact that women have remained stagnant in political and governmental leadership positions for more than a decade.

APPENDIX II

The following text is derived from the Department of the Treasury's Web site.

Top 10 Reasons to Work for Treasury[34]

Distinguished Mission: Treasury has a distinguished history dating back to the founding of our nation. Today, as the steward of U.S. economic and financial systems, Treasury is a major and influential participant in the global economy.

Influence on Policy: Treasury employees research, analyze and inform policy decision-makers on current and emerging economic issues facing the Nation. They collect the taxes that make government work, print the money, issue the checks, and keep track of the nation's debt. Your work plays a role in shaping the economy of our country.

Professional Work Environment: Our primary goal is to maintain the trust of the American people. Our work environment offers open communication and respect of individual contributions so employees are motivated and empowered to perform their job.

Public Service: Treasury challenges you—on your very first day—to ask yourself, "What can I do today to improve the lives of the American people?" Treasury employees work together to face and meet the economic challenges of our nation and serve the American people.

1. Learning and Growth: Energetic and talented employees work together to collaborate with one another to create a continuous environment of learning. As the nature of our work continues to change and grow, we work to ensure our employees are prepared to meet the challenge. You will have the opportunity to hit the ground running, learning and gaining experience every day.

2. Multi-Stage Career Opportunities: The Department and its bureaus have unique opportunities for professionals at any career level. Whether you're just starting out in your career or looking for a later career challenge as a bridge to retirement, we have a place for you.

3. Location, Location, Location: Treasury's headquarters is located in the heart of Washington, D.C., with offices on 15th and Pennsylvania, next door to the White House, a few blocks from the McPherson Square and Metro Center metro stations, and close to shops, museums, and restaurants. We have offices in most major cities across the country.

4. Flexible Schedules and Work/Life Balance: We recognize that each employee has unique personal interests and responsibilities to balance with a busy work schedule. In addition to 10 paid holidays, 13–26 vacation days (depending on service), and 13 days of sick leave each year, your manager may be able to offer you flexible work schedules and/or telework options to help you balance work and family.

5. Competitive Salaries and Benefits: We provide competitive salaries and benefits to include great health coverage and retirement plans, 401(k)-type investment plans including matching options, life and long-term care insurance, and flexible spending accounts. In addition to our salary and benefits package, we offer generous transit subsidies, on-site health offices, fitness centers, and child care programs.

6. Diversity: We recognize the value of a diverse workforce and strive to ensure an environment where every individual can advance to his or her full potential.

Diversity

A diverse workforce increases productivity and enhances the Department's ability to maneuver in an increasingly competitive market. To that end, the Department is committed to creating the conditions that allow its programs and activities to perform efficiently and effectively, while continuing to drive results through performance and cost-based decision-making, aligning resources to deliver outcomes, investing in, securing and leveraging information technology, closing skill gaps, recruiting and retaining a high performing workforce, and developing effective leadership. Therefore, managing diversity at the Department of the Treasury involves creating and maintaining a work environment that:

• Attracts the widest pool of talent;
• Provides opportunities for all employees to maximize their potential and contribute to the agency's mission; and
• Ensures all employees are treated with dignity and respect.

The Office of Civil Rights and Diversity (OCRD) in conjunction with the Office of Human Capital Strategic Management is charged with ensuring the recruitment and retention of a well-qualified diverse workforce to meet the current and emerging mission-related needs of the Department of the Treasury.

NOTES

1. Fox, R., and J. Lawless. (May 2008). "Why Are Women Still Not Running for Public Office?" *Brookings.* Accessed at http://www.brookings.edu/research/papers/2008/05/women-lawless-fox.

2. Anzia, S., and C. Berry. (2011). "The Jackie (and Jill) Robinson Effect: Why Do Congresswomen Outperform Congressmen?" *American Journal of Political Science* 55(3): 478–493.

3. Ibid., 484.

4. Ibid., 490.

5. Ibid.

6. Center for American Women and Politics. (2008). *Fact Sheet on Gender Differences in Voter Turnout.* Retrieved June 2012 from http://www.cawp.rutgers.edu/fast_facts/voters/documents/genderdiff.pdf.

7. File, Thom. (May 2013). "The Diversifying Electorate—Population Characteristics." *U.S. Census Bureau.* Accessed at http://www.census.gov/prod/2013pubs/p20-568.pdf.

8. Center for American Women and Politics. (2012a). Women of Color in Elective Office 2012. Accessed at http://www.cawp.rutgers.edu/fast_facts/levels_of_office/documents/color.pdf

9. Center for American Women and Politics. (2012a). Women of Color in Elective Office 2012. Accessed at http://www.cawp.rutgers.edu/fast_facts/levels_of_office/documents/color.pdf

10. National Conference of State Legislatures. (May 2012). *Women in State Legislatures: 2012 Legislative Session.* Accessed June 2012 from http://www.ncsl.org/legislatures-elections/wln/women-in-state-legislatures-2012.aspx

11. Ibid.

12. National Association for Women Justices. (2012). *2012 Representation of United States State Court Women Judges.* Accessed June 2012 at http://www.nawj.org/us_state_court_statistics_2012.asp

13. Center for American Women and Politics. (2012a). Women of Color in Elective Office 2012. Accessed June 2012 at http://www.cawp.rutgers.edu/fast_facts/levels_of_office/documents/color.pdf.

14. National Governors Association. (2013). Past Election Information. Accessed at http://www.nga.org/cms/elections.

15. Center for American Women and Politics. (2012a). Women of Color in Elective Office 2012. Accessed June 2012 at http://www.cawp.rutgers.edu/fast_facts/levels_of_office/documents/color.pdf.

16. Inter-Parliamentary Union. (2012). *Women in National Parliaments.* Accessed June 2012 at http://www.ipu.org/wmn-e/classif.htm.

17. Center for American Women and Politics (CAWP). (January 2012b). Women Mayors in U.S. Cities 2012. Accessed http://www.cawp.rutgers.edu/fast_facts/levels_of_office/Local-WomenMayors.php#Bypopulation.

18. U.S. Senate. (2012). *Nominations.* Accessed June 2012 at http://www. senate.gov/artandhistory/history/common/briefing/Nominations.htm#10; Women in Congress. (2012). *Historical Data: Women of Color in Congress.* Accessed June 2012 at http://womenincongress.house.gov/historical-data/women-of-color. html.

19. U.S. Courts. (2012). *History of the Federal Judiciary.* Accessed at http:// www.whitehouse.gov/administration/cabinet.

20. The White House. (2012). *The Cabinet.* Accessed at http://www.white-house.gov/administration/cabinet.

21. Associated Press. (2010). *Christina Romer Resigning: Top Obama Adviser Leaving Economic Council.* Accessed at http://www.huffingtonpost. com/2010/08/06/christina-romer-resigning_n_672984.html.

22. The White House. (2013). *The Cabinet.* Accessed at http://www.white-house.gov/administration/cabinet

23. Office of Personnel Management (OPM). (2011). *Federal Employment Viewpoint Survey.* Accessed at http://www.fedview.opm.gov/2011/Published/

24. Ibid.

25. Ibid.

26. Stateline. (April 2011). *On Average, Governors' Salaries Show Decline in Pay.* The Pew Charitable Trusts. Accessed at http://www.pewstates. org/projects/stateline/headlines/on-average-governors-salaries-show-decline-in-pay-85899375094.

27. Opensecrets.org. (2012a). *Top PAC Recipients.* Retrieved June 2012 from http://www.opensecrets.org/overview/toppac.php?cycle=2012&Display=S&Type=C2.

28. Ibid.

29. Opensecrets.org. (2012b). *Top 20 Recipients of Party Committee Funds.* Accessed at http://www.opensecrets.org/overview/pty2cand.php.

30. Ibid.

31. Ibid.

32. Opensecretes.org (2012c). *Top Recipients of Contributions from Lobbyists, 2012 Cycle.* Accessed at http://www.opensecrets.org/lobby/lobby_contribs. php.

33. Ibid.

34. U.S. Treasury. "Top Ten Reasons to Work for the Treasury." Accessed at http://www.treasury.gov/careers/Pages/Working-For-Treasury.aspx.

7

Military

The U.S. military's responsibilities have expanded and grown exponentially since the 1990s, and yet, its forces have shrunk in size. The U.S. military reflects just 1 percent of the total population, the smallest in several decades. Soldiers and troops, who once prepared for land, sea, and air defenses, now prepare for land, sea, air, terrorist, cyberspace, and border offenses and defenses. With declining rates of male volunteers, women's distinctive contributions have become even more critical on and off the battlefield abroad, domestically, locally, and in cyberspace. The percentage of female enlistees has quadrupled, and the percentage of female officers has tripled since 1979.

The interesting demographic shift among military officers may be the result of shifting warfare tactics. Warfare has shifted from hand-to-hand combat and battles on land to electronic (e) war. The term "e-war" reflects the role of technology in war, and in particular, how technology advances war with little hand-to-hand engagement with the enemy, which the military prohibited women from engaging in. In e-war soldiers carry out military operations from their desks.

In interviewing female officers in the military, they expressed their belief that very few military women were concern about combat restrictions, primarily because they believed women were already engaged in combat. Instead, their preference centered on a change in climate and prescribed gender roles overtly and covertly assumed by informal and formal policies; these are addressed in the conclusion at the end of this chapter. Nonetheless, it will be curious to examine how the lift on the combat prohibition for women affects women's leadership, if at all.

Another interesting facet to this chapter is the growing presence of women of color in the military, particularly African American women. While male enlistees and officers have decreased overall, women of color have steadily increased. Latina and Asian American women reflect a roughly equal representation compared to their male counterparts. A military recruiter explaining this trend indicated that the military has restricted enlistee requirements and is now prohibiting visible tattoos and those with criminal records. The recruiter posited that such restrictions had a particular impact on African American males, and proffered that the military provides a stable career trajectory, which appealed to many women of color, particularly African Americans.

HISTORY IN THE MAKING: WOMEN IN THE MILITARY FROM 1976 TO 2012

In 1976, the armed services permitted women to reach the rank of general and admiral. Two years later, the Marine Corps promoted the first woman to the rank of general. Nearly 20 years thereafter, in 1996, the Marine Corps selected the first woman for promotion to three-star rank, Lieutenant General Carol Mutter. Simultaneously, navy Vice Admiral Patricia Tracey was also selected for three-star rank and was promoted before Lieutenant General Mutter. In 2008, the first woman was promoted to a four-star general rank in the army, more than 10 years after the first three-star promotion occurred. Only in 2012 were the first African American females promoted to general rank, 36 years after women were permitted to serve as general and admiral.

The Air Force is the only branch of the Department of Defense in which nearly all jobs are open to women, and thus it leads the armed services with the largest percentage of females. Unlike the other branches, the Air Force does not have a ceiling on the number of women it can recruit. However, despite having the largest number of women recruits, the Air Force has the smallest percentage of female senior leaders of any of the military branches.

The following timeline captures a historical overview of significant military events that have allowed positions and opportunities to open up for women.

- **1976**
  - Women become eligible to become generals and admirals.
  - Women admitted to three major service academies.

- **1978**
  - First woman named brigadier general, General Margaret Brewer of the Marine Corps. It is important to note that General Brewer was promoted just one year after the Marine Corps disbanded the Women Marines Office.
- **1986**
  - First women test pilots in the U.S. Navy.
- **1991**
  - Congress repeals the ban against women serving in combat aviation, but not all services comply.
- **1993**
  - President Bill Clinton signs "Don't Ask, Don't Tell" policy into law, both forbidding the military from asking personnel about their sexual orientation and forbidding personnel from disclosing it.
- **1996**
  - First two women selected for and promoted to three-star rank in navy and Marine Corps.
- **1999**
  - First woman makes lieutenant general in air force.
- **2005**
  - First woman promoted to Air Force Academy Commandant of Cadets.
- **2006**
  - First woman makes vice commandant of Coast Guard.
- **2007**
  - First woman becomes commander of Naval Fighter Squadron.
  - First Latina woman promoted by Marine Corps as general, General Angelina Salinas.
- **2008**
  - Army promotes first woman, General Ann Dunwoody, to four-star general.
- **2011**
  - President Barack Obama repeals the "Don't Ask, Don't Tell" policy, which prohibited gays and lesbians from serving openly in the military.
  - Coast Guard admiral, Rear Admiral Sandra Stosz, becomes first female rear admiral in Coast Guard history.
- **2012**
  - Pentagon loosens restrictions on women in combat.

- The Marine Corps invited women to join in infantry training.
- Army promotes first openly gay woman, General Tammy Smith, as brigadier (one star) general.
- Air force promotes first four-star general, General Janet Wolfenbarger.
- Vice Admiral Michelle Howard becomes first African American woman promoted to vice admiral in the navy.
- First African American woman, Major General Marcia Anderson, promoted to rank of general by army.
- **2013**
  - Department of Defense removes the combat ban on women.

Positional Leadership and Influence

The military is composed of two distinct groups: officers and enlisted personnel. To become officers, individuals usually attend one of the service academies, enter an ROTC program in college, or go to officer candidate school. Enlisted personnel who decide to become officers must attend officer candidate school. Not many enlisted personnel choose to pursue careers as officers. Since 1973 when the draft ended, women's participation in the military has increased. The number of enlisted women rose from 2 percent to 14 percent, and commissioned officers have quadrupled from 4 percent to 17 percent.

In 2011, women still comprised 14 percent of active duty personnel but 17 percent of officers.[1] As shown in figure 7.1, from 1973 to 2010, active-duty enlisted women went from 42,000 to 167,000. The number of

Figure 7.1   Women in the Military, 1973–2010

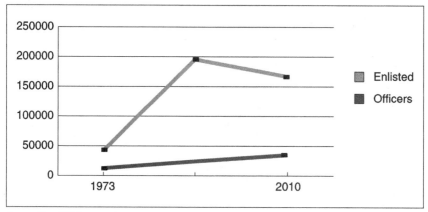

Source: Pew 2010.

Figure 7.2   Women's Military Rank and Grade, All Branches[2]

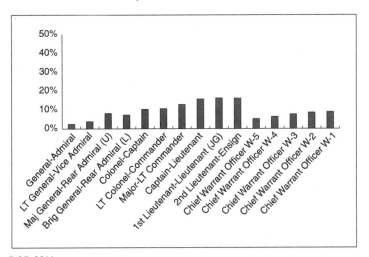

Source: DOD 2011.

women commissioned officers is greater in comparison to male commissioned officers (17 percent of women compared to 15 percent of men). As shown in figure 7.2, women comprise 5.38 percent of all generals and admirals in the armed services and 10 percent of all colonels. On average, women comprise 12.35 percent of leadership roles in the armed services, which includes all generals, admirals, colonels, *and* senior agency leaders.

In 2010, women comprised 8 percent of all veterans. However, among the veterans of post-terrorist attacks of September 11, 2001, women comprise 19 percent. By 2035, the number of female veterans is expected to grow another 15 percent to 34 percent.[3]

The military reports the demographics of its forces (figure 7.3) based on black, white, Asian, mixed/other races, and Hispanic or non-Hispanic ethnicities. In 2008, among males on active duty, 29 percent were men of color, and 46 percent of active duty females identified as non-white. Among officers, 32 percent of women identified themselves as non-white compared to 18 percent of male officers. In 2011, the percentage of active-duty females continued to be more racially diverse than the male force:

- 31 percent of women in service were African American compared to 16 percent of males
- 53 percent of active duty women were white compared to 71 percent of men.

Figure 7.3   Women in the Military Based on Race, 2010

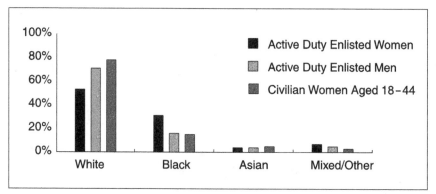

Source: Pew 2010.

Figure 7.4   Latina/Latino Ethnicity in the Military, 2010

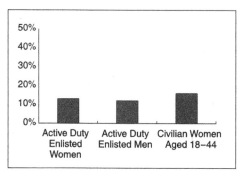

Source: Pew 2010.

Additionally, the percentage of men of color, like their white counterparts, has declined slightly.

The military distinguishes between race and ethnicity. Therefore, those who identify as Latina/Latino (figure 7.4) fall into a different category and are not included in the race percentages above.

Figure 7.5 shows that there exists a slightly higher *proportional* percentage of female than male commissioned officers in all branches of the military, with 17 percent of women versus 15 percent of men. It is important to note that while the percentage of female officers is higher than males, there exist more men because there are more male enlistees. This is most noticeable in the Army, where 18 percent of women are commissioned officers in comparison to 13 percent of men. In all other branches,

Figure 7.5   Women Officers in the Military, 2010

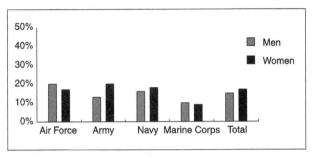

Source: AWV 2011.

Figure 7.6   Occupations in the Military, 2010

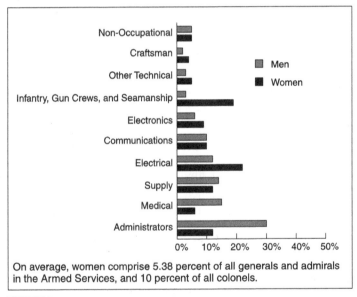

Source: AWV 2011.

the numbers show almost equal representation in the number of male and female commissioned officers.

According to figure 7.6, 30 percent of women serve in administrative roles.[4] Women's occupations within the military determine their salary and advancement. Following the trends seen in other sectors, female participation is quite low in areas such as infantry, which may have been due to the Department of Defense restrictions on women serving in combat roles.

The Department of Defense, under Secretary Leon Panetta, loosened restrictions on woman in combat in 2012, primarily as tank mechanics and field artillery radar operators. The Pentagon lifted its ban on women serving in combat in January 2013. This offers women the possibility of jobs previously denied to them for lack of frontline experience, which results in higher pay scale ranges and more opportunities for leadership. Some combat jobs immediately opened, while others are still being debated. Special operations detail, such as Navy SEALS and Army Delta Force, are still not open; however, the armed services must provide a ruling on those roles by January 2016.[5]

The Joint Chiefs of Staff recommended the new rule, which "overturns a 1994 rule prohibiting women from being assigned to smaller ground combat units."[6] This decision could open more than 230,000 jobs for women, most of them in the Army and Marine infantry units. As a result, the lifted restriction may stimulate more female enlistees and the proportional percentage of female leaders may be affected.

The impact of this decision on the advancement of females as military leaders is unclear at this time. When the military prohibited women from participating in combat occupations, they were unable to be promoted into top leadership roles that required combat service. Therefore, theoretically, this decision should have a positive effect on women's advancement. As an aside, women have been engaged in combat-related service, injuries, and so on spanning many decades, yet the military did not recognize this service. Women's career advancement had been restricted by the military's combat policy, which prevented women from serving in direct combat roles. Though women have been serving in combat-related roles, they have not been recognized as serving in combat, because of the ban.

As in other sectors, the lack of diversity and inclusion affects the overall effectiveness of the military. Table 7.1 captures the total number of women and men of color serving in the military. The Departments of Homeland Security and Veterans Affairs have the highest percentage of senior women leaders. In 2009, President Barack Obama appointed Arizona Governor Janet Napolitano to lead the Department of Homeland Security. This agency is a military-related agency charged with targeting domestic terrorism and security, and it remains the only agency with any military-related responsibilities to ever be led by a woman. Perhaps most noteworthy is that this cabinet secretary position is last of eighteen positions in line for succession to the presidency. The Department of Veterans Affairs is also a military-related agency charged with the management of military veterans' benefits. This cabinet secretary is second from the bottom.

Table 7.1 2006 Demographics on Military Leadership[7]

Military Department	Total # Senior Women	Total # Senior Men	Senior People of Color	Senior Women of Color	Senior Men of Color	Total % Senior Women	2001 Agency Head a Woman	2006 Agency Head a Woman?	2012 Agency Head a Woman?
Air Force	38	248	25	1	24	15%	No	No	No
Army	65	339	35	5	30	19%	No	No	No
Navy	109	656	66	9	57	17%	No	No	No
Defense	376	1786	188	38	150	21%	No	No	No
Homeland Security	115	398	71	16	55	29%	No	No	Yes
Veterans Affairs	249	868	179	53	126	29%	No	No	No
Total Average Agency Representation						22%			

Source: OPM 2009.

A closer examination of the two military-related agencies with the highest percentage of senior women leaders reveals three important points. First, among all executive agencies, the secretaries of Homeland Security and Veterans Affairs are the least powerful positions. Second, both agencies are civilian, which is arguably a reason why women are entrusted in senior leadership roles.

Third, there are two types of leadership positions: top executive and senior leaders. Department of Homeland Security has 41 top executives, including former Secretary Napolitano. Among the 41 leaders, 10 are women (24 percent). Conversely, the Department of Veterans Affairs, a department that has never had a women head, has 19 top executives, including the secretary, one of whom is a woman, or 5 percent. Having a woman leader seems to make a significant difference in the overall female representation among the senior leadership. This same correlation existed in other federal agencies as well. Each of these departments should be more closely examined to better understand existing practices and policies that may have contributed to female promotions in senior leadership positions.

Performance and Compensation

Collectively, armed services and other federal agencies were among the first employers to give women equal pay for equal work. Since 1901, when women began serving in the military, they have received the same compensation as men, based on rank and time in service (table 7.2). This is not to suggest that gender and/or family status does not play an indirect yet consequential role in promotion and, therefore, compensation. However, as with other business and professional sectors, the higher one rises, the more one earns. Because women are typically not reaching the top ranks, they are not earning top salaries. A relatively small number of women are promoted to the upper ranks of the military.[8]

Research shows that serving in the military offers women a better chance at obtaining a college degree than the civilian population. It is likely that a college education, in tandem with serving in the military, equates to fewer women living in poverty and being uninsured at almost every stage in their lives.[9]

CONCLUSIONS

The culture of the military transcends the armed services and impacts civilian culture. The military helps to define masculinity, and in many ways, has been at the forefront of many societal issues, including addressing sexual assault against women. The military has a responsibility to

Table 7.2   Monthly Salary by Rank, 2011[10]

Rank	Level	Monthly Pay with over 20 Years of Service
0–10	General/Admiral	$15,401
0–9	Lieutenant General/Vice Admiral	$13,470
0–8	Major General/Rear Admiral (U)	$12,762
0–7	Brigadier General/Rear Admiral (L)	$11,541
0–6	Colonel/Captain	$9,223
0–5	Lieutenant Colonel/Commander	$8,070
0–4	Major/Lieutenant Commander	$7,049
0–3	Captain/ Lieutenant	$6,039
0–2	First Lieutenant/ Lieutenant (Junior Grade)	$4,439
0–1	Second Lieutenant/Ensign	$3,503
Warrant Officers		
W-5	Chief Warrant Officer	$6,821
W-4	Chief Warrant Officer 4	$6,190
W-3	Chief Warrant Officer 3	$5,685
W-2	Chief Warrant Officer 2	$4,988
W-1	Warrant Officer 1	$4,702
Enlisted Personnel		
E-9	Sergeant Major/Master Chief Petty Officer/ Chief Master Sergeant /Master Gunnery Sergeant	$5,195
E-8	First Sergeant /Senior Chief Petty Officer/ Senior Master Sergeant /Master Sergeant/ Senior Chief Petty Officer	$4,568
E-7	Sergeant First Class/Chief Petty Officer/ Master Sergeant /Gunnery Sergeant/Chief Petty Officer	$4,189
E-6	Staff Sergeant /Petty Officer First Class/Tech Sergeant	$3,533
E-5	Sergeant /Petty Officer Second Class/Staff Sergeant	$2,966
E-4	Corporal/Specialist/Petty Officer Third Class/ Senior Airman	$2,326
E-3	Private First Class/Seaman/Airman First Class/Lance Corporal	$1,950
E-2	Private/Seaman Apprentice/Airman/Private First Class	$1,645
E-1	Private/Seaman Recruit/Airman Basic	N/A

Source: BLS 2011.

not only create a world-class institution but also to help set standards of culture and norms in U.S. civilian society. Moreover, women leaders are essential to the long-term sustainability and ingenuity of the U.S. armed services. To establish a critical mass of women in the military, the services must work to attract and retain women in significantly larger numbers.

- First and foremost the Department of Defense's Advisory Committee on Women should be heeded and recommendations offered need to be adopted accordingly.
- The Department of Defense should open all units and military occupations to women as well as men. Build qualifications on certain physical skills and intellectual requirements based on the needs of the position rather than a blanket exclusion of a gender. This recommendation will only be useful if promotion is used proportionally for both males and females. Females, despite performance to the contrary, often have to overcome presumptions and biases against them as able leaders.
- As military leaders are promoted, the expectations and demands of spouses, or more accurately wives, creates an uneven playing field for female leaders. Male spouses do not have the same expectations and duties as female spouses, which inherently places women leaders at a disadvantage. A culture needs to be created that does not assume the male or female leader is married, which will also help to address the disadvantages presented to single parents.
- Direct public appeals to join military service toward young women, as well as men. While the active duty military is predominantly male, women should be encouraged to choose military service as a career and should be actively recruited.
- Navy, Air Force, and ROTC should increase the number of both scholarships and placements offered to women at service academies. Whereas a balanced gender demographic is important, do not restrict placements based on gender. Develop new outreach efforts to encourage more women to apply to the service academies and seek ROTC scholarships.
- Each of the armed services should foster a military culture that demands respect for all service members and punishes those who violate sexual harassment and assault rules. Military leaders must hold all violators of laws and policies against sexual assault and harassment strictly accountable and foster a culture in which peer pressure helps to uphold

these rules. New reporting procedures for sexual assault in 2005 have encouraged more women to report violence against them to the proper authorities than in prior years. The effectiveness and continued improvement of the procedures, from accusation to prosecution, needs review accordingly.

- The Department of Defense should ensure that both military women and men receive a full range of benefits and health care services, including attention to and treatment for post-traumatic stress disorder; full access to reproductive health care services, including abortion; and appropriate attention to their health care needs as veterans. Additionally, servicemen should be allowed the same amount of leave time as servicewomen receive for maternity leave. The current paternity leave is only 10 days. This is a disservice to our men, but also disadvantages women, because women are seen as putting in less time in active duty because they get more maternity leave time than their male counterparts.

- The armed services need to continue studying ways to better accommodate parenting and family issues, such as taking a pause in service, without career penalties for both women and men.

- To better track and understand the rate of promotion, a qualitative study needs to be conducted focused on each career field within each branch. Only in this way will a clearer picture emerge in understanding the rate of promotion for servicewomen compared to servicemen.

- Finally, the armed services should continue to work to eradicate sexual assault and harassment within the various military entities.

NOTES

1. Patten, E., and K. Parker. (2011). "Women in the U.S. Military: Growing Share, Distinctive Profile." *Pew Social and Demographic Trends.* Accessed at www.pewsocialtrends.org.

2. Department of Defense (DOD). (2010). Population Representation in the Military Forces Fiscal Year 2010. *U.S. DOD.* Accessed at http://prhome.defense.gov/rfm/MPP/ACCESSION%20POLICY/PopRep2010/summary/PopRep-10summ.pdf.

DOD. (September 2011). Female Active Duty Military Personnel by Rank/Grade. *U.S. DOD.* Accessed at http://siadapp.dmdc.osd.mil/personnel/MILITARY/rg1109f.pdf.

3. America's Women Veterans (AWV). (2011). "Military Service History and VA Benefit Utilization Statistics." *National Center for Veterans Analysis and*

Statistics. Accessed at www.va.gov/vetdata/docs/SpecialReports/Final_Womens_
Report_3_2_12_v_7.pdf.

4. Ibid.

5. Baldor, L. (January 23, 2013). "Women in Combat: Leon Panetta Removes Military Ban, Opening Front-Line Positions." *The Huffington Post*. Accessed at http://www.huffingtonpost.com/2013/01/23/women-in-combat_n_2535954.html.

6. Ibid.

7. Office of Personal Management (OPM). (2006). Race/National Origin Distribution of Federal Civilian Employment. *Office of Personal Management*. Accessed at http://www.opm.gov/feddata/demograp/Table2mw.pdf and http://www.opm.gov/feddata/demograp/table2w.pdf.

8. Bureau of Labor Statistics (BLS). (August 2011). Military Rank and Employment for Active Duty Personnel, April 2011. Table 3. *Occupational Outlook Handbook*. United States Department of Labor. Accessed at http://www.bls.gov/ooh/military/military-careers.htm#pay.

9. Service Women's Action Network (SWAN). (February 2011). Women in Combat: The Facts. Accessed at http://servicewomen.org/wp-content/uploads/2011/01/97-WIC-fact-sheet.pdf.

10. BLS. (August 2011). Military Rank and Employment for Active Duty Personnel, April 2011. Table 3. *Occupational Outlook Handbook*. United States Department of Labor. Accessed at http://www.bls.gov/ooh/military/military-careers.htm#pay.

8

Academia

In the United States, more women and white males are attending college and obtaining degrees than ever before. Female students comprised 57 percent of all enrollments and received 59 percent of all degrees conferred in 2009–2010.[1] The representation of white males in higher education continues to grow, as well. Men of color and older males, however, are not attaining degrees at the same rate as their white and female counterparts. The rate of women's participation in colleges and universities exceeds the rate of males because women of color and older women are obtaining degrees at higher rates than their male counterparts. In 2010, women of color comprised approximately 20 percent of total female enrollments.[2] Women of color also comprised 17.6 percent of post-baccalaureate enrollment.[3] Additionally, the "knowledge economy" has precluded the ability of many to earn a sustainable wage without a degree. Women typically cannot earn as much as men without a college degree, causing more women to pursue higher education to increase their earning capacity.

The percent of women completing college and graduate school has increased significantly since 1969–1970, when women received 43 percent of the undergraduate degrees (associate and bachelor's), 40 percent of the master's degrees, 5 percent of the first professional doctoral degrees (primarily law and medicine), and 13 percent of the research doctoral degrees.[4] In 2009–2010, women received 62 percent of associate degrees, 57 percent of bachelor's degrees, 60 percent of master's degrees, and 52 percent of doctoral and first professional degrees.[5]

Recent years have yielded great and in many instances fair criticisms of the growing costs of higher education. Many critics debate whether the cost of a degree outweighs the intended benefit. Yet, it remains that earning a college degree increases the salaries of both men and women considerably. However, the pay gap between males and females with a college degree is greater. In fact, the pay gap between males and females without a high school diploma is $98 per week, while the pay gap between male and female college graduates is $344 per week on average.[6]

POSITIONAL LEADERSHIP AND IMPACT

This high level of participation in education among women does not translate to comparable representation in leadership roles or compensation in academia, as other sectors have also demonstrated. Women still lag significantly behind men.

Academic leaders can have far-reaching influences on the universities they represent, as well as within other institutions where their scope of research and knowledge can affect much of society. In particular, female academicians can influence many arenas outside their home institutions in their pursuit of generating knowledge and educating leaders of tomorrow. Like all educators, their reach surpasses a discipline or field. The perspectives brought by diverse women, representing various socioeconomic, racial, and ethnic backgrounds, encourage a breadth and depth of ideas that cannot be found in a homogeneous pool.

Studies have shown that when prominent female academics are involved in research, for example, it can affect the nature of both the questions that are asked and the findings.[7] Women in tenured faculty positions and top-level leadership positions in academia provide all students, faculties, and staff with an important opportunity to work with talented women. In addition, women serve as powerful role models and mentors to younger women beginning their path to leadership. Thus, these leaders will foster the best and brightest of not only this generation but for several generations to come.

The academic institutions in the United States are vastly different, varying from public and private community colleges, to for-profit and nonprofit baccalaureate, master, and doctoral universities. The data in this chapter measuring women's leadership in academia focus on doctoral, nonprofit institutions, which have historically been the most influential in the industry (see table 8.1).

Measuring performance across sectors proved a challenging task. Academia presents one of the more uniformed and comprehensive sectors where high-level performance indicators were widely available and

Table 8.1   Overview of Academic Leadership

Position at Nonprofit Doctoral Institutions	% of Women	% of Men
Full Professors	8%	27.4%
Board Trustees	28.4%	71.6%
Presidents	22%	78%
Chief Academic Officers	32%	68%
Average % of Women Leaders in Academia	**24.53%**	**64.7%**

accessible for comparison. Doctoral institutions with "very high research activities" as classified by the Carnegie Foundation for the Advancement of Teaching also appear among most, if not all, university rankings. Such institutions maintain their prestige by securing national, highly selective grants and awards through faculty research. In comparing the national research grants and awards, we found that women outperform men 55.88 percent to 44.12 percent in national research awards and grants, despite their low positional representation among the faculty ranks.

FACULTY

Table 8.2 and figures 8.1 and 8.2 track women and men by both faculty rank and institution type. There are four types of institutions: doctoral granting (herein after doctoral), master's degree granting (master's), baccalaureate granting (baccalaureate), and associate's degree granting (associate's). There are five faculty ranks: lecturer, assistant professor, associate professor, professor, and other, including instructor and adjunct. By examining faculty ranks, a closer, more nuanced examination reveals where women sit in leadership. At first glance, the percentage of women appears to have nearly reached parity with men in faculty positions. A closer examination reveals that the types of institutions and the positions women occupy differ from men. Women have high representation among community college and baccalaureate institutions. However, female faculty representation declines significantly among doctoral institutions, particularly in tenure and tenure-track positions.

Additionally, women are more likely than men are to have entry-level faculty positions, such as lecturers and/or instructors. Among instructors and lecturers, women comprise 50 percent, which has remained virtually unchanged since 2006.[8] Since 2006, there has also been a slight increase in women joining faculties at most institution types (an average increase of 2.7 percent).[9]

Table 8.2 Distribution of Faculty by Rank, Gender, and Institution Type, 2010–2011 (Percent)

Institution/ Academic Rank	Doctoral		Master's		Baccalaureate		Associate's with Ranks		Associate's without Rank		Total (except Associate's without ranks)	
	Men	Women	Men	Women	Men	Women	Men	Women	Men	Women	Men	Women
Professor	27.4	8	19.2	9.1	19.1	9.6	14.9	14	N/A	N/A	23.1	8.9
Associate	16.1	10.4	15.5	12.3	16.1	12.8	11.9	12.9	N/A	N/A	15.7	11.4
Assistant	12.3	10.7	13.6	15	15.2	16.3	11.6	14.7	N/A	N/A	13.1	13
Instructor	2.1	3.1	2.4	4.3	2.5	4	6.8	8.3	N/A	N/A	2.5	3.9
Lecturer	3.5	4.3	3.1	3.9	1.4	1.7	1.6	2.2	N/A	N/A	3	3.7
No Rank	1	1.1	0.7	0.8	0.7	0.6	0.4	0.6	47.4	52.6	0.9	0.9
TOTAL	62.4	37.6	54.6	45.4	55	45	47.3	52.7	N/A	N/A	58.2	41.8

Source: AAUP 2011, p. 33.

At *all* degree-granting institutions, women account for 43 percent of the full-time faculty, up from 32 percent in 1991.[10] While this increase may suggest substantial progress on its face, the disaggregation of data depicts a more accurate picture. Women are underrepresented among the more prestigious faculty ranks, particularly among tenure-track, doctoral institutions. As was found in all other sectors, the number of women steadily declines as they move up the ranks. Moreover, these nontenure-track jobs often exclude women from attaining the top ranks of academia because, historically, universities have tended to pull from tenured faculty to fill top administrative positions. Stated differently, the representation of women at colleges and universities differs significantly by institution type. Women make up 38 percent of faculty at doctoral institutions, 45 percent of faculty at master's and baccalaureate institutions, and 53 percent of faculty at associate institutions. Overall, there are more male faculty members than female ones in all categories, except among associate degree-granting institutions. In this category—often the least paid and least recognized—women outnumber men 52.7 percent to 47.3 percent.

Figure 8.1   Distribution of Faculty by Rank, Gender and Institution Type, 2010–2011

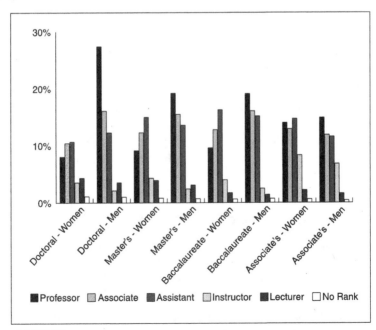

Source: AAUP 2011.

Figure 8.2   Average Faculty Distribution by Rank, Gender and Institution Type, 2010–2011

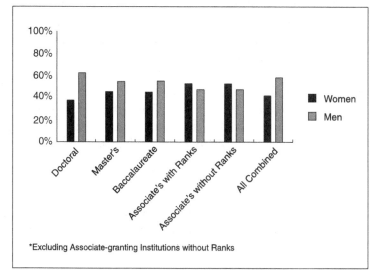

Source: NCES 2011.

At the most valued and rewarded tenure-track positions within doctoral, nonprofit or public institutions, women comprise just 29.1 percent compared to 55.8 percent of men. The remaining percentage of faculty includes nontenured faculty, such as lecturers. Typically, institutions will promote from within these ranks to university administrators, leaving women at a strong disadvantage for advancement.

In 2009, women of color accounted for 11.4 percent of instructors (up from 10.7 in 2007), 10.6 percent of assistant professors (up from 9.9 percent in 2007), and only 3.7 percent of professors (compared to 3.4 percent in 2007).[11] Overall, women of color accounted for 8.1 percent of all faculty members in 2011, a slight increase from 7.5 percent in 2007.[12]

Faculty Compensation and Performance

Women's salaries not only lag behind their male counterparts in academia, the gap has remained virtually unchanged since the 1980s. Again, this finding becomes apparent when the data is disaggregated. In 1980–1981, women faculty earned 81.6 percent of the salary of men, compared to 82.4 percent in 2010–2011.[13] Looking more closely, a notable difference exists in the wage gap between two- and four-year institutions. At both public and private four-year institutions, women make close to 20 percent less than their male counterparts (18.4 percent for public and 18.9 percent for private institutions), which has not changed significantly over the last three decades. By contrast, at two-year public institutions, women make 4 percent less than their male counterparts, and at two-year private institutions, women actually make slightly more (2.2 percent) than their male counterparts.[14]

The pay gap for women also differed between types of institutions. Doctorate-granting institutions showed the greatest pay gap between women and men, while the smallest showed among the associate's degree-granting institutions. This finding is not unlike the pay discrepancies in other sectors, where women earn less as the power and influence of the position grows.

At doctoral institutions, female faculty members earn 78 percent of their male counterparts' pay, compared to 88 percent at master's-granting institutions, 90.2 percent at baccalaureate-granting institutions, and 95.9 percent at associate's-granting institutions.[15] The pay gap among doctoral institutions mirror the disparity found in the 1980s, and in some cases, the gap was wider in 2010 than in 1989.[16] More specifically, as figure 8.3 shows, in 2010–2011, female professors earned an average of 85.8 percent of male earnings regardless of institution type. Female associate and assistant professors fared better, earning 93 percent of what their male counterparts earned (figure 8.4). When institution type is not considered, the pay gap between women and men narrows.

Figure 8.3   Average Faculty Salary by Gender and Institution Type, 2010–2011[17]

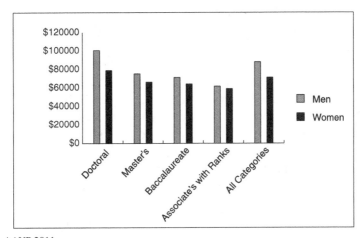

Source: AAUP 2011.

Figure 8.4   Female's Salaries as Percent of Men's Salaries by Academic Rank[18]

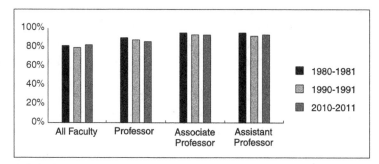

Source: NCES 2011.

There exists a larger pay gap between men and women in four-year institutions than in two-year institutions. In fact, the gap is greatest among women in public, four-year doctoral institutions. This is unusual compared to other sectors. Typically salaries in public institutions and entities are regulated by policy and monitored accordingly, thereby creating fewer discrepancies. Yet, in academia, greater discrepancies exist for women.

One erroneous justification could be made that women at public institutions hold fewer top faculty positions and therefore, in total, did not earn as much as men. This is an invalid comparison because my team and I compared apples to apples, meaning similar faculty ranks and institutions were compared. The status of women in four-year doctoral institutions is particularly concerning and should continue to be monitored.

To measure industry performance standards, my team and I collected 2011–2012 data on the top 60 largest awards from six national entities shown in figure 8.5: National Institutes of Health (NIH), National Science Foundation (NSF), National Endowment for the Humanities (NEH), Institute for Education Sciences (IES) and the National Education Association (NEA), and the Social Science Research Council (SSRC). By examining award recipients and grantees, we sought to understand which gender could claim national recognition on meritorious grounds. Tenure-track faculty at doctoral institutions comprises the vast majority of award recipients and grantees, and women have the lowest representation among those positions. Therefore, what the data uncovered is particularly surprising and noteworthy as evidenced in figure 8.6. Women researchers comprised 55.88 percent of top grantees in academia's prestigious national awards in education, health, humanities, and science. Despite the underrepresentation

Figure 8.5   Top Ten Funded Researchers in 2011–2012[19]

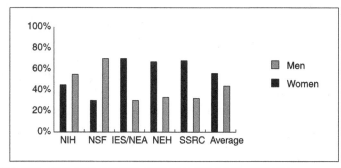

Source: NSF 2012a; NEA 2012; IES 2012; NEH 2012; SSRC 2012; NIH 2012.

Figure 8.6   2012 Gender Comparison of Tenure Faculty and Actual Grants/Awards Recipients

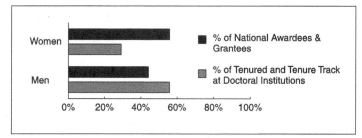

Source: AAUP 2011; NSF 2012a; NEA 2012; IES 2012; NEH 2012; SSRC 2012; NIH 2012.

of women in tenure-track positions at doctoral institutions, they claim the majority of the nation's top academic accolades and emerge as the nation's leaders in academic awards and recognition.

Women researchers comprised the lowest percentage among the NIH (45 percent) and the NSF (30 percent) awardees. However, when considering the low percentage of female tenured and tenure-track faculty in such disciplines at doctoral institutions (29.1 percent), women's science and health contributions exceed expectations.

COLLEGE AND UNIVERSITY PRESIDENTS

Approximately two-three decades ago, women began climbing to the top leadership position in higher education—the presidency or the chancellorship. During the last five years, the number of female presidents remained constant at about 500. Women's representation increased from 23 percent of presidents in 2006 to 26.4 percent in 2011.[20] However, the percent at types of institutions shifted slightly. As shown in figure 8.7, women presidents at associate's degree-granting institutions rose from 29 percent in 2006 to 33 percent in 2011. At doctoral-granting institutions, women gained 22 percent in 2011, up from 15 percent in 2006.

Currently, women lead five of the eight Ivy League institutions: Brown, Dartmouth, Harvard, Princeton, and University of Pennsylvania. All of the Ivies, except for Cornell, were chartered before the American Revolution, and it took more than 200 years to name a woman to the top position. University of Pennsylvania was the first to take this significant step in 1994 and again in 2008. Brown earns the distinction of naming the first African American female president among the Ivies.

When examining the source of college and university presidents, a couple of key facts emerge. First, more than a third of presidents typically come from provost or chief academic officer positions (CAOs). In fact, several studies support the finding that chief administrative officer positions are a primary way in which women attain the presidency.[21] Among all college and university presidents, 52 percent of female presidents and 42 percent of males were previously provosts or CAOs.[22]

In other words, CAO positions are the primary way in which women attain the presidency, and therefore, it is more important for women to emerge through the traditional faculty ranks than men. Yet, on average, women make up only 40 percent of CAOs, with fewer women CAOs in the higher paid, more influential institutions. More specifically, women comprise 50 percent of CAOs at community colleges, 38 percent at the master's level, 37 percent at baccalaureate institutions, and 32 percent at doctorate-granting institutions.[23]

Figure 8.7   Female Presidents by Academic Institution Type[24]

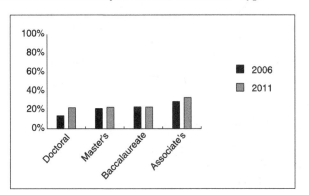

Source: COOK 2012.

Second, sitting presidents are most likely to fill presidential vacancies at other institutions. Based on these facts, some apparent disadvantages emerge for women. The number of presidents 61 years of age and older has significantly increased to approximately 60 percent.[25] A convergence of retirees could bring a wave of presidential retirements in 5 to 10 years, and as a result, present more opportunities for women. However, because the most common candidates for the presidency are other presidents and women comprise only one quarter of all sitting presidents, there exists another obvious disadvantage for women, when and if, such an opportunity presents itself in 10 years.

Women of color have made significant strides in attaining college presidencies, comprising 17 percent of all positions in 2011 compared to 4.4 percent in 2006. Among African American presidents, 34 percent are women, topping the 25 percent who are female among white presidents. Women are 39 percent of all Hispanic presidents, 20 percent of all Asian American presidents, and 54 percent of all other or multiple races. Racial discrepancies become more evident when salaries are examined.

Historically, women without families were often perceived to be better able to manage leadership responsibilities. Caution should be exercised, however, whenever attempting to understand why women are not adequately represented in leadership roles, as the previous two sources for hiring presidents showed. Demographic information, such as marital status, does not adequately explain the makeup or motivation of presidents, particularly those who also identify as lesbian or gay. In a recent survey, 71.6 percent of female academic institution presidents reported being married, presumably to men (an increase from 63 percent in 2006) compared with 90.1 percent of male presidents, presumably to women. Of female presidents, 72 percent have children compared to 90 percent of males.[26]

Presidential Compensation and Performance

Neither private nor public institutions pay women comparably to their male counterparts. Only one female appeared in each of the top 10 lists for highest paid presidents in private institutions and in public institutions. The only woman on the public institutions list, Mary Sue Coleman of the University of Michigan, ranked number five. On the list of top paid presidents from private institutions—and the only person of color on either list—Shirley Ann Jackson of Rensselaer Polytechnic Institute ranked number seven.[27]

INDUSTRY DISTINCTIONS

The disaggregation of data shows that it is not enough to examine how many female professors, CAOs, presidents, and trustees exist in the United States. When understanding where women sit in leadership, it is essential to understand the institutions that hold power and influence and how well women are performing compared to their male counterparts in those positions. Moreover, academic institutions foster power and influence through research distinctions. The most prestigious of those distinctions includes an invitation from the Association of American Universities (AAU). AAU invites a discrete number of research universities into its membership ranks, and all of the distinguished or high performing universities identified are AAU members. Among the 11-member AAU executive cabinet, only two are women (18 percent).[28] The NIH and the NSF distribute highly sought after research dollars and are among the largest of such entities. For these reasons, women's leadership roles at institutions with the largest NIH and NSF funding were examined (see tables 8.3 and 8.4).

Table 8.3   Gender of Leadership Positions of Top NIH-funded Academic Institutions, 2012

Institution	President/ Chancellor	Provost/CAO	Average % of Female Leaders
Johns Hopkins University	Male	NA*	
University of California– San Francisco	Female	Male	
University of Michigan, Ann Arbor	Female	Male	
University of Pennsylvania	Female	Male	
University of Washington	Male	Female	
University of Pittsburgh	Male	Female	
University of California– San Diego	Male	Male	
University of North Carolina at Chapel Hill	Male	Male	
Yale University	Male	Male	
% Female Leaders	**33.33%**	**22.22%**	**27.78%**
National % Females Leaders	**22%**	**32%**	**27%**

Source: NIH 2012.

Table 8.4   Gender of Leadership Positions of Top NSF-funded Academic Institutions, 2012

Institution	President/ Chancellor	Provost/CAO	Average % of Female Leaders
University of Illinois at Urbana-Champaign	Female	Male**	
University of California–Berkley	Male	Male	
Cornell University	Male	Male	
California Institute of Technology	Male	Male	
University of Texas at Austin	Male	Male	
University of Wisconsin–Madison	Female	Male	
University of Washington	Male	Female	
University of Michigan, Ann Arbor	Female	Male	
Columbia University	Male	Male	
Massachusetts Institute of Technology	Male	Male	
% Female	**30%**	**20%**	**25%**
National % of Female Leaders	**22%**	**32%**	**27%**

** The only male who appears to be a man of color.
Source: NSF 2012b.

On average, the percentage of female leaders in each of the top funded institutions is higher than the overall percentage of female presidents nationally. For example, women comprise 33 percent of presidents among the top NIH-funded institutions and 30 percent at NSF-funded institutions compared to the national average at doctoral institutions of 22 percent. Yet, the percentage of female CAOs or provosts among the top-funded NIH and NSF institutions was lower.

For the purposes of determining women's leadership among the top 10 institutions in the United States, researchers of this report relied on *U.S. News and World Report* and the *Washington Monthly.* There exist many more third-party reviewers. Yet the public relies most frequently on the *U.S. News and World Report* college and university rankings, and the *Washington Monthly* ranks institutions based on their societal and

Table 8.5   **Gender of Leadership Positions in Top 10 Ranked Academic Institutions in the United States by** *U.S. News and World Report,* **2012**[29]

Institution	President/ Chancellor	Provost	Average
Harvard University	Female	Male	
Princeton University	Female	Male	
Yale University	Male	Male	
Columbia University	Male	Male	
University of Chicago	Male	Male	
Massachusetts Institute of Technology	Male	Male	
Stanford University	Male	Male	
Duke University	Male	Male	
University of Pennsylvania	Female	Male	
California Institute of Technology	Male	Male	
Dartmouth College	Female*	Male	
% of Female	**36%**	**0%**	**16.11%**
National % of Female	**22%**	**32%**	**27%**

* In July 2013, Dartmouth's president was replaced by a man.

Source: US News 2012.

student impact. Among third-party reviewers such as these, the percentage of noted institutions with women leaders varies compared to the national averages. It is important to note that at the time of the rankings release, female chancellors and/or presidents comprised 36 percent of *U.S. News and World Report*'s rankings (table 8.5), nearly 10 percentage points higher than the national average. In the *Washington Monthly's* rankings (table 8.6), women leaders fell below the national average, an unusual trend for in the majority of sectors, women were better represented among the top industry performers than in the industry as a whole.

BOARDS OF TRUSTEES

Women are still a distinct minority among college and university boards of trustees, where the responsibility and power to hire and fire key academic leaders and determine the strategic direction of an institution rests. As shown in figure 8.8, since 2004, the percentage of women on boards has

Table 8.6   Gender of Leadership Positions in Top 10 Ranked Academic Institutions in the United States by *Washington Monthly*, 2012[30]

Institution	President/ Chancellor	Provost	Average Female %
University of California– San Diego	Male	Male	
Texas A&M	Male	Female	
Stanford University	Male	Male	
University of North Carolina at Chapel Hill	Male	Male	
University of California–Berkeley	Male	Female	
University of California–Los Angeles	Male	Male	
Case Western Reserve University	Female	Male	
University of Washington	Male	Female	
University of California–Riverside	Male	Male	
Georgia Institute of Technology	Male	Male	
% of Female	**10%**	**30%**	**20%**
National % of Female	**22%**	**32%**	**27%**

Source: Washington Monthly 2012.

Figure 8.8   Percent of Female Board Members by Year

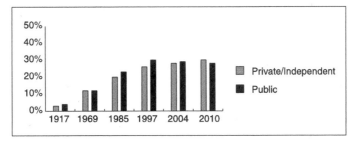

Source: AGB 2004; AGB 2010a; AGB 2010b.

decreased slightly from 29 percent to 28.4 percent in 2010.[31] There has been a steady decline since 1997, when college and university boards reached their high of 30 percent women.[32] Although women's representation on private boards has increased by 1.8 percent since 2004, men still outnumber women on private college and university boards by more than two to óne, or 69.8 percent to 30.2 percent as of 2010.[33] Since 1997, the percentage of women on public boards has decreased from a high of 30 percent to 28 percent in 2010.

Conversely, people of color were better represented on public boards than on private boards in 2010, and they are steadily increasing on both. The percentage of trustees of color on private boards has increased from 11.9 percent in 2004 to 12.5 percent in 2010.[34] A similar increase can be found on public boards, with people of color representing 23.1 percent in 2010, up from 21.3 percent in 2004.[35]

CONCLUSIONS

- The governing board and the senior staff should annually review the institution's commitment to diversity to see how well it is working.
- Identify, support, and advance women to become CAOs, provosts, and senior executives. These positions are stepping-stones to the presidency for women.
- Look beyond sitting presidents in order to increase the pool of potential presidential selections. Because women are more likely to have followed a nontraditional career path, the best candidates may come from farther afield.
- Review hiring, promotion, and tenure policies to ensure they are fair and equitable and do not disproportionately encumber women. For example, if the majority of nontenure-track positions do not have equal standing in promotion, and women predominantly occupy these positions, then the university must critically evaluate its hiring process.
- Evaluate the lack of tenure-track hires and consider how promotion may not be uniformly administered.
- Insist that pools of candidates for faculty and senior leadership positions be highly qualified *and* diverse. Women cannot get hired if they are not in the pool of candidates.
- Diversify search committees for presidential, senior leadership, and faculty positions. Often diversification on the committee helps ensure a search will be expanded to the broadest range of qualified candidates.
- Make certain search committees have data on the status and benefits of diverse candidates.

- If universities hire search firms, they should ensure the firms have a reputation for providing diverse pools of candidates.
- Public institutions should pay particular attention to the declining number of women leaders. Among all the sectors, academia is the only one that has this trend. Typically, public organizations, entities, and offices have a better representation of women overall.
- Private, two-year colleges had a virtually non-existent pay gap. The only parity that existed among any institutional type, and in any sector. These institutions, however few, should be examined to learn more about their equitable approaches.

NOTES

1. National Center for Education Statistics (NCES). (2012). Digest of Educational Statistics 2011, p. 289. U.S. Department of Education, Washington, D.C. Accessed at http://nces.ed.gov/pubs2012/2012001.pdf.

2. NCES. (2011). The Condition of Education 2011. U.S. Department of Education, Washington, D.C. Accessed at http://nces.ed.gov/pubs2011/2011033.pdf.

3. Ibid.

4. U.S. Census Bureau. (2012). Statistical Overview of the United States: 2012. Accessed atwww.census.gov/compendia/statab/cats/labor_force_employment_earnings/labor_force_status.html.

5. NCES. (2012). Digest of Educational Statistics 2011, p. 289. U.S. Department of Education, Washington, D.C. Accessed at http://nces.ed.gov/pubs2012/2012001.pdf.

6. Bureau of Labor Statistics (BLS). (2011). Household Data Annual Averages 11: Employed persons by detailed occupation, sex, race, and Hispanic or Latino ethnicity. Accessed at http://www.bls.gov/cps/cpsaat11.pdf.

7. Curtis, J., and M. West. (2006). AAUP Faculty Gender Equity Indicator 2006, p. 4. American Association of University Professors. Accessed at http://www.aaup.org/NR/rdonlyres/63396944-44BE-4ABA-9815-5792D93856F1/0/AAUPGenderEquityIndicators2006.pdf.

8. American Association of University Professors (AAUP). (2011). "It's Not over Yet: The Annual Report on the Economic Status of the Profession 2010–2011." Retrieved from http://www.aaup.org/NR/rdonlyres/17BABE36-BA30-467D-BE2F-34C37325549A/0/zreport.pdf.

9. Ibid.

10. NCES. (2011). The Condition of Education 2011. U.S. Department of Education, Washington, D.C. Accessed at http://nces.ed.gov/pubs2011/2011033.pdf.

11. Ibid.

12. Ibid.

13.   Ibid.

14.   Ibid.

15.   AAUP. (2011). "It's Not over Yet: The Annual Report on the Economic Status of the Profession 2010–2011." Retrieved from http://www.aaup.org/NR/rdonlyres/17BABE36-BA30-467D-BE2F-34C37325549A/0/zreport.pdf.

16.   Ibid.

17.   Ibid.

18.   NCES. (2011). The Condition of Education 2011. U.S. Department of Education, Washington, D.C. Accessed at http://nces.ed.gov/pubs2011/2011033.pdf.

19.   Institute for Education Science. (2012). U.S. Department of Education, Washington, D.C. Accessed at http://ies.ed.gov/funding/grantsearch/index.asp?mode=1&sort=1&order=1&searchvals=University&SearchType=or&checkaffiliation=on&checkprincipal=on&slctAffiliation=0&slctPrincipal=0&slctYear=2012&slctProgram=0&slctGoal=0&slctCenter=0&FundType=1&FundType=2.

National Education Association (NEA). (2012). Grantees. NEA. Accessed at http://www.neafoundation.org/pages/past-grantees/?tab=1&grades=Higher+Education.

National Endowment for Humanities (NEH). (2012). Accessed at http://www.neh.gov/search/content/2012%20grants.

National Institutes of Health (NIH). (2012). NIH Reporter. U.S. Department of Health and Human Services. Accessed at http://projectreporter.nih.gov/reporter_SearchResults.cfm?icde=13931503.

National Science Foundation (NSF). (2012a). Discoveries Search Results. National Science Foundation. Accessed at http://www.nsf.gov/discoveries/disc_search_results.jsp?queryText=&date_slct=3&fromDate=01%2F01%2F2012&award=&nsf_org=all&subj=0&prio_area=0&prog_slct=0&prog=&begin_year=&end_year=&investigator=&inst_slct=1&inst=University&rsch_loc=&st_code=any&beenhere=yes&Submit.x=20&Submit.y=5.

NSF. (2012b). Award Summary: Top 50 Institutions FY 2011. National Science Foundation. Accessed at http://dellweb.bfa.nsf.gov/Top50Inst2/default.asp.

Social Science Research Council. (2012). SSRC Fellows around the Globe. Social Science Research Council. Accessed at http://www.ssrc.org/fellowships/map/.

20.   Cook, S. (May 2012). Women Presidents: Now 26.4% but Still Under-represented. Women in Higher Education, 21(5):1–3. Accessed at http://www.wihe.com/printBlog.jsp?id=36400.

21.   American Council on Education (ACE). (March 2009). *ACE Survey: Few CAOs Wannabe President*.18(3).

22.   Cook, S. (May 2012). Women Presidents: Now 26.4% but Still Under-represented. Women in Higher Education 21(5): 1–3. Accessed at http://www.wihe.com/printBlog.jsp?id=36400.

23.   ACE. (March 2009). *ACE Survey: Few CAOs Wannabe President* 18(3).

24.   Cook, S. (May 2012). Women Presidents: Now 26.4% but Still Under-represented. Women in Higher Education, 21(5): 1–3. Accessed at http://www.wihe.com/printBlog.jsp?id=36400.

25. Ibid.

26. Ibid.

27. Chronicle of Higher Education. (2009). Highest Paid Private College Presidents, 2009. Accessed at http://chronicle.com/article/Public-Pay-Landing/131912/; Chronicle of Higher Education. (2011). Highest-Paid Public-College Presidents, 2011 Fiscal Year. Accessed at http://chronicle.com/article/Executive-Compensation/129979/.

28. American Association of Universities, AAU Leadership. Accessed at https://www.aau.edu/about/article.aspx?id=8376.

29. U.S. News and World Report. (2012). *Best Colleges and Universities Rankings 2012*. Accessed at http://colleges.usnews.rankingsandreviews.com/best-colleges/rankings/national-universities

30. Washington Monthly. *National University Rankings* 2012. Washington, D.C. Accessed at http://washingtonmonthly.com/college_guide/rankings_2012/national_university_rank.php.

31. Association of Governing Boards (AGB). "2011 Policies, Practices, and Composition of Institutionally Related Foundation Board: Executive Summary." Accessed at http://agb.org/sites/agb.org/files/u3/AGB_Foundation_Board_Exec_Summary.pdf.

32. AGB. (2010a). "2010 Policies, Practices, and Composition of Governing Boards of Public Colleges and Universities: Executive Summary." Accessed at http://agb.org/sites/agb.org/files/u3/2010PublicBoardCompositionSurveySumm ary.pdf.

33. AGB. (2010b). "2010 Policies, Practices, and Composition of Governing Boards of Independent Colleges and Universities: Executive Summary." Accessed at http://agb.org/sites/agb.org/files/u3/2010IndependentBoardCompositionSur vey%20Summary.pdf.

34. Ibid.

35. AGB. (2010a). "2010 Policies, Practices, and Composition of Governing Boards of Public Colleges and Universities: Executive Summary." Accessed at http://agb.org/sites/agb.org/files/u3/2010PublicBoardCompositionSurveySumm ary.pdf.

9

K–12 Education

It is no surprise that women dominate primary and secondary education (K–12), holding the majority of teacher positions across most subject areas. As shown in figure 9.1, since 1961, the percentage of male and female teachers has remained relatively constant. Women have outnumbered men 70 percent to 30 percent. Over the last decade, the number of teachers in the United States has steadily increased. Among the 3.7 million teachers,[1] public schools employ the vast majority. Among all teachers (table 9.1), 83 percent were white, 14 percent were black or Hispanic, 1 percent identified as Asian, and 2 percent as other.[2] When just examining secondary schools, the difference between male and female teachers is not as great. In fact, figure 9.2 shows that the percentage of men exceeds the percentage of women in certain teaching professions, such as physical education and social studies. There exist more female teachers in mathematics and science than males.[3] Specific demographic breakdowns follow with 2011 statistics shown in figures 9.3 and 9.4.

There are an estimated 1,884,000 elementary teachers in the United States and 1,344,000 secondary teachers.[4] In 2003–2004, there were 3.3 million teachers.[5] Among private schools, women comprised 74 percent of teachers, 39 percent were under the age of 40, and 38 percent had a master's degree or higher.[6] In public schools, women comprised 59 percent of secondary teachers, an increase from 57 percent in 2003–2004.[7] In 2007–2008, 76 percent of public school teachers were female, or 2,584,000 women to 821,000 men.[8] Among the 76 percent, 44 percent were under the age of 40, and 52 percent had a master's degree or higher.[9] In private secondary schools, females represented 53 percent of teachers, or 362,000 women to 127,000 men.[10]

Yet, as positions rise in stature and power, the number of women leaders declines. Often the erroneous assumption is that women also make up the majority of K–12 leadership—a logical conclusion, since women make up roughly 76 percent of teachers. Women hold approximately 44 percent of public school principal positions.[11] In other words, men comprise 56 percent of the leadership and 24 percent of the workforce.

Figure 9.1   Gender Distribution of Public School Teachers, 1961–2006 (Percent)

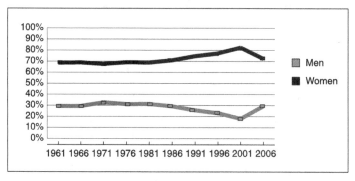

Source: Synder and Dillow 2011.

Figure 9.2   Gender of Public School Teachers (Grades 9–12) by Field of Main Teaching Assignment, 2007–08

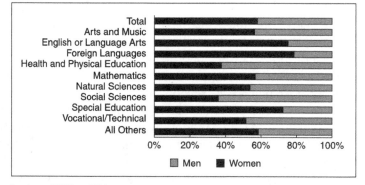

Source: Synder and Dillow 2011.

Table 9.1　K–12 Teachers by Gender and Race, 2011

Position	Total Employed in Thousands	% Women	% Black or African American	% Asian	% Hispanic or Latino
Education Administrators	853	65.2%	13.3%	2.9%	6.5%
Postsecondary Teachers	1.355	46.2%	7.3%	10.1%	4.8%
Preschool & Kindergarten Teachers	707	97.7%	14.5%	2.8%	12.7%
Elementary & Middle School Teachers	2.848	81.7%	9.8%	1.6%	8.0%
Secondary School Teachers	1.136	58.0%	7.4%	2.1%	6.9%
Special Education Teachers	388	85.4%	8.0%	1.8%	6.8%
Other Teachers & Instructors	812	62.6%	8.0%	3.9%	7.3%
Librarians	198	86.2%	10.1%	2.6%	3.9%
Teacher Assistants	950	92.2%	14.3%	2.6%	14.9%

Source: BLS 2012a.

Figure 9.3   Percentage of Male and Female Teachers, 2011

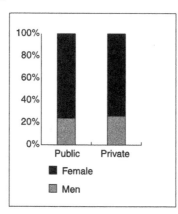

Source: U.S. Census 2012c.

Figure 9.4   Percentage of Women in Teaching Occupations, 2011

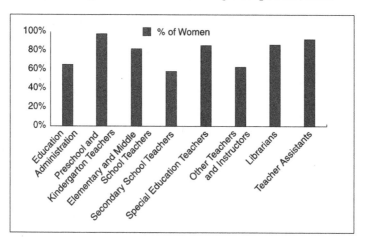

Source: BLS 2012a.

TEACHER COMPENSATION

On average, male teachers earn only slightly more than female teachers in public schools. Figure 9.5 shows the average male salary was $50,560 compared to $49,230 for women.[12] In private schools, the pay gap is much greater (a common finding throughout most sectors), with the average annual male salary of $40,380 compared to the average female salary of $34,700.[13]

In the public schools, the pay gap is greatest among teachers classified as "other teachers," meaning they are entry-level, temporary, and/or

Figure 9.5   Average Annual Teacher Salaries, 2010

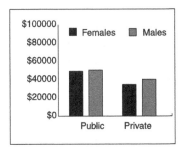

Source: U.S. Census 2012a.

Figure 9.6   Female Educator's Earnings as a Percentage of Men's, 2010

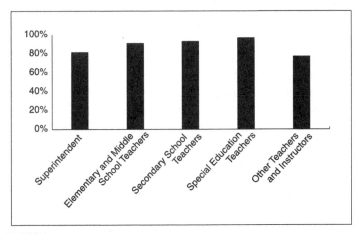

Source: BLS 2011.

Figure 9.7   Median Weekly Earnings of Educators by Year

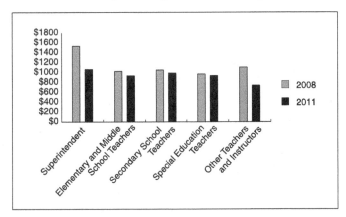

Source: BLS 2012b.

assistant teachers. I posit that this salary inequity is the result of discretion-ary pay, unlike the permanent, full-time teachers represented by unions and/or standard salary prescription. There is the greatest parity among the elementary, middle, and secondary school teachers (figures 9.6 and 9.7), confirming the role of unions in ensuring greater salary equity. It is impor-tant to emphasize that while the salary gap is not as great as some indus-tries, it is still not equitable.

POSITIONAL LEADERSHIP AND INFLUENCE

By averaging the total number of school board members, principals, superintendents, and chief state education officers (tables 9.2–9.6), women comprise 30 percent nationally. A closer examination of the last decade in the teaching profession reveals that women have inched up in leadership roles. From 1999–2000 to 2007–2008, the percentage of female principals increased from 52 to 59 percent at public elementary schools and from 22 to 29 percent at public secondary schools.[14] Female superintendents increased from 13.2 percent in 2000 to 24.1 percent in 2010.[15] In the public schools, the pay gap is greatest among superinten-dents. Women superintendents earn just 81.4 percent of what their male counterparts earn.

Among the largest school districts, there exists greater gender parity than in medium or small districts. This is a similar finding to other indus-tries, such as radio and business, suggesting that larger markets embrace

Table 9.2   Female Principals, 2000 vs. 2008

School Level	1999–2000	2007–2008
Public Elementary	52%	59%
Public Secondary	22%	29%

Source: Aud et al. 2012.

Table 9.3   Superintendents by Gender, 2000 vs. 2010

Gender	2000	2010
Male	86.8%	75.9%
Female	13.2%	24.1%

Source: AASA 2010.

Table 9.4   Gender of School Boards, 2002[16]

Gender	Percentage
Male	61.1%
Female	38.9%

Source: Hess 2002.

Table 9.5   Gender Composition of School Boards, 2002

Gender	Large Districts (25,000+)	Medium Districts (5,000–24,999)	Small Districts (less than 5,000)	All Districts
Male	55.6%	60.1%	63.3%	61.1%
Female	44.4%	39.9%	36.7%	38.9%

Source: Hess 2002.

Table 9.6   Chief State School Officers by Gender, 2013[17]

	Name
Alabama	Thomas Bice
Alaska	Mike Hanley
Arizona	John Huppenthal
Arkansas	Tom Kimbrell
California	Tom Torlakson
Colorado	Robert Hammond
Connecticut	Stefan Pryor
Delaware	Mark Murphy
District of Columbia	Hosanna Mahaley*
Florida	**Pam Stewart**
Georgia	John Barge
Hawaii	**Kathryn Matayoshi**
Idaho	Thomas Luna
Illinois	Christopher Koch
Indiana	Tony Bennett
Iowa	Jason Glass
Kansas	**Diane DeBacker**
Kentucky	Terry Holliday
Louisiana	John White
Maine	Stephen Bowen
Massachusetts	Mitchell Chester

(Continued)

Table 9.6   Chief State School Officers by Gender, 2013 (*Continued*)

	Name
Michigan	Michael Flanagan
Minnesota	**Brenda Cassellius**
Mississippi	**Lynn House**
Missouri	Chris L. Nicastro
Montana	**Denise Juneau**
Nebraska	Roger Breed
Nevada	James Guthrie
New Hampshire	**Virginia Barry**
New Jersey	Christopher Cerf
New Mexico	**Hanna Skandera**
New York	John King
North Carolina	**June Atkinson**
North Dakota	Wayne Sanstead
Ohio	Michael Sawyers
Oklahoma	**Janet Barresi**
Oregon	Rudy Crew
Pennsylvania	Ronald Tomalis
Rhode Island	**Deborah Gist**
South Carolina	Mick Zais
South Dakota	Melody Schopp
Tennessee	Kevin Huffman
Texas	Robert Scott[1]
Utah	Larry Shumway
Vermont	Armando Vilaseca
Virginia	Patricia Wright
Washington	Randy Dorn
West Virginia	James Phares[2]
Wisconsin	Tony Evers
Wyoming	Cindy Hill
% Female	**29%**

* Hosanna Mahaley stepped down in 2013, and therefore, was not included in the overall numbers.
[1] Texas has withdrawn from the Council of Chief State School Officers (Cavanagh 2011).
[2] Phares replaced fired state chief Jorea Marple in January 2013.
Source: CCSSO 2012.

women leaders more readily than smaller ones. Perhaps a similar mentality exists in smaller districts and private schools. When insulated, less diverse markets cannot shift paradigms as quickly, and as a result, are still operating from antiquated modalities.

PERFORMANCE

Female leaders are better represented among the top-performing elementary (figure 9.8), middle, and high school principals in the United States as a whole. As shown in table 9.7, *U.S. News and World Report* determined the highest performing high schools by examining state proficiency standards, how well schools prepared students for college, and the performance of historically marginalized and low-income students. The National Association of Elementary School Principals (NAESP) also evaluated the performance of principals across the United States.[18] As shown in figure 9.9, on average, female principals outperform their male counterparts by 55 percent to 45 percent among the top 10 performing schools in the United States.

Figure 9.8   Class of 2012 Most Distinguished Elementary School Principals

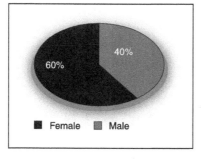

Source: NAESP 2012.

Figure 9.9   Comparison of Top Principals to All Principals by Gender, 2012

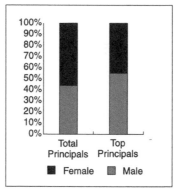

Source: US News 2012.

Table 9.7 Top 10 Performing High Schools in the United States, 2012[19]

School	Location	Principal	School District Superintendent	# Members on Board of Trustees/ Education	# Women on Board of Education	% Women on Board of Education
School for the Gifted & Talented	Dallas, TX	F. Michael Satarino	Mike Miles	9	4	44.4%
Thomas Jefferson High School for Science & Technology	Alexandria, VA	Evan Glazer	Jack D. Dale	12	8	66.7%
School of Science and Engineering Magnet	Dallas, TX	**Jovan G. Wells** (woman of color)	Mike Miles	9	4	44.4%
University High School	Tucson, AZ	**Elizabeth Moll**	John J. Pedicone	5	1	20.0%
International Academy	Bloomfield Hills, MI	**Lynne Gibson**	**Vickie L. Markavitch**	7	4	57.1%
BASIS Tucson	Tucson, AZ	Jason Shorbe (Head of School)	John J. Pedicone	5	1	20.0%

School	Location	50% Female Principals	20% Female District Superintendents			School Boards are Female
Oxford Academy	Cypress, CA	Kathy Scott	Elizabeth I. Novack	5	3	60.0%
Pacific Collegiate School	Santa Cruz, CA	Archie Douglas	Gary Bloom	6	3	50.0%
International School	Bellevue, WA	Jennifer Rose	Justin (Tim) Mills	5	2	40.0%
High Technology School	Lincroft, NJ	Kevin D. Bals	Timothy M. McCorkell	4	0	0.0%
Totals/Average		50% Female Principals	20% Female District Superintendents	67	30	44.8% School Boards are Female

Source: *US News* 2012.

CONCLUSIONS

- Private schools need to pay particular attention to the pay disparity between their male and female teachers and set forth actionable goals to improve the discrepancy.
- All schools need to remedy the pay disparity between male and female superintendents.
- Hiring firms and search committees need to acknowledge that only 30 percent of leaders are female, in light that 75 percent of teachers are female, is grossly disproportionate. Such firms and committees must begin to help guide schools and districts to more equitable hiring and promotion practices. Even when considering the misleading explanations as to why there are not more female leaders (i.e., lifestyle preferences and choices) does not even begin to account for the disproportionate percentage and gap in leadership.
- Districts should adopt performance-based measurements to drive salaries and promotions, thus lessening the influence of gender bias.
- Every district should assess the salaries of their male and female leaders to ensure pay remedies and equities.
- The education sector lacks recent school board demographic information. The most recent study was conducted in 2002, and therefore, is more than 10 years old.

NOTES

1. National Center for Education Statistics (NCES). (2009). Common Core of Data (CCD). *NCES*. Accessed at http://nces.ed.gov/ccd/

2. NCES. (2009). CCD. *NCES*. Accessed at http://nces.ed.gov/ccd/

3. Snyder, T., and S. Dillow. (2012). Digest of Education Statistics 2011. *National Center for Education Statistics, Institute of Education Sciences*, p. 62. U.S. Department of Education. Washington, D.C. Accessed at http://nces.ed.gov/pubsearch/pubsinfo.asp?pubid=2012001

4. Snyder, T., S. Dillow, and C. Hoffman. (2008). Digest of Education Statistics 2007. *National Center for Education Statistics, Institute of Education Sciences*. U.S. Department of Education. Washington, D.C. Accessed at http://nces.ed.gov/pubsearch/pubsinfo.asp?pubid=2008022

5. NCES. (2009). CCD. *NCES*. Accessed at http://nces.ed.gov/ccd/

6. Snyder, T., and S. Dillow. (2012). *Digest of Education Statistics* 2011, p. 61. National Center for Education Statistics, Institute of Education Sciences.

U.S. Department of Education. Washington, D.C. Accessed at http://nces.ed.gov/pubsearch/pubsinfo.asp?pubid=2012001.

7. Aud, S., Hussar, W., Johnson, F., Kena, G., and Roth, E. (2012). *The Condition of Education 2012 (NCES 2012-045)*. National Center for Education Statistics. U.S. Department of Education. Washington, D.C. Accessed at http://nces.ed.gov/pubsearch

8. Bureau of Labor Statistics (BLS). (2011). Table 18. Median usual weekly earnings of full-time wage and salary workers by detailed occupation and sex, 2010 annual averages. U.S. Bureau of Labor Statistics. Accessed at http://www.bls.gov/cps/wlf-table18-2011.pdf.

BLS. (2012a). BLS Household Data Annual Averages. Table 11. Employed Persons by Detailed Occupation, Sex, Race, and Hispanic or Latino Ethnicity. U.S. Bureau of Labor Statistics. Accessed at http://www.bls.gov/cps/cpsaat11.pdf.

BLS. (2012b). Table 39. Median weekly earnings of full-time wage and salary workers by detailed occupation and sex. U.S. Bureau of Labor Statistics. Accessed at http://www.bls.gov/cps/cpsaat39.pdf.

9. Snyder, T., and S. Dillow. (2012). *Digest of Education Statistics 2011*, p. 59. National Center for Education Statistics, Institute of Education Sciences, U.S. Department of Education. Washington, D.C. Accessed at http://nces.ed.gov/pubsearch/pubsinfo.asp?pubid=2012001.

10. BLS. (2011). Table 18. Median usual weekly earnings of full-time wage and salary workers by detailed occupation and sex, 2010 annual averages. U.S. Bureau of Labor Statistics. Accessed at http://www.bls.gov/cps/wlf-table18-2011.pdf.

BLS. (2012a). BLS Household Data Annual Averages Table 11. Employed Persons by Detailed Occupation, Sex, Race, and Hispanic or Latino Ethnicity. U.S. Bureau of Labor Statistics. Accessed at http://www.bls.gov/cps/cpsaat11.pdf

BLS. (2012b). Table 39. Median weekly earnings of full-time wage and salary workers by detailed occupation and sex. U.S. Bureau of Labor Statistics. Accessed at http://www.bls.gov/cps/cpsaat39.pdf.

11. Snyder, T., and S. Dillow. (2012). *Digest of Education Statistics 2011*, p. 61. National Center for Education Statistics, Institute of Education Sciences, U.S. Department of Education. Washington, D.C. Accessed at http://nces.ed.gov/pubsearch/pubsinfo.asp?pubid=2012001.

12. U.S. Census Bureau. (2012a). Table 255. Public Elementary and Secondary School Teachers—Selected Characteristics: 2007 to 2008. U.S. Census Bureau. Accessed at http://www.census.gov/compendia/statab/2012/tables/12s0256.pdf.

U.S. Census Bureau. (2012b). Table 256. Public Elementary and Secondary Schools—Number and Average Salary of Classroom Teachers, 1990 to 2009, and by State, 2009. U.S. Census Bureau. Accessed at http://www.census.gov/compendia/statab/2012/tables/12s0255.pdf.

13. U.S. Census Bureau. (2012c). Table 266. Private Elementary and Secondary School Teachers—Selected Characteristics: 2007 to 2008. U.S.

Census Bureau. Accessed at http://www.census.gov/compendia/statab/2012/tables/12s0265.pdf.

14. American Association of School Administrators (AASA). (December 2010). The American School Superintendent: 2010 Decennial Study. Accessed at http://www.aasa.org/content.aspx?id=458.

15. The gender differences in leadership style were highlighted in a meta-analysis of gender and the effectiveness of leaders in a study by Eagly and Johnson in 1990. They concluded: "The strongest evidence we obtained for a sex difference in leadership style occurred on the tendency for women to adopt a more democratic or participative style and for men to adopt a more autocratic or directive style" (247). The study found that female principals:

- Decrease when going from elementary to middle to high school among both private and public schools: elementary (73.5%), middle school (41.3%), high school (29.8%).
- Provide more instructional support than males, who were focused on management issues.
- Are concerned with student achievement and have an inclination to listen to others.

Another important finding is that regardless of gender, students of male teachers perform worse than students of female teachers on high stakes test scores in reading, mathematics, and writing among fourth graders in the State of Washington (Guramatunhu-Mudiwa and Bolt 2012).

16. Hess, F. (2002). School Boards at the Dawn of the 21st Century. National School Boards Association. Accessed at http://www.nsba.org/Board-Leadership/Surveys/SchoolBoardsattheDawnofthe21stCentury.pdf.

17. Cavanagh, S. (June 22, 2011). Texas Pulling Out of Council of Chief State School Officers. *Education Week.* Accessed at http://blogs.edweek.org/edweek/state_edwatch/2011/06/post_5.html; Council of Chief State School Officers (CCSSO). (2012). Meet the Chiefs. *CCSSO.* Accessed at http://www.ccsso.org/Who_We_Are/Meet_the_Chiefs.html.

18. National Association of Elementary School Principals (NAESP). (2012). Class of 2012 National Distinguished Principal. Accessed at http://www.naesp.org/class-2012-national-distinguished-principals.

19. U.S. News and World Report. (2012). National Rankings: Best High Schools. *U.S. News.* Retrieved from http://www.usnews.com/education/best-high-schools/national-rankings; Information on school officials and board members is taken from each school district's Web site.

10

Nonprofits and Philanthropy

The nonprofit sector consists of an entity or organization that is neither part of government nor generates a profit. In general, nonprofit organizations comprise voluntary, independent, or nongovernmental agencies, associations, and foundations.[1] Most nonprofits fall into one of the following categories: charitable, advocacy, political, religious, educational, scientific, or literary. Some of the nonprofit fields, such as education, are so large and influential that we analyzed them separately in this book.

The nonprofit sector is one of the fastest-growing parts of the economy representing the third largest employing industry "behind only retail trade and manufacturing."[2] In 1994, there were 1.1 million recognized nonprofits, employing 5.4 million people. By 2007, the number of nonprofits had grown by more than 50 percent to 1.64 million nonprofits, employing 8.7 million people.[3] In 2010, 1.96 million nonprofits were employing 10.7 million paid workers, accounting for 10.1 percent of private employment in the United States.[4] By 2011, however, the economic crisis impacted the nonprofit sector, resulting in nonprofit numbers falling to 1.63 million in total. More specifically, health professionals, educators, other professionals, health technicians, administrative support workers, and service occupations account for the majority of paid workers in the nonprofit sector. Women continue to dominate the nonexecutive staffing of the nonprofit sector, with no significant change in the last five years.[5] In 2005, women made up nearly 75 percent of the 8.4 million employees.[6] Despite their overwhelming presence in staff positions, women are underrepresented in the top leadership positions, holding only 45 percent of all

CEO positions in 2009. As shown in figures 10.1 and 10.2, when examining the largest organizations with budgets in excess of $25 million, women represent only 21 percent of leaders.[7] In addition, women CEOs continue to earn less than their male counterparts.

NONPROFITS

Positional Leadership and Influence

Women form a majority of the workers in development, education, human resources, marketing, and public relations. But that dominance disappears in the higher ranks of nonprofits. In 2008, only 1 in every 10 females in nonprofit organizations held a senior leadership role, compared with 1 in 5 males.[8] Women's representation at the top is significantly less than their

Figure 10.1   CEOs Budgets Under $25 Million, 2011

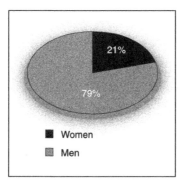

Source: GuideStar 2011.

Figure 10.2   Percent Female and Male Employees

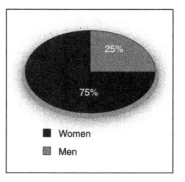

Source: GuideStar 2011.

presence in the nonprofit sector as a whole. The smallest organizations saw the largest percentage of female leaders, with that number quickly declining as budgets grew. In 2008, women held more than 63.7 percent of the top positions (executive/senior staff) in organizations with budgets under $250,000; 50 percent with budgets below $1 million; less than 32 percent with budgets between $5–$10 million; 26 percent with budgets between $11–$50 million, and only 16 percent in nonprofits with budgets more than $50 million.[9]

Table 10.1 shows that between 2006 and 2009, the overall percentage of women leaders in the nonprofit sector has decreased more than two percentage points—from 46 percent to 43.9 percent. There was a decrease in 11 out of the 14 top leadership positions, or approximately 79 percent of leadership positions. Additionally, there was a decrease in CEOs in six out of the nine budget sizes (table 10.2), or 67 percent of the budget categories. Figures 10.3–10.5 show that female representation and compensation in CEO positions decline as budget size increases. In no categories do females earn comparable salaries to their male counterparts.

Compensation and Performance

Women in nonprofit CEO positions receive, on average, 80 percent of their male counterpart's salary. Of the 26 nonprofit executives with salaries higher than $1 million in 2006, not one was a woman. The average annual salary for a female CEO was $73,244, while the comparable figure for a male CEO was $111,273—a 34.2 percent pay gap. In 2009, the gap noticeably decreased but still lingered, with the average CEO salary for women at $166,410 compared to a male's salary of $210,305—an approximate 20 percent pay gap.[10] Female CEOs managed to shrink the pay gap even though there were fewer female CEOs overall.

Yet, when examining organizations by budget size, women's pay has decreased. The pay gap has increased in four out of the nine budget categories. Specifically, at nonprofits with budgets in excess of $50 million, women CEOs made an average of $293,672 in 2006, compared with $395,886 for male CEOs—a difference of more than $100,000 or a gap percentage of 23 percent. In 2009, the difference in pay gap grew slightly, with women earning $507,447 compared to men's average salary of $658,713, or 24.6 percent. The pay gap in organizations with budgets between $1 million to $2.5 million increased from 16 percent in 1999 to 22 percent in 2009. The pay gap among organizations with budgets between $250,000 and $500,000 increased from 13.4 to 14.8 percent in 2009. Even among the smallest nonprofits, with budgets of $250,000 or less, where female

Table 10.1 Top Positions in Nonprofits by Gender, 2006–2009

Position	# Females in 2006	# Males in 2006	% Females in 2006	# Females in 2009	# Males in 2009	% Females in 2009	Decrease Between 2006 and 2009?
CEO/Executive Director	20,456	25,148	45%	30,292	38,219	44%	Yes
Top Administrative Position	1,910	1,980	49%	2,753	3,776	42%	Yes
Top Business Position	389	763	34%	615	1194	34%	No
Top Development Position	1,483	868	63%	1,370	1105	55%	Yes
Top Education Position	256	187	58%	218	239	48%	Yes
Top Facilities Position	21	227	8%	6	353	2%	Yes
Top Financial Position	3,452	4,691	42%	6,846	9,352	42%	No
Top Human Resources Position	605	260	70%	881	523	63%	Yes
Top Legal Position	188	302	38%	367	646	36%	Yes
Top Marketing Position	380	248	61%	440	401	52%	Yes
Top Operations Position	1,244	1,650	43%	2,250	3,128	42%	Yes
Top Program Position	1,333	862	61%	1,112	693	62%	No
Top Public Relations Position	274	163	63%	305	272	53%	Yes
Top Technology Position	158	645	20%	201	1088	16%	Yes
Total	**32,149**	**37,994**	**46%**	**47,656**	**60,989**	**44%**	**Yes**

Source: GuideStar 2011.

Table 10.2   CEOs by Gender and Budget Size, 2009

Nonprofit Budget Size	Female CEOs	Males CEOs	% Female CEOs	Decrease since 2006?
$250,000 or less	2,882	1,642	63.7%	No
$250,000 to $500,000	6,151	4,378	58.4%	No
$500,000 to $1M	6,312	5,223	54.7%	No
$1M to $2.5M	6,857	8,553	44.5%	Yes
$2.5M to $5M	3,423	5,721	37.4%	Yes
$5M to $10M	2,142	4,605	31.7%	Yes
$10M to $25M	1,543	4,040	27.6%	Yes
$25M to $50M	517	1,663	23.7%	Yes
Greater than $50M	465	2,394	16.3%	Yes
Total Average			**40%**	**67% Categorical Decrease**

Source: GuideStar 2011.

Figure 10.3   Females in Top Positions by Budget Size

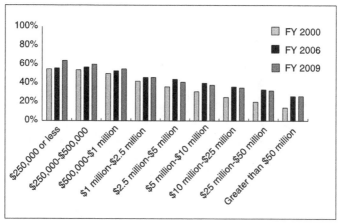

Source: GuideStar 2002; GuideStar 2008; GuideStar 2011.

employees outnumber male employees in most positions, women CEOs earn 22 percent less, nearly 10 percentage points increase since 2009. The wage gap extends beyond CEOs to nearly all the top positions. Women CEOs took home 72 percent of male CEOs' pay in 2000—only 65.8 percent in 2006 and 80 percent in 2009 (table 10.3 and figures 10.5–10.7).[11]

As organizational budgets increase, women's representation decreases—from a high of 51 percent for nonprofits with budgets under $500,000 to

Figure 10.4   Percent of CEOs by Gender and Budget Size, 2009

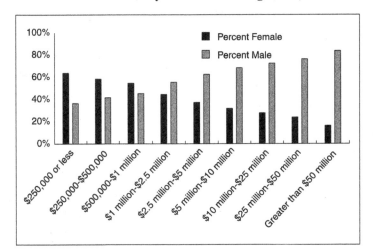

Source: GuideStar 2011.

Figure 10.5   Number of CEOs by Budget Size and Gender, 2009

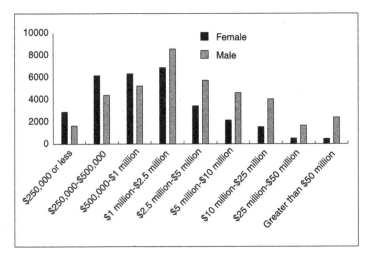

Source: GuideStar 2011.

a low of 33 percent for budgets over $25 million. When examining all nonprofit boards, women make up 43 percent on average, according to a Boardsource survey of more than 1,000 nonprofits in the United States. Women have the largest representation on the boards of smaller arts, cultural, health, human services, environmental, and educational organizations.[12] Yet, among the top 10 nonprofits, measured by the *Chronicle of*

Table 10.3   Average Nonprofit CEO Compensation by Gender and Budget, 2009

Nonprofit Budget Size	Female CEO Salary	Male CEO Salary	Females' Salary as % of Males'	Gap Increase Since 2006?
$250,000 or less	**$42,951**	**$54,735**	**78.5%**	**Yes**
$250,000 to $500,000	**$54,547**	**$64,041**	**85.2%**	**Yes**
$500,000 to $1 million	$70,192	$83,252	84.3%	No
$1 million to $2.5 million	**$92,917**	**$118,930**	**78.1%**	**Yes**
$2.5 million to $5 million	$121,147	$154,219	78.6%	No
$5 million to $10 million	$151,918	$192,435	78.9%	No
$10 million to $25 million	$189,437	$240,358	78.8%	No
$25 million to $50 million	$267,136	$326,066	81.9%	No
Greater than $50 million	**$507,447**	**$658,713**	**77.0%**	**Yes**
Average Percentage			**80%**	**44% Categorical Increase**

Source: GuideStar 2008; GuideStar 2011.

Figure 10.6   Average Nonprofit CEO Compensation by Gender and Budget, 2009

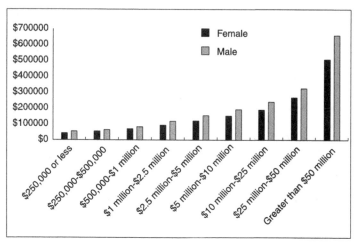

Source: GuideStar 2011.

Philanthropy Philanthropy 400, women comprised approximately 52 percent of the boards, a significant difference.

As shown in tables 10.4 and 10.5, of the top 10 largest nonprofit organizations, measured by the *Chronicle of Philanthropy* Philanthropy 400, three of the CEOs are female (30 percent), and five of the board chairs

Figure 10.7   Nonprofit CEO Pay Female Relative to Male's by Budget Size, 2009

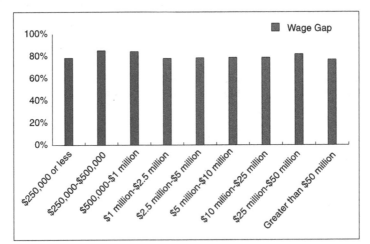

Source: GuideStar 2011.

Table 10.4   Leadership of *Chronicle of Philanthropy* Top 10 Nonprofits

Nonprofit	CEO	Board Chair
United Way Worldwide	M	M
Salvation Army	M	F
Fidelity Charitable Gift Fund	F	M
Task Force for Global Health	M	F
American Red Cross	F	F
Food for the Poor	M	M
Schwab Charitable Fund	F	F
American Cancer Society	M	F*
AmeriCares Foundation	M	M
Catholic Charities USA	M	M

*American Cancer Society Board Chair is a male as of 2012–2013.

Source: Chronicle of Philanthropy 2012; www.cancer.org.

are female (50 percent). Two of these nonprofits—Fidelity Charitable Gift Fund and Catholic Charities USA—have a majority of women on their boards. Only half of the charities, or 50 percent, have women of color on their boards. On nonprofit boards, only 4.5 percent of directors are women of color.

Table 10.5   Board Members of *Chronicle of Philanthropy* Top 10 Nonprofits

Nonprofit	# Board Members	# Women	% Women	# Women of Color	% Women of Color
United Way Worldwide	10	2	20.0%	0	0.0%
Salvation Army	42	14	33.3%	3	7.1%
Fidelity Charitable Gift Fund	7	4	57.1%	0	0.0%
Task Force for Global Health	7	3	42.9%	0	0.0%
American Red Cross	17	6	35.3%	1	5.9%
Food for the Poor	12	3	25.0%	0	0.0%
Schwab Charitable Fund	5	2	40.0%	1	20.0%
American Cancer Society	24	8	33.3%	1	4.2%
AmeriCares Foundation	16	4	25.0%	0	0.0%
Catholic Charities USA	27	14	51.9%	2	7.4%

Source: Chronicle of Philanthropy 2012.

PHILANTHROPY

Philanthropic Giving

Two types of philanthropic foundations were assessed: private and community foundations with the largest accumulated assets in the United States. Of the private foundations with the largest assets (table 10.6), 30 percent have a female president or CEO. Representation of women increases among the largest community foundations (table 10.7), with women in 40 percent of the leadership positions. In sum, women hold 35 percent of positions in philanthropic organizations.

My team and I found little difference in women's representation when considering both the foundations with the largest assets and those foundations that give the most money. Women's overall representation in leadership positions did not change among community foundations with the largest giving compared to community foundations with the largest assets.[13]

Social Entrepreneurs and Funding Organizations

Measuring the top social entrepreneurs is a challenge because profits—a somewhat objective and easily obtained data set—are not the prime factor in determining success. While some companies, such as *Businessweek,* identify businesses that were for-profit and sought to fulfill a global, national, and/or local need, others, such as *Fast Company Magazine* and

Table 10.6   Leadership of Private Foundations with Largest Assets

Foundation	2010 Assets	CEO/ President	Board Chair	# Board Positions	# Females on Board	% Females on Board
Bill & Melinda Gates Foundation	$37,430,150,458	Male	Male/**Female** Co-Chairs	15	4	26.67%
Ford Foundation	10,344,933,000	Male	**Female**	13	4	30.77%
J. Paul Getty Trust	9,584,879,219	**Female**	**Female**	14	**5**	35.71%
Robert Wood Johnson Foundation	9,199,687,456	Female	Male	14	4	28.57%
W.K. Kellogg Foundation	7,696,627,040	Male	N/A	12	4	33.33%
The Hewlett Foundation	7,377,220,546	Male	Male	13	5	38.46%
The Packard Foundation	6,100,637,478	**Female**	**Female**	15	8	53.33%
The MacArthur Foundation	5,737,270,334	Male	**Female**	12	5	41.67%
Gordon and Betty Moore Foundation	5,585,288,763	Male	Male	12	3	25.00%
The Andrew Mellon Foundation	5,490,877,291	Male	Male	11	3	27.27%
Total		**70% Male, 30% Female**	**50% Male, 50% Female**	**116**	**45**	**38.79%**

Source: Foundation Center 2012a.

Forbes Magazine, focus on not-for-profits that seek to do the same. For the purposes of this book, we assessed nonprofit enterprises.[14] In 2009, the staff of *Fast Company Magazine* identified the top 10 social entrepreneurs of 2009, and 7 of the top 10 founders were women, or 70 percent.[15]

In 2011, *Forbes Magazine* identified a different set of social entrepreneurs, and yet the same percentage of women emerged. *Forbes* identified the top-30 social entrepreneurs in the world. My team and I then limited those identified by Forbes to those focused on U.S. problems and

Table 10.7   Leadership of Community Foundations with Largest Assets

Community Foundation	2010 Assets	CEO/ President	Board Chair	# Board Positions	# Females on Board	% Females on Board
Tulsa Community Foundation	$4,022,451,000	Male	Male	26	5	19.23%
The New York Community Trust	1,877,885,562	**Female**	**Female**	12	7	58.33%
Silicon Valley Community Foundation	1,830,140,000	Male	Male	20	9	45.00%
The Cleveland Foundation	1,816,947,057	Male	Male	15	4	26.67%
The Chicago Community Trust	1,595,765,501	Male	Male	15	5	33.33%
California Community Foundation	1,242,402,000	**Female**	Male	23	11	47.83%
Marin Community Foundation	1,207,464,129	Male	Male	9	4	44.44%
Greater Kansas City Community Foundation	1,189,480,459	**Female**	Male	14	6	42.86%
The San Francisco Foundation	1,101,069,000	**Female**	Male	12	6	50.00%
The Columbus Foundation and Affiliated Organizations	1,061,039,486	Male	Male	9	2	22.22%
Total		**60% Male, 40% Female**	**90% Male, 10% Female**	**155**	**59**	**38.06%**

Source: Foundation Center 2012b.

eliminated others focused on capital and/or investment funds. Only 17 entrepreneurs remained. Among those 17, seven are women (41.2 percent). When eliminating the nonprofits with revenues or budgets less than $7 million and fewer than 1,000 people positively impacted, the top 10 remained. Among those top 10, 7 founders were women, or 70 percent,[16] a significant percentage of leading entrepreneurs.

Capital investment firms provide a vital component to social entrepreneurship, much like for-profit entrepreneurship. Among for-profit entrepreneurship, capital investment firms provided start-up and growth funding. Capital investment firms serve a similar function for social entrepreneurs. Social capital firms support entrepreneurs financially, educationally, and/or encourage networking. Among the 10 largest social capital firms, 50 percent of the CEOs and/or founders were female or majority female. I defined "majority female" as females who comprise 50 percent or more of the founders and/or presidents.

Women are well represented as social entrepreneurs and those who invest in social entrepreneurs. One explanation suggests that women investors are more likely to fund other women, as the for-profit entrepreneurship field also suggested. There exists a correlation between the presence of women in a field and the likelihood of other women participating. For example, a high percentage of females in social capital firms illustrate that when more women are present, more women succeed. Another explanation is that social entrepreneurship lacks structural or institutional barriers. Women dominate in an industry when innovative performance with little "paved pathways" exist, arguably because there are fewer, if any, gatekeepers. This explanation may also explain the presence of women in some aspect of the media industry, where blogging and tweeting have little or no gatekeeping.

Conclusions

- Foundation leaders must ensure that strategic investment, both in terms of social impact and sustainability, are present in philanthropic activities.
- All nonprofits should educate about the gender gap, and assist girls and women in overcoming obstacles in attaining leadership positions and reducing the salary gap.
- Boards of directors and executive nonprofit staff should recruit, train, and retain people of color across all levels of the nonprofit organization.
- Boards of directors should widen the search criteria for top positions, including board leadership, and look within the organization to promote.

RELIGION

Because trends in religion cannot compare to trends in other nonprofits, religion is treated separately, and a distinct set of recommendations will follow accordingly. To begin, religion is as much part of political and governmental discourse as democracy, elections, and voting. Whether overt or subtle, religion often inspires debates, policy, laws, and protests. Religious views and institutions drive social agendas, wars, diplomacy, and can be a source of tremendous political influence. Some may argue that religious fanatics are predominantly responsible for the contrived moral panic plaguing some parts of the United States and abroad. To a large extent, religious institutions are often legally unaccountable bastions of gender inequality. Many religious feminists, such as Blu Greenberg, members of the Episcopal Church, Ray Bourgeois, Reza Aslan, and Naylene McBaine, have worked to effectuate the public's wide support for women religious leaders. In fact, more than 80 percent of the U.S. public welcomes prominent roles for female religious leaders.[17]

Despite the support of parishioners and followers nationally, leaders of most religious institutions have actively rejected prominent leadership roles of and for women. Understanding the current leadership of religious institutions will prepare religious feminists and their supporters for change. Therefore, the presence and absence of women religious leaders will be explored in this section.

While several institutions and research centers seek to measure U.S. religious affiliation, it is important to note that there exists a tremendous gap in data about affiliation, practices, and leadership in the United States. For example, the U.S. Census Bureau does not ask people about their religious affiliation, and religious organizations lack transparency in leadership. Additionally, religion is much like race in terms of self-identification and self-appraisal, and therefore, varying measurements of identity. With this stated, I have sought to capture the religious makeup of the United States and religious leaders overall with little available data. This section explores seven major religions that exist in the United States (table 10.8); three of the seven are Christian-based and comprise the majority of religious participants.

Table 10.8   U.S. Religious Participation, 2012

Religion	% of U.S. Population
Protestant*	48–51.3%
Roman Catholic	23.9%
Mormon	1.7%
Christian	1.6%
Jewish	1.7%
Buddhist	.7%
Muslim	.6%
Other/Unspecified	2.5%
Unaffiliated*	12.1–20%
None	4%

*According to Pew Research Center, fewer Protestants (48 percent) and more unaffiliated (20 percent) exist than compared to the percentage estimated by the U.S. Central Intelligence Agency.

Source: CIA World Factbook 2012a; Pew 2012a.

Among the United States' more popular religions, women followers comprise more than half of each faith as shown in figures 10.8 and 10.9. Among Jewish, Muslim, Buddhist, and Hindu faiths, women followers comprise less than 50 percent.[18] The number of Americans who do not consider themselves affiliated with any religion has grown from 15 percent to almost 20 percent since 2007, which is the highest percentage ever recorded by the Pew Research Center.[19] Forty-six percent of women identify as following an "other" faith, and 41 percent identify as unaffiliated. Women's religious affiliation has remained virtually unchanged during the last decade.

Figure 10.8   Gender by Religious Affiliation, 2012

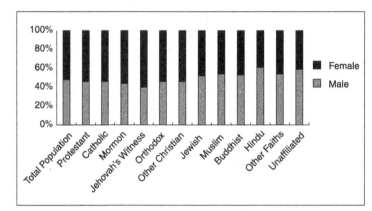

Source: Pew 2012b.

Figure 10.9   Gender by Religious Affiliation, 2012

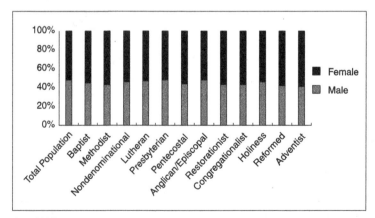

Source: Pew 2012b.

The number of unaffiliated Americans has grown over the last 5 years among white Americans, and the number of Protestants decreased from 53 percent in 2007 to 48 percent in 2012. While the number of whites identifying as unaffiliated has risen by 5 percent, the number of blacks and Hispanics who identify as unaffiliated has remained unchanged.[20] The racial composition of former Protestants is unknown but can be assumed that whites comprise the majority of those who left the Protestant faith.

The percentage of women attending seminary averages 33 percent.[21] The greatest gender gap exists among non-U.S. students (i.e., visa students), followed by Asians and then Latinos and whites. There were considerable gender differences in seminary attendance among most racial groups, except blacks and natives. Among natives, the gender gap was less than 20 percent; black males and females attended seminary at nearly equal percentages.[22] However, when just doctoral seminary students are examined, there are far fewer women. This is likely to be the result of limited opportunities for female leaders in most major religions in the United States.

Positional Leadership and Influence

Female religious leaders compare to nonprofit and philanthropic leadership in that women are far more likely to lead small and moderate size religious organizations, as the size of the organization grows the percentage of female leaders shrinks. To illustrate the average attendance of protestant services led by a male is 103 adults, compared to 81 led by a female. In 2009, there were twice as many women senior pastors as there were in 1999, yet this still equates to only 1 in 10 of U.S. religious organizations that employs a female senior pastor.[23] Since 2009, the percentage of female leaders has remained virtually unchanged. What the researchers of this report were unable to uncover about women's religious leadership is far greater than what was discovered. For example, it appears that some Pentecost churches permit women leaders and some do not. Virtually no data is available on the status of the church's leadership, particularly the role of women. Because no creditable data source could be found, the Pentecost Church has been excluded from this section.

As in other sectors, the impact of women-led and -founded religious organizations has had a positive impact on the overall number of female leaders within the organization. Consider the following: six females have been credited with the founding of several modern world religions, all of which are part of the New Thought Movement of the 19th and 20th centuries. The original founder of the New Thought Movement was Emma Curtis Hopkins, Mary Baker Eddy founded Christian Science, Divine Science was founded by Malinda E. Cramer, Helen Blavatsky founded Theosophy,

Unity Church was founded by Myrtle Fillmore and her husband, and Ellen White founded the Seventh Day Adventist.[24] These religions have many commonalities, including inclusivity, self-realization, and human universalism. Not surprisingly, more women comprised the leadership of these organizations in 2012 than the major religions covered in detail in this section. Data on the leadership of New Thought religious organizations is also widely accessible to the public. Again, these relatively newer religions have fewer gatekeepers and traditional, impeding structures.

Baptist   While some religious groups have expanded the role of women in leadership roles, others have curtailed women's abilities to hold leadership positions. The Baptist Church, the largest Protestant denomination in the United States, has prohibited women pastors since 2000.[25] The Baptist Church is also an illustration of an apparent division within many Christian religions, particularly as it pertains to gender roles and responsibilities in the church. In 2010, 53 women were ordained as ministers in Baptist churches, and the church maintains that thousands of women have served in ministry without being ordained.[26] In 2010, more women served as pastors than in 2005, despite the fact that women are not officially permitted to do so.

I expect that women pastors will rise despite the church's gender prohibition because female students and missionaries continue to rise. Enrollment at Baptist-affiliated schools dropped in 2010, and yet, the percentage of female students increased from 38.5 percent to 39.4 percent. Women also made up 54 percent of all field missionaries in 2012.[27] Additionally, the percentage of female chaplains and counselors has increased slightly over the last five years or so. The steady but small increases of visible female Baptist leaders also suggest that the percentage of women leaders will rise slowly and steadily.

Catholicism   The Catholic Church is the oldest established Western Christian church, and is also the world's largest religious structure. Perhaps its rigor for traditionalism explains why it maintains gender disparity, particularly within its leadership (figure 10.10). For example, nuns are not ordained, but they live a life "consecrated to God."[28] In 2010, the Vatican decreed that ordaining women is a sin of the same magnitude as pedophilia.[29]

Figure 10.11 shows that Catholicism in the United States has been decreasing significantly since 1975. While the number of graduated seminarians and parishes has remained constant over the years, the number of priests and sisters has declined steadily. Perhaps it is no coincidence

Figure 10.10   Catholic Leadership in the United States, 2012

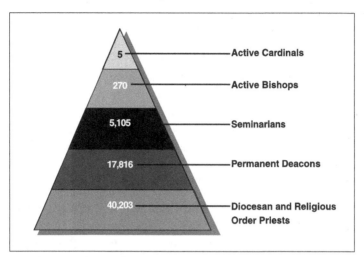

Source: United States Conference of Catholic Bishops (USCCB) 2012.

Figure 10.11   Catholic Leadership Participation

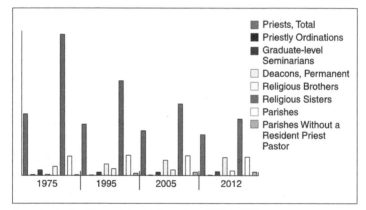

Source: Center for Applied Research in the Apostolate (CARA) 2012.

that, as the number of priests has declined, the number of deacons has risen. Women cannot be ordained as deacons, priests, or bishops, and the ordained ministry is a necessary step to institutional leadership.[30] The church also prohibits women from leading mass or giving communion. The Catholic Church appears to enforce these policies consistently and unilaterally, unlike the policies of the Baptist Church, which likely contributes to the church's overall decline.

Aside from that which has already been stated, there exists virtually no data on Catholic women or religious sisters. A secondary analysis reveals that there has been a steady decline of Catholic nuns in the United States. To illustrate, the Leadership Conference of Women Religious, a "mainstream organization that represents approximately 80 percent of the 57,000 nuns in the U.S." explains that Catholic Churches have alienated nuns.[31] Some have speculated that the decline of priests is due to the vow of celibacy and prohibition of marriage, although the decline of priests has not been as drastic as the decline of nuns. Since the Church prohibits nuns from being ordained leaders, approximately 3,000 out of 17,000 Catholic Churches in the United States are operating without such a leader.[32] The gap in Catholic leadership in the United States has forced some churches to close.

Episcopalian   Unlike the Catholic Church, the Episcopal Church has been ordaining females as deacons, priests, and bishops since 1976. The church is one of the most transparent major religious organizations in the United States. The Episcopal Church has also a church-led women's organization devoted to equality; some key points from the Episcopal Women's Caucus include:

- Advocating for equal pay for work of equal value in the church and in the world.
- Working for increased appointment or election of women to leadership roles, including the episcopate.
- Work for inclusion of women and minorities in the church calendar and Sunday lections.[33]

The Episcopalian Church is divided into two houses: the House of Bishops and the House of Deputies. Each house shares governing power equally. The president of the House of Bishops, Dr. Katherine Jefferts Schori, presides over the House of Bishops and its 300 bishops. The president of the House of Deputies is Rev. Gay Clark Jennings—the first ordained woman to hold the position.[34] The vice president of the House of Deputies is Byron Rushing. In the House of Deputies is the Council of Advice, which is comprised of nine appointed members. In 2012, two of the nine members are women or 22.2 percent.[35]

Episcopalians claim the highest percentage of female leaders among any of the major religions in the United States. In fact, as figure 10.12 shows, 31 percent of rectors and vicars, or parish priests, are female. This is an increase of females compared to 2007 when women represented 29 percent of priests. The Episcopalian Church also elected a woman, Dr. Katherine Jefferts Schori, as the Presiding Bishop in 2006.[36]

Figure 10.12   2010 Vicars and Rectors (Parish Priests)

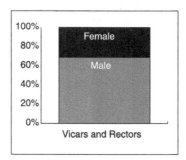

Source: Episcopal Church 2010.

Islam   Islamic interpretations vary as widely as Christian interpretations, perhaps more so. Unlike Islamic countries whose interpretations are sanctioned by law, in the United States interpretations are left to the individual, family, and community practices and beliefs. Unlike the various Christian denominations, there is not one national Muslim authority; instead, several communities exist and even work together. Because there is not one national authority, we were unable to include any national leadership representation.

It is important to note that in some Islamic countries Muslim women are permitted to serve as scholars of the Quran and muftis, which are authoritative teachers of the religion. For example, the United Arab Emirates announced in 2009 that it would appoint the world's first state-sanctioned female muftis and have them trained and in service by the end of 2010.[37] However, there have been no updates on this since 2009. Even with more liberal interpretations of the Quran, religious leaders maintain that women cannot become imams or lead prayers of mixed-gender services. Women usually have segregated areas for prayers and separate rooms for services.[38] These same interpretations can be widely found in the United States as well, and suggest that it is unlikely that there exists female leaders in the Islamic faith.

Muslims who conduct Eid prayers in a mosque form the basis for measuring of total mosque participants in the Bagby study (table 10.9). More female converts in mosques were recorded in a 2011 survey than in the 2000 survey. Whereas, in 2000, only 32 percent of all converts were female, in 2011, 41 percent of converts were female.[39]

Judaism   Generally, Judaism allows women rabbis in Conservative, Reform, and Reconstructionist traditions, but Orthodox Judaism does not allow women.[40] Since 1972, 600 women have become Reformed rabbis,

Table 10.9   States with Largest Attendance at Eid Prayers

State	# of Mosques	Eid Average/Total
Texas	166	2.542/421,972
New York	257	1,529/392,953
Illinois	109	3,296/359,264
California	246	1,109/272,814
Virginia	62	3,436/213,032
Florida	118	1,397/164,846
New Jersey	109	1,474/160,666
Michigan	77	1,563/120,351
Pennsylvania	99	813/ 80,487
Georgia	69	762/ 52,578

Source: Bagby 2012.

and as of 2012, there are a total of 200 Reformed rabbis serving in North America.[41] A newly ordained female senior or solo rabbi serving a congregation of 300 families earns $97,746 while her male counterpart earns $102,934. Female senior or solo rabbis with five to eight years of experience serving congregations with 600 or more families earn $180,870 and their male counterparts earn $217,079.[42] The salary gap grows as the size of the congregation grows, which is not unlike the disparity found in most of the other sectors.

Lutheranism   The Evangelical Lutheran Church of America (ELCA) embraces the idea of their founder, Martin Luther, that things must be called what they really are. Perhaps for this reason, at least in part, the Justice for Women organization within the ELCA calls the "sustainment of male privilege in the church and society sexism."[43]

The ELCA does ordain women as pastors and their hymnal includes gender-neutral invocations and benedictions. The ELCA has been ordaining women for at least 40 years. In 2010, 21 percent of clergy were women and approximately 86 percent of ordained women and 83 percent of men were actively serving in congregations.[44] Less than 20 percent of ordained females comprised the clergy in 2008; women experienced a slight increase within two years.

Membership in the Lutheran Church has been on the downward trend since 1991, with the largest decrease between 2009 and 2010, when membership fell by 3.29 percent.[45] Yet, the percentages of ordained women (86 percent) to ordained men (83 percent) serving have remained unchanged.

The discrepancy between ordained women to female clergypersons continues to be grossly disproportionate. It is important to note that not all Lutheran synods ordain women. Some specifically prohibit women in the clergy, such as the Missouri and Evangelical synods.[46]

Methodist The United Methodist Church (UMC) has ordained women since 1968. The Methodist Church, like the Lutheran Church, has an internal organization for women: the General Commission on the Status and Role of Women, formed in 1972. The church publically states that 5 percent of its largest and most influential churches are lead by women pastors.[47] The number of senior female pastors (7 percent) has remained unchanged since 2003. This sector should commend the Methodist Church for its transparency in leadership and look to it for lessons gleaned. However, in reviewing figures 10.13 and 10.14, women and men of color are more likely to hold a probationary role within the church.

Figure 10.13   Clergy Status by Gender United Methodist Church 2008

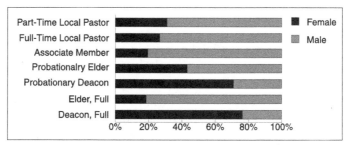

Source: GCSRW 2011.

Figure 10.14   Clergy Status by Race/Ethnicity United Methodist Church, 2008

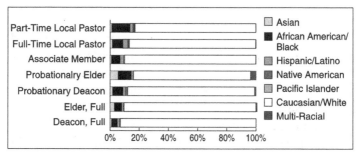

Source: GCSRW 2011.

Mormonism   Approximately 56 percent of the Mormon population is female,[48] and no women exist in the top leadership of the Church. Like many other religions, Mormonism maintains a hierarchical religious structure, and it excludes women from leadership ranks. The church excludes women from ordained priesthoods; therefore, they cannot participate in church rites, such as baptizing. The church permits women to serve as missionaries and teachers; therefore, they may preach to the congregation and lead prayers during service. The Mormon Church places special emphasis on women as mothers, so Mormon women are encouraged to make motherhood "their first priority ... and achieve prominence in later life in business, education, medicine, and other endeavors."[49]

Mormon women have formed an organization within the church, the Relief Society. Founded in 1842, membership is more than 5.5 million women aged 18 and older. The Relief Society meets once a week for one hour and instructs women on furthering the teachings of Jesus Christ within their own homes and families. The church assigns two women from the Relief Society to "visit her [another woman's] home each month to give a religious message and offer help if needed."[50]

Presbyterianism

The Presbyterian Church's official policy has permitted women to become ordained ministers since 1956, although many individual churches prohibit the ordination of women.[51] Each church is autonomous and can elect its own officers and ordain women as it chooses.[52] With this stated, women comprise 27 percent of pastors, 52 percent of elders, and 45 percent of "other ministers."[53] This is the extent of the data available for the Presbyterianism Church.

Sikhism

In 2012, Sikhism received national attention when opponents, who had mistaken Sikhs for Muslims, executed a mass shooting at a temple in Wisconsin. Originating from India in the 19th century, Sikhism emphasizes "equality of humankind and disavows caste, class, or gender discrimination."[54] In fact, the Sikh religion emphasizes gender equality. "Female subordination, the practice of taking a husband or father's last name and practicing rituals that subordinate women are alien to Sikh principles."[55] "Seeker of truth," Sikhs believe they were given human bodies to experience the Divine Light within themselves and everything around them by meditating to recognize the Divine Light and being of service to others.[56]

More specifically, non-Punjabi Sikhs living in the United States are referred to as Gora (white) Sikhs. Gora Sikhs practice gender egalitarianism. Sikhism allows women to lead ceremonies and may now wear a turban like the men, as opposed to the traditional scarves. In 2012, Pew Research Center reported that roughly 200,000 Sikhs live in the United States, which the center describes as a conservative estimate.[57]

Compensation

Only general information can be attained about salaries and earnings. Albeit isolated and limited in nature, data were obtained from Bureau of Labor Statistics (BLS). As of May 2011, the BLS estimated that chief executives of religious organizations earn $176,550 on average, and senior-level executives earn $114,490 annually.[58] The salary breakdown based on gender is unknown but will, in all likelihood, be grossly disproportional, particularly as the size of the organization grows. Women are rarely in senior executive positions and, therefore, would not attain the same pay opportunities.

Conclusions

- Religion is one of the few sectors that allow and condone overt gender discrimination. Little will change unless constituents push for and demand transparency in leadership.
- Religious sects must strength its female clergy by allowing more female leaders, amplifying their voices, and position them as spiritual thought leaders.
- Constituents should encourage search committees, congregation leaders, and others to follow their egalitarian mission and make diversity in top leadership a high priority. Search committees should examine their selection process, not only for candidates, but also for the "experts" they rely on who recommend candidates. Rethinking evaluation methods and interview processes would provide more complete measures by which to assess candidates. Religious leaders who are trying to avoid controversy by primarily or exclusively recruiting men need to realize that their congregations are probably receptive to women clergy.
- Because there is very little data on religion in the United States, any quantitative or descriptive data capturing the number of religious women leaders would aid in better understanding religious leadership.

NOTES

1. O'Neill, M. (2002). *Nonprofit Nation*, p. 2. San Francisco, CA: Jossey Bass.

2. IRS. (2011). 2011 Data Book. Internal Revenue Service. Accessed at http://www.irs.gov/pub/irs-soi/11databk.pdf; Salamon, Sokolowski, and Geller (2012).

3. Butler, A. (2009). Wages in the Nonprofit Sector: Management, Professional, and Administrative Support Occupations. Bureau of Labor Statistics. Accessed at http://www.bls.gov/opub/mlr/cwc/wages-in-the-nonprofit-sector-management-professional-and-administrative-support-occupations.pdf.

4. Internal Revenue Service (IRS). (2011). 2011 Data Book, p. 56. Internal Revenue Service. Accessed at http://www.irs.gov/pub/irs-soi/11databk.pdf.

5. Nonprofit HR Solutions. (2010). 2010 Nonprofit Employment Trends Survey, p. 11. Accessed at http://www.nonprofithr.com/wp-content/uploads/2013/03/2010-Employment-Trends-Survey-Report.pdf.

6. Schmitz, P. and K. Stroup. (July 21, 2005). "Building Tomorrow's Nonprofit Work Force." *The Chronicle of Philanthropy*. Accessed at http://www.publicallies.org/atf/cf/%7BFBE0137A-2CA6-4E0D-B229-54D5A098332C%7D/COP%207-21-05.pdf.

7. GuideStar. (2011). 2011 GuideStar Nonprofit Compensation Report. Accessed at http://www.guidestar.org/rxg/products/nonprofit-compensation-solutions/guidestar-nonprofit-compensation-report.aspx.

8. Butler, A. (2009). Wages in the Nonprofit Sector: Management, Professional, and Administrative Support Occupations. Bureau of Labor Statistics. Accessed at http://www.bls.gov/opub/cwc/cm20081022ar01p1.htm.

9. GuideStar. (2011). 2011 GuideStar Nonprofit Compensation Report. Accessed at http://www.guidestar.org/rxg/products/nonprofit-compensation-solutions/guidestar-nonprofit-compensation-report.aspx.

10. GuideStar. (2008). 2008 GuideStar Nonprofit Compensation Report. Accessed at http://www.guidestar.org/rxa/news/articles/2008/2008-guidestar-nonprofit-compensation-report-now-available.aspx; GuideStar. (2011). 2011 GuideStar Nonprofit Compensation Report. Accessed at http://www.guidestar.org/rxg/products/nonprofit-compensation-solutions/guidestar-nonprofit-compensation-report.aspx.

11. GuideStar. (2011). 2011 GuideStar Nonprofit Compensation Report. Accessed at http://www.guidestar.org/rxg/products/nonprofit-compensation-solutions/guidestar-nonprofit-compensation-report.aspx.

12. BoardSource. (2010). Nonprofit Governance Index 2010. Accessed at http://www.boardsource.org/dl.asp?document_id=884.

13. Foundation Center. (2012a). Top 100 U.S. Foundations by Asset Size. Accessed at http://foundationcenter.org/findfunders/topfunders/top100assets.html.

Foundation Center. (2012b). 25 Largest Community Foundations by Asset Size. Accessed at http://foundationcenter.org/findfunders/topfunders/top25assets.html.

Foundation Center. (2012c). 25 Largest Community Foundations by Total Giving. Accessed at http://foundationcenter.org/findfunders/topfunders/top25giving.html.

14. Some groups sought to measure the top social entrepreneurs by popularity among the public. For example, *Businessweek* asked readers to vote for the top social enterprises of 2012. Among 25 enterprises, women were either founders or cofounders of 10 businesses or 40 percent (http://images.businessweek.com/slideshows/2012-06-21/americas-most-promising-social-entrepreneurs-2012#slide26). The results of the public vote had not been released in time for the study's release; therefore, the *Businessweek* tally will not be included in the overall averages.

15. Fast Company. (2009). The 10 Best Social Enterprises of 2009. Accessed at http://www.fastcompany.com/1093657/10-best-social-enterprises-2009.

16. Forbes. (2011). "Impact 30." *Forbes.* Accessed at http://www.forbes.com/impact-30/list.html.

17. Center for Applied Research in the Apostolate (CARA). (2012). Frequently Requested Church Statistics. Georgetown University. Accessed at http://cara.georgetown.edu/caraservices/requestedchurchstats.html.

18. Pew Research Center. (2012c). "Nones on the Rise." *Pew Forum on Religion and Public Life.* Accessed at http://www.pewforum.org/2012/10/09/nones-on-the-rise.

19. Ibid.

20. Ibid.

21. Ibid.

22. Ibid.

23. Barna Group. (2009). Number of Female Senior Pastors in Protestant Churches Doubles in Past Decade. Barna Group. Accessed at http://www.barna.org/leadership-articles/304-number-of-female-senior-pastors-in-protestant-churches-doubles-in-past-decade?q=one+ten+pastors+women.

24. American Academy on Religions (AAR). (2012). American Academy of Religions. Accessed at http://www.aarweb.org; Fiedler, M. (Oct. 18, 2010). "Women as Religious Leaders: Breaking through the Stained Glass Ceiling." *Huffington Post.* Accessed at http://www.huffingtonpost.com/maureen-fiedler/women-religious-leaders_b_766006.html.

25. Fairchild, M. (2012). "Southern Baptist Church Beliefs and Practices." *About.com.* Accessed at http://christianity.about.com/od/denominations/a/baptistdenom.htm; Fiedler, M. (Oct. 18, 2010). "Women as Religious Leaders: Breaking through the Stained Glass Ceiling." *Huffington Post.* Accessed at http://www.huffingtonpost.com/maureen-fiedler/women-religious-leaders_b_766006.html.

26. Durso, P. (2010). The State of Baptist Women. *Baptist Women in Ministry.* Accessed at http://www.bwim.info/files/State%20of%20Women%20in%20Baptist%20Life%202010.pdf.

27. Ibid.

28. Catholic Pages. (2012). Church Hierarchy. *Catholic Pages.* Accessed at http://www.catholic-pages.com/church/hierarchy.asp.

29. Hooper, J. (July 15, 2010). "Catholics Angry as Church Puts Female Ordination on Par with Sex Abuse." *The Guardian.* Accessed at http://www.guardian. co.uk/world/2010/jul/15/vatican-declares-womens-ordination-grave-crime.

30. Fiedler, M. (Oct. 18, 2010). "Women as Religious Leaders: Breaking through the Stained Glass Ceiling." *Huffington Post.* Accessed at http://www. huffingtonpost.com/maureen-fiedler/women-religious-leaders_b_766006.html.

31. Cary, M. (May 11, 2012). "The Catholic Church's Treatment of Nuns Is Polarizing and Alienating." *US News.* Accessed at http://www. usnews.com/opinion/articles/2012/05/11/the-catholic-churchs-treatment-of-nuns-is-polarizing-and-alienating.

32. Ibid.

33. Episcopal Women's Caucus. (2012). Issues for Today. *The Episcopal Women's Caucus.* Accessed at http://www.episcopalwomenscaucus.org/issues.htm.

34. Episcopal Church. (2010). Episcopal Overview Fact 2010. *Episcopal Church.* Accessed at http://www.episcopalchurch.org/sites/default/files/episcopal_overview_fact_2010.pdf.

Episcopal Church. (2012a). Biography—Rev. Gay Clark Jennings. *Episcopal Church.* Accessed at http://www.episcopalchurch.org/page/ gay-clark-jennings-biography.

Episcopal Church. (2012b). Presiding Bishop. *Episcopal Church.* Accessed at http://www.episcopalchurch.org/page/presiding-bishop.

35. House of Deputies. (2012). About the President. *House of Deputies of the Episcopal Church.* Accessed at http://houseofdeputies.org/about-the-president. html

36. Episcopal Church. (2010). Episcopal Overview Fact 2010. *Episcopal Church.* Accessed at www.episcopalchurch.org/sites/default/files/episcopal_overview_fact_2010.pdf.

Episcopal Church. (2012a). Biography—Rev. Gay Clark Jennings. *Episcopal Church.* Accessed at http://www.episcopalchurch.org/page/gay-clark-jennings-biography.

Episcopal Church. (2012b). Presiding Bishop. *Episcopal Church.* Accessed at http://www.episcopalchurch.org/page/presiding-bishop.

37. Elass, R. (Nov. 3, 2009). Women Muftis by End of 2010. *The National.* Accessed at http://www.thenational.ae/news/uae-news/women-muftis-by-end-of-2010.

38. Fiedler, M. (Oct. 18, 2010). "Women as Religious Leaders: Breaking through the Stained Glass Ceiling." *Huffington Post.* Accessed at http://www. huffingtonpost.com/maureen-fiedler/women-religious-leaders_b_766006.html.

39. Bagby, I. (Jan. 2012). The American Mosque 2011. *Council on American-Islamic Relations: US Mosque Study 2011.* Accessed at http://www.cair.com/ american-muslims/reports-and-surveys.html.

40. Fiedler, M. (Oct. 18, 2010). "Women as Religious Leaders: Breaking through the Stained Glass Ceiling." *Huffington Post.* Accessed at http://www. huffingtonpost.com/maureen-fiedler/women-religious-leaders_b_766006.html.

41. Jewish Telegraphic Agency (JTA). (June 20, 2012). Reform Female Rabbis Are Paid Less Than Male Counterparts. *Jewish Telegraphic Agency.* Accessed at http://www.jta.org/news/article/2012/06/20/3098691/reform-female-rabbis-earn-less-than-male-rabbis-study-finds.

42. Ibid.

43. Evangelical Lutheran Church in America (ELCA). (2012a). Justice for Women. *ELCA.* Accessed at http://www.elca.org/Our-Work/Publicly-Engaged-Church/Justice-for-Women/Sexism-and-Patriarchy. One woman recounts her experience. "I stood up and said, 'You cannot use language like that in the church. You are welcome to your opinions, but your language is unacceptable. You'll need to leave if you cannot keep your comments appropriate.' He told me, 'You need to sit down, little lady. I can say whatever I want.' No one in the room came to my defense. I sat down because there was nothing else I could do." Our Voices, Our Stories (ELCA 2012a).

44. ELCA. (2012b). Welcome to the ELCA: Quick Facts. *ELCA.* Accessed athttp://www.elca.org/News-and-Events/ELCA-Facts.

45. Ibid.

46. Christians for Biblical Equality (CBE). (2007). US Denominations and Their Stances on Women in Leadership. *CBE International* 6(2). Accessed at http://www2.cbeinternational.org/new/E-Journal/2007/07spring/denominations%20first%20installment--FINAL.pdf.

47. United States Conference of Catholic Bishops. (2012). Clergy and Religious. *USCCB.* Accessed at http://www.usccb.org/about/media-relations/statistics/clergy-religious.cfm.

48. Pew Research Center. (2009). A Portrait of Mormons in the U.S. *Pew Forum on Religion and Public Life.* Accessed at http://www.pewforum.org/Christian/Mormon/A-Portrait-of-Mormons-in-the-US.aspx#2.

49. The Church of Jesus Christ of Latter-Day Saints. (2012). Women in the Church. Accessed at http://www.mormonnewsroom.org/article/women-in-the-church.

50. Ibid.

51. CBE. (2007). US Denominations and Their Stances on Women in Leadership. *CBE International* 6(2). Accessed at http://www2.cbeinternational.org/new/E-Journal/2007/07spring/denominations%20first%20installment--FINAL.pdf.

52. Evangelical Presbyterian Church. (1984). Position Paper on the Ordination of Women. Accessed at http://www.epc.org/about-the-epc/position-papers/ordination-of-women/.

53. Hodges, S. (Feb. 11, 2010). One in Four Presbyterian Pastors Is Female, and Nearly Half the Membership Is 65 or Older. *Dallas News.* Accessed at http://religionblog.dallasnews.com/2010/02/one-in-four-presbyterian-pasto.html/.

54. CIA. (2012a). The United States. *CIA World Factbook.* Accessed at https://www.cia.gov/library/publications/the-world-factbook/geos/us.html.

CIA. (2012b). Religion. *CIA World Factbook.* Accessed at https://www.cia.gov/library/publications/the-world-factbook/fields/2122.html).

55. Fiedler, M. (Oct. 18, 2010). "Women as Religious Leaders: Breaking through the Stained Glass Ceiling." *Huffington Post.* Accessed at http://www.huffingtonpost.com/maureen-fiedler/women-religious-leaders_b_766006.html.

56. The Path of Sikh Dharma. Accessed at http://www.sikhdharma.org/content/path-sikh-dharma).

57. Pew Research Center. (2012a). Ask the Expert: How Many U.S. Sikhs? *Pew Research Center.* Accessed at http://pewresearch.org/pubs/2323/how-many-sikhs-us-population-religion-temple-wisconsin-shooting.

58. Bureau of Labor Statistics. (2011). National Industry-Specific Occupational Employment and Wage Estimates. Accessed at http://www.bls.gov/oes/current/naics4_813100.htm.

11

Arts and Entertainment

Whether art imitates life or life imitates art, few would dispute the impact of film and television on societal culture. On camera, roles depicting women and men reflect public consciousness and/or foster dialogue about values and beliefs. Since its inception, television has captured and shaped gender stereotypes and cultural beliefs, from separate marital beds in *I Love Lucy* to the cancellation of the first lesbian character in the once successful situational comedy *Ellen* to sex-driven men in *Two and Half Men*, (which has also boasted the highest paid actors in television history). A few productions have bucked male and female stereotypes, such as the 1997 production of *G.I. Jane* and the short-lived 2005 *Commander in Chief* series about the first American woman president.

The significance of the portrayal and acceptance of on-screen women cannot be overstated. The American palate seems to lack an appetite for a strong female protagonist, let alone a female hero who is not sexualized. Little has changed in arts and entertainment regarding women's leadership in the last 10 years, although a woman has reached a noteworthy milestone as a director. In 2010, a woman won an Oscar for best director for the first time—Kathryn Bigelow for *The Hurt Locker*.[1] Two years later, Ava DuVernay won the best director award for a dramatic film at the Sundance Film Festival for *Middle of Nowhere*—the first African American woman to earn such an honor.[2] Aside from these two noteworthy events, women have not gained or lost any significant representation in arts and entertainment, except in television, where women have lost ground in almost every area.

Top-performing artists help to better understand women's leadership in arts and entertainment in the United States. Women's strong performance in music and literature among the top-selling artists conveys much about the industry and how it recognizes, or fails to recognize, women's leadership. This section examines leading musical artists, authors, actors, and those behind the scenes, including their salaries. Key findings include top women artists still earning less than or the same as the lowest paid male artists, and women bestselling authors earn less than male authors who are not best sellers. These findings illustrate the great subjectivity that exists throughout this sector in awarding both recognition and salaries. Women in the arts and entertainment sector have not been rewarded based on talent or contributions in their respective fields. When subjectivity exists in an industry, all women are poorly represented and often receive disparate salaries. The arts and entertainment sector is illustrative of this finding. In the film industry, two major pieces of data stand out: the disparate earnings between top male and female actors and the overall stagnation of women in all roles over the last 15 years. A positive trend in film may be emerging with an upward climb among women in some key positions behind the scenes.

WOMEN IN FILM

Positional Leadership and Influence

In 2011, women comprised an average of 10 percent of all leadership roles in the top films in front of the camera, behind the scenes, and at the studios. More specifically, as seen in tables 11.1 and 11.2, women held approximately 8 percent of key behind-the-scene positions and 15 percent (5 positions) out of the 33 executive positions available in the major, independent, and mini-major studios. Interestingly, when just the top 10 highest grossing films were analyzed, women were better represented with 13 percent.

From 2008–2011, women constituted 7 percent of all directors, 36 percent of executive producers, 63 percent of producers, 16 percent of writers, 3 percent of cinematographers, and 19 percent of editors. Since 2008 women have declined in the roles of director and editor in general. The decline is modest, yet it may point to a trend similar to the overall decline seen in television and radio.

On the other hand, women have gained modest ground as executive producers and writers. This trend continued throughout 2012.

For the purposes of this report and in better understanding leadership, researchers examined five key roles in behind-the-scenes positions in all major films in 2011. As shown in figure 11.1, on average, women comprised 8 percent of behind-the-scenes roles in films in 2011.

In examining the percentage of women in just the top 10 highest grossing films of 2011, figure 11.2 shows that women's representation

Table 11.1   Major Film Studio Executives by Gender, 2012

Studio	Positions	Gender
Paramount Pictures	Chairman and CEO	Male
	Vice Chairman	Male
Sony Pictures Entertainment	Chairman	Male
	Cochairman	**Female**
	Head of Production	Male
20th Century Fox Entertainment	Chairman and CEO	Male
	Executive Vice President	Male
Universal Studios	Cochair	Male
	Cochair	Male
Walt Disney Studios Motion Pictures	Chairman	Male
	Head of Production	Male
Warner Brothers	Chairman and CEO	Male
	Head of Production	Male
	Executive VP of Communications & Public Affairs	**Female**
Total	**14**	**14%**

Source: Compiled from each company's public records.

Table 11.2   Independent and Mini-Major Film Studio Executives by Gender, 2012

Studio	Position	Gender
MGM	Chairman and CEO	Male
	COO	Male
Lionsgate Entertainment	CEO and Cochairman	Male
	Vice-Chair	Male
	President and CO-COO	Male
Fox Searchlight Pictures	Copresidents	Male, **Female**
Sony Pictures Classics	Copresidents	Male, Male, **Female**
Magnolia Pictures	CEO	Male
Miramax Films	CEO	Male
	President	Male
Overture Films	Senior Vice-President	**Female**
	CEO	Male
Weinstein Company	Cochairs	Male, Male
DreamWorks Films	CEO	Male
	President and CFO	Male
	COO	**Female**
Total	**20**	**20%**

Source: Compiled from each studio's Web site.

Figure 11.1   Trends in Key Behind-the-Scenes Positions in Film

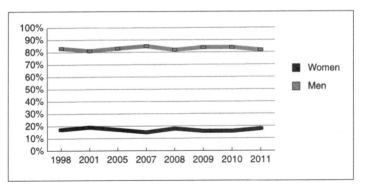

Source: IMDB 2012.

Figure 11.2   Gender Comparison in Behind-the-Scenes Roles in 10 Highest Grossing Films of 2011[3]

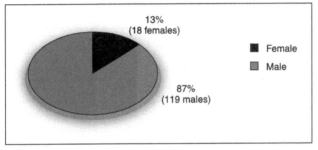

Source: IMDB 2012.

improved with 13 percent in behind-the-scene roles compared to just 8 percent when all films are examined. As this study illustrates, this trend has emerged in most sectors across the United States, where women are often better represented among the top organizations, companies, and entities than in the industry as a whole. The presence of women among the top echelon suggests that either these companies select women to maintain and/or increase their standing, or that women directly help to improve and bolster these companies.

The first half of 2012 showed that women were better represented than in 2011. There was a 5 percent increase among executive producers and editors and a 7 percent increase among writers. Other positions have remained virtually unchanged, except for the role of director, which has continued to decrease slightly.[4] On average, women experienced a slight increase in the

Table 11.3   Top-Grossing Films of 2011[5]

Rank	Film	Lead Role	Studio	Earnings of Film in $ Millions
1	*Harry Potter and the Deathly Hallows Part 2*	M	Warner Bros	$381,011,219
2	*Transformers: Dark of the Moon*	M	Paramount	$352,390,543
3	***The Twilight Saga: Breaking Dawn Part 1***	**F**	**Summit Entertain.**	**$281,287,133**
4	*The Hangover Part 2*	M	Warner Bros.	$254,464,305
5	*Pirates of the Caribbean: On Stranger Tides*	M	Disney	$241,071,802
6	*Fast Five*	M	Universal	$209,837,675
7	*Mission: Impossible—Ghost Protocol*	M	Paramount	$209,397,903
8	*Sherlock Holmes: A Game of Shadows*	M	Warner Bros.	$186,848,418
9	*Thor*	M	Marvel	$181,030,624
10	*Rise of the Planet of the Apes*	M	20th Century Fox	$176,760,185

Source: Box Office Mojo 2012.

film industry over a four-year period. In 2008, 24.5 percent of films had women leaders, and in 2012, 27 percent had women leaders.

According to table 11.3, among the leading on-screen roles available in the 10 highest grossing films of 2011, just one female character was represented, or 10 percent. Women leaders have declined in film both as the protagonist and in some key behind-the-scenes positions. It is unclear to the researchers what caused this decline and whether the decline will continue.

Compensation and Performance

Salary comparisons help to better understand gender disparity in any given industry. Salaries also convey value placed on individuals and positions. Throughout all sectors, women are underpaid regardless of their performance and achievement. In fact, often there is not a correlation between performance and compensation. Two important facts about the top-earning actors from 2010 to 2011 highlight the gender disparity in this sector. First, shown in tables 11.4 and 11.5, the lowest paid male actors earn almost as much as the top-earning female actors.[6] And figure 11.3 shows that

Table 11.4   Top Earning Actors, 2010–2011

Rank	Actor	Earnings in $ Millions
1	Leonardo DiCaprio	$77
2	Johnny Depp*	$50
3	Adam Sandler	$40
4	Will Smith	$36
5	Tom Hanks+	$35
6	Ben Stiller	$34
7	Robert Downey Jr.*	$31
8	Mark Wahlberg	$28
9	Tim Allen (tie)	$22
10	Tom Cruise (tie)*	$22

Source: Pomerantz 2011a.

Table 11.5   Top Earning Actresses, 2010–2011

Rank	Actress	Earnings in $ Millions
1	Angelina Jolie+ (tie)	$30
2	Sarah Jessica Parker (tie)	$30
3	Jennifer Aniston (tie)	$28
4	Reese Witherspoon (tie)	$28
5	Julia Roberts+ (tie)	$20
6	Kristen Stewart* (tie)	$20
7	Katherine Heigl	$19
8	Cameron Diaz	$18
9	Sandra Bullock+	$15
10	Meryl Streep+	$10

*Starred in top-grossing films.

+Earned an Academy Award at some point in his or her career.

Source: Pomerantz 2011b.

women earn approximately one-third of what male actors earn. Second, no correlation exists between the highest paid actor and the top-grossing films. Nor is there a correlation between the highest paid actors and recipients of the Academy Award.

This subjectivity also exists among other industries in arts and entertainment, and points to the subjectivity of earned salaries in the sector. When subjectivity exists in an industry, women often experience the poorest positional representation and disparate salaries. In fact, there were no women of color represented among the top-earning actors of 2011.

Figure 11.3   Film Actor Earnings by Gender, 2010–2011

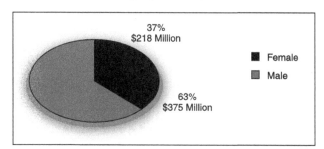

Source: Pomerantz 2011a; Pomerantz 2011b.

WOMEN IN TELEVISION

Positional Leadership and Influence

In general, women are better represented in leadership roles in television than in film, with 31 percent representation on average, and yet female leaders in television have been steadily declining. Like the film industry, women hold more roles as producers than any other position. Women gained a modest (and arguably, statistically insufficient) increase as executive producers in 2011. This finding may be explained by the fact that more women are television producers. However, women have experienced a decline since 2008 in a number of other roles, including producer, writer, editor, and creator. In the roles of director and director of photography, women also continue to experience incremental losses and remain grossly underrepresented.

Unlike film, 2012 was an even more disappointing year for women in television than 2011. It signaled a 15-year low, with declines across all positions, except executive producer (figure 11.4). If this trend continues, which is highly likely, women will be virtually absent in all leadership roles.

The steady and sharp descent of women in television demonstrates that this decline is likely to remain persistent for some time. Women are currently experiencing the lowest representation in television since 1997–1998. Women make up 32 percent of all behind-the-scene roles in television, with the majority occupying producer and executive producer positions. Conversely, women comprised 36 percent of behind-the-scene leadership roles in all television shows in 2008, and 42 percent in 2012.[7] It is unclear what is drawing and/or keeping more women in the production aspect of television when all other roles are at their lowest representation since 1997, and this may be an area of future research worth further investigation. Such findings may help to better explain trends in all sectors, particularly where there is a larger concentration of women.

Figure 11.4   Women in Key Behind-the-Scenes Positions in TV, 1998–2011

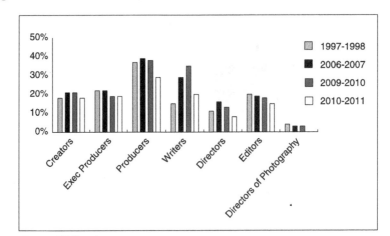

Source: Lauzen 2012b, p.1.

Other factors, such as ratings and earnings, were explored in an attempt to determine if television has the level of subjectivity that film appears to have, and to better understand the industry's top performers. Women comprised approximately 23 percent of the highest-paid television actors in 2011 and 28 percent of the highest-paid television hosts.[8] These earnings are consistent with other industries in arts and entertainment, which suggests that gender bias exists in television as well. Women represent 30 percent of the highest-paid television actors.

In examining the most watched television programs, the findings were inconclusive, and researchers of this report were unable to report ratings with any certainty. Often, popular sporting events or particular episodes would usurp regularly syndicated programs. However, of the television programs with Nielsen's highest ratings, only *Two and a Half Men* and *CSI* claim the highest ratings,[9] and also claim the highest-paid television actors in 2012. Therefore, in television, the most watched programs had some correlation to actors' salaries (table 11.6 and figure 11.5).

Though included in other statistics concerning top television hosts (table 11.7), when analyzing the earnings, in figure 11.6 researchers excluded Oprah Winfrey, who is an exceptional media mogul. Winfrey's earnings expand beyond a typical television host and include multimedia syndication and ownership. We also excluded similar moguls in other sectors. Holding 4 of the 10 positions, or 40 percent, women represent more than one-third of the top television hosts and, excluding Winfrey, earn 28 percent of what men earn as hosts. The disparity between men and women in television is not as great as in film.

Table 11.6   Highest-Paid TV Actors, 2010–2011 (in millions)

Actor	Earnings	Gender
Charlie Sheen	$40 million	Male
Ray Romano[+]	$20	Male
Steve Carell	$15	Male
Mark Harmon	$13	Male
Tina Fey[+]	**$13**	**Female**
Eva Longoria	**$13**	**Female**
Jon Cryer[+]	$11	Male
Laurence Fishburne[+]	$11	Male
Patrick Dempsey	$10	Male
Marcia Cross	**$10**	**Female**

[+]Won Emmy award(s).

Source: Pomerantz 2011c; Pomerantz 2011d.

Figure 11.5   TV Actor Earnings by Gender in 2011 (sum in millions)

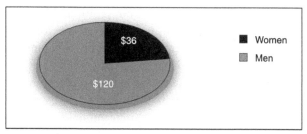

Source: Pomerantz 2011c; Pomerantz 2011d.

Table 11.7   Highest Paid TV Hosts

Rank	Host	Earnings (millions)
1	**Oprah Winfrey[+]**	**$290**
2	Simon Cowell	$90
3	Dr. Phil McGraw	$80
4	Ryan Seacrest	$61
5	Donald Trump	$60
6	**Bethenny Frankel**	**$55**
7	**Ellen Degeneres (tie)[+]**	**$45**
8	David Letterman (tie)	$45
9	**Judge Judy Scheindlin (tie)**	**$45**
10	Glenn Beck	$40

[+]Won Emmy award(s).

Source: Pomerantz 2011e.

Figure 11.6   Earnings among Top Television Hosts (sum in millions) *excluding Oprah Winfrey*

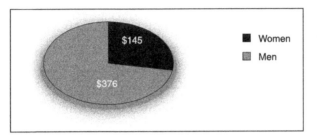

Source: Pomerantz 2011e.

WOMEN IN MUSIC

Positional Leadership and Influence

Researchers of this report were unable to access comparable data to determine the representation of women leaders throughout the music industry. Privately held music companies are not required to disclose earnings and revenues, and have not done so voluntarily. Therefore, public access to the data is limited. Of the publicly owned music companies, including those in table 11.8, *all* of the executives are male. If all data were accessible, researchers would expect that women's representation in music would be considerably lower than in other industries in arts and entertainment. Unfortunately, we were unable to determine an average percentage of women leaders in music with certainty. The pieces of data that were accessible will be analyzed and compared accordingly.

According to figure 11.7, of the top 10 music labels, there were three women and 40 men in executive roles, or 7 percent of women executives.

Billboard ranked the top 25 most influential musical artists, shown in figure 11.8, based on *Billboard* charts, revenue, and decision makers at each company. Among those ranked, more than 99.5 percent of those listed as the most influential in the music industry were men. According to *Billboard*, nearly 85 percent of white male artists were most influential, and 14 percent of men of color. No white woman is ranked among the top 25 influential musicians, and just one female of color is listed, or 0.42 percent.[10]

Compensation and Performance

Among the top-selling albums of 2012, women began to close the leadership gap significantly. Figures 11.9 and 11.10 show that women produced

Table 11.8   Top-Selling Music Labels of 2011[11]

Top 10 Music Labels	# Top-Selling Titles
Sony Music	265
RCA	113
Interscope Geffen A&M	102
Universal Republic	138
Island Def Jam Music Group	86
Atlantic Group	82
Capitol	113
Warner Bros.	99
Sony Music Nashville	47
Capitol Nashville	33

Source: Billboard 2011.

Figure 11.7   Top 10 Music Labels Executives by Gender in 2011

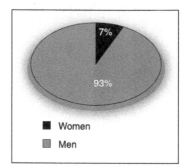

Source: Billboard 2011.

Figure 11.8   Top 25 Influential People in Music Industry, 2011

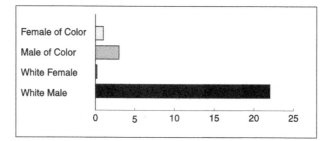

Source: Billboard 2012.

Figure 11.9   Top-Selling Albums of 2012[12]

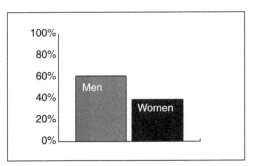

Source: Caulifield 2012.

Figure 11.10   Earnings of Top 10 Male and Female Artists in the Music Industry, 2011[13]

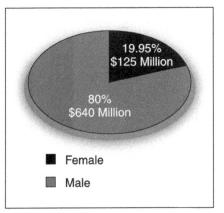

Source: O'Malley Greenburg 2011; Caulifield 2012.

39 percent of the top-selling albums but only 20 percent of salary earnings, as explained in the following section. It is important to note that there exists tremendous variation in reported salaries; however, the top 10 artists can be universally confirmed among various sources. Women of color and white women were equally represented among the top-selling albums. Men of color comprised 25 percent of top-selling male artists, compared to white men at 36 percent. Not surprisingly, women artists earned approximately 75 percent of what their male counterparts earned on average. Among the top-earning artists, women averaged $60 million, while men average $80 million. Despite the fact that women musicians perform well, they do not earn comparable salaries.

WOMEN IN LITERARY PUBLISHING

Positional Leadership and Influence

The trend in music, where women do not earn a proportionate salary to their sales, also exists in the literary publishing industry. Women authors experience a discrepancy between earned income and success on the top sellers' lists. Women account for 20 percent of CEOs in the publishing industry and 60 percent of the best-selling authors. Two out of 10 chief executive officers (CEOs) of publishing companies in 2012 were women (table 11.9), or 20 percent, a drop from 30 percent in 2011. A male replaced Jane Friedman at Harper Collins.[14]

Compensation and Performance

As shown in table 11.10, more female authors (60 percent) claimed a position among the top 10 best sellers in 2011. When examining the 2012 awardees of the National Endowment for the Arts, women outperformed men 80 percent to 20 percent for literary works as shown in figure 11.11. Yet, figure 11.12 shows female authors' earnings are significantly below their male counterparts' earnings. Top women authors earn approximately 27 percent of industry earnings, despite the fact that women produce 60 percent of the best sellers (figure 11.13).[15]

Table 11.9   Top 10 Publishing Company CEOs, 2012

Publishing Company	CEO	Company's Earnings (in millions)
Thomson Reuters	James Smith	$5,435
McGraw-Hill Education	Terry McGraw-Hill	$2,292
Scholastic	Richard (Dick) Robinson	$1,906
Cengage Learning	Michael Hansen	$1,876
Wiley	Steve Smith	$1,743
Reader's Digest	Robert Guth	$1,438
Houghton Mifflin Harcourt	**Linda Zecher**	**$1,295**
HarperCollins	Jane Friedman (2011) Brian Murray (2012)	$1,100
Simon and Schuster	**Carolyn Reidy**	**$787**
Perseus Books	David Steinberger	$350
% Women	**20%**	

Source: DeBarros 2012.

Table 11.10   Top 10 Best Sellers in 2011[16]

Author	Book
1. Kathryn Stockett	*The Help*
2. Suzanne Collins	*The Hunger Games*
3. Todd Burpo	*Heaven Is for Real*
4. Sara Gruen	*Water for Elephants*
5. Suzanne Collins	*Catching Fire*
6. Jeff Kinney	*Diary of a Wimpy Kid: Cabin Fever*
7. Suzanne Collins	*Mockingjay*
8. Walter Isaacson	*Steve Jobs: A Biography*
9. Stieg Larsson	*The Girl with the Dragon Tattoo*
10. Laura Hillenbrand	*Unbroken*
% of Women Top Sellers in 2011	**60%**

Source: DeBarros, Cadden, & Schnaars 2012.

Figure 11.11   2012 Literary Awardees[17]

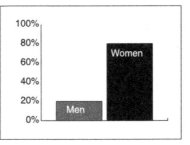

Source: NEA 2012a.

Figure 11.12   Top 10 Best-Selling Authors by Gender, 2011

Figure 11.13   Percentage of Earnings by Gender for Top Authors, 2011 (in millions)

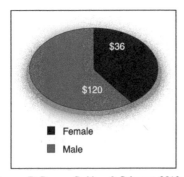

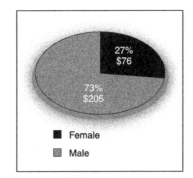

Source: DeBarros, Cadden, & Schnaars 2012.

Source: Bercovici 2011.

Figure 11.14   National Medal of the Arts, 2009–2011[18]

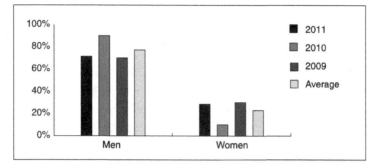

Source: NEA 2012a.

In closing, women entertainers and artists are undercompensated for their success across several industries. The subjectivity that exists in salaries among top-performing women has become much more evident.

However, the percentage of women leaders recognized by the federal government from 2009 to 2011 for the National Medal of the Arts (figure 11.14), a nationally publicized event, is much lower on average than the industry-specific accolades. Women averaged less than 23 percent over the last three years among the National Medal of the Arts recipients. This study has uncovered that it is relatively common for women to excel in production and performance, while failing to be recognized among traditionally structured entities, such as the Academy Awards and the National Medal of the Arts, suggesting that gatekeeping may be one explanation.

CONCLUSIONS

- Arts and entertainment, in addition to other sectors, requires performance-driven criteria for determining earned salaries.
- In negotiating salaries, women should base their earnings on the success and performance of their respective art. Women should also calculate the industry's overall average when considering their salaries.
- Women and men in television should consider ways in which they can attract more women to their industry. With declining numbers in creative and administrative roles, women's overall leadership will be expected to decline as well. If trends continue as projected, women will have faced nearly five years of steady declines.

- While most industries within this sector could improve their data collection, music and the performing arts were particularly void of substantial data on their performers and executives. Leaders in music should insist that data are collected. Similarly, leaders in theatre and other performing arts should also insist on data collection to determine the overall equity and representation in each industry. The performing arts were not included in this study because little, if any, data were found.

- Additionally, fewer movie and television roles exist for white women and even fewer for women of color. Presumably the industry has shied away from female protagonists for fear of poor box office ticket sales and/or inherent male-centric perspectives. It would be interesting to better understand the type of protagonists that drive sales, and whether women protagonists are unwelcomed by the public or need to be better crafted.

- Another methodology should be considered to adequately capture all top performers in the arts and entertainment sector. The vast amount of subjectivity in this chapter begs for a better set of performance measurements. One method, for example, could be to examine top-grossing sales, expansion of the artist's brand in other industries, and a sum total calculation of all national awards.

- More research is suggested in attempting to determine the relationship, if any, between compensation and top performance.

- Finally, as with many sectors, there lacks comprehensive data on women and men of color. As Lord Kelvin once stated, and many thereafter adapted, "If you cannot measure it, you cannot prove it."

SPORTS

Professional and amateur sports consume much of American culture. Whether parents are spending evenings and weekends supporting their young athletes or friends gather on a Sunday afternoon to cheer for their hometown team, sports pervade and inform societal conversations and perceptions. When police arrest a professional athlete, or a sports commission suspends another for drug use, the conversation immediately turns to examining the kind of role model *he* represents for our youth. Much like the way actors serve, albeit inadvertently at times, as role models and community spokespersons, so do athletes. Spectator sports are also a major industry in the United States, representing $25 billion annually with continued growth even during economic recessions.[19] Sports significantly inform and influence American culture and economy. How, if at all, women represent this industry helps to understand their role in society.

Largely, the industry locks women out despite their vast participation at all levels. In schools across America, the number of female athletes soared after the passage in 1972 of Title IX, which made it illegal to exclude anyone from participating in any education program or activity that received federal financial assistance. In 2008, an estimated 8 million girls in grades 3 through 12 participated in an organized sport.[20] In 2010, there were over 3 million females participating in high school athletics, along with more than 186,000 women in NCAA college sports.[21]

Overall, approximately 69 percent of girls in grades 3 through 12 participate in youth sports, compared to 75 percent of their male counterparts. These numbers vary significantly depending on community types. Participation is highest for both boys and girls in suburban communities, where 81 percent of third- through fifth-grade girls and 89 percent of boys participate. By contrast, in urban communities, only 59 percent of third-through fifth-grade girls participate in sports compared to 68 percent of boys.[22] Participation rates are highest at the elementary age and decrease as they reach high school. Girls are more likely to join sports later and quit earlier than boys. This shortened length of participation is especially true for girls of color from low-income families.[23]

Women's participation rates in intercollegiate athletics are at their highest in history. The average number of women's teams at colleges and universities more than tripled from 2.5 per school in 1972 to 8.73 per school in 2012,[24] while the total number of women's teams offered at NCAA member schools jumped from 6,346 in 1998 to 9,660 in 2010. Although there are more women's teams (9,660) than men's teams (8,530), male college athletes (249,307) continue to surpass the number of female athletes (186,460).[25]

NCAA COACHES AND ATHLETIC DIRECTORS

Positional Leadership and Influence

Women's leadership in college coaching has declined since the passage of Title IX. In 1972, 90 percent of coaches of women's teams were women.[26] The massive rise in participation by women in sports, after Title IX, transferred the governance of women's sports from the Association of Intercollegiate Athletics for Women to the National Collegiate Athletic Association (NCAA).[27] Despite the increase to an average 8.73 teams per school in 2012, women coaches in women's sports dropped by more than half, to 42.9 percent. Furthermore, women comprised only 51.7 percent of paid assistant coaches of women's teams, and less than 3 percent of men's teams today are coached by women (figure 11.15).[28]

Figure 11.15   NCAA Female Head Coaches of Women's Teams, 2011

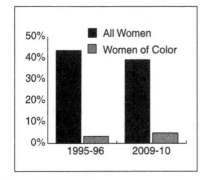

Source: NCAA 2011.

Figure 11.16   Percent NCAA Female Head Coaches by Division

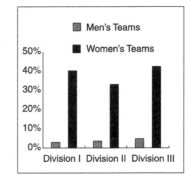

Source: NCAA 2011.

This drastic drop of women coaches since the passage of Title IX should raise a great deal of concern, and yet few are making a concerted effort to address the discrepancy. Little explanation can be offered to effectively attribute the reason for the discrepancy other than gender bias.

The number of female coaches of women's teams does not vary significantly by division. Women make up 42 percent of coaches of women's teams in Division III schools, compared to 40 percent of Division I schools. For men's teams, women are less likely to coach at Division I schools than Division III, 2.9 percent versus 4.8 percent, respectively (figure 11.16).[29]

In administrative leadership, women have made scant progress. The presence of a female collegiate athletic director increases the chances of having female coaches. However, in 2009–2010, only 19.2 percent of collegiate athletic directors, to whom all college coaches report, are female. This is a slight increase from 1995–1996, when women accounted for 16 percent of athletic directors, and yet it is a decrease from 2008 when women made up 21.3 percent of all athletic directors.[30]

Administrative representation of women within the various divisions does matter. Females accounted for only 9.4 percent of athletic directors at Division I schools in 2009–2010, compared to 7.7 percent in 1995–1996. Division III schools have the largest female representation for athletic directors, where women held 28.8 percent of these positions in 2009–2010, compared to 25.5 percent in 1995–1996.[31] Approximately 9.2 percent of athletic departments have no women in any part of their administration. This is a slight improvement from 2010, when 13.2 of departments had no women.[32]

During the 2009–2010 academic year, only 2.4 percent of all athletic directors identified as women of color. By comparison, in 1995–1996, women of color accounted for 1.1 percent of athletic directors. Unlike their white counterparts, women of color fare slightly better at Division I schools (2.3%) than at Division III schools (1.6%).[33]

AMATEUR SPORTS GOVERNANCE ORGANIZATIONS: THE OLYMPICS AND PARALYMPICS

The London Olympics 2012 saw female participation of approximately 44 percent, which was the highest ever at the Olympic Games. In fact, 34 National Olympic Committees (NOCs) representing the various countries had more female athletes than males.[34] The United States was one of these countries, as 51 percent of U.S. athletes were female,[35] which is an increase from 2004 when it was 48 percent. Women also won 55.8 percent of all medals for the United States, including 63 percent of gold medals.[36]

However, the proportion of women leaders in international sports governance does not keep pace with participation levels. As of June 2012, 20 women (19 percent) are active members of the International Olympic Committee (IOC). The highest leadership body of the IOC consists of an executive board that includes the president, four vice presidents and 10 members. Two women are members of that IOC executive board, including Gunilla Lindberg, who is also acting as chairperson for the IOC Coordination Commission for the 2018 Winter Games. On the U.S. Olympic Committee (USOC), women make up 37.5 percent (6 out of 16) of the board of directors and 35.3 percent of the executives.[37] This is a slight decrease from 2008, when women made up 44 percent of the board of directors and 36 percent of the executive team.[38]

In the 2012 Paralympics, 41.2 percent of the athletes were female. On the International Paralympic Committee (IPC), women constituted 13.3 percent of the governing board, which was an increase from 6.7 percent in 2009. By contrast, women occupied half (4 out of 8) of the executive positions and managed 55.6 percent of the sports.[39]

PROFESSIONAL SPORTS LEADERSHIP

In professional sports, a similar pattern emerges. Women make up a minority of leadership positions in professional women's sports, and they are scarcely seen in the men's professional sports arena. Female representation is the greatest at the office management level, though the NBA, MLS, and MLB have seen a slight decrease since 2009, and the NFL has remained unchanged. As shown in figure 11.17, the NBA has the greatest

Figure 11.17   Women in Office Management

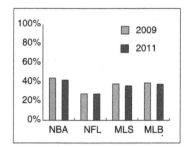

Source: Lapchick 2011; Lapchick 2012.

Figure 11.18   Female Presidents and Vice Presidents of Professional Men's Sports Teams

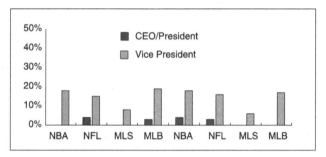

Source: Lapchick 2011; Lapchick 2012.

representation of women at the office management level with 42 percent women, and the NFL has the least with 28 percent.[40]

Of the 62 NBA referees, one was a woman; Shannon Eastin became the first female to officiate a regular season NFL game in 2012,[41] after she was hired as a replacement referee during the lockout of the regular game officials in a labor dispute.[42] Only 4 of the 12 Women's National Basketball Association (WNBA) teams currently have female head coaches, or 33 percent, while 12 of the 20 (60 percent) assistant coaches are female. Only two WNBA teams have female majority owners.[43] Nancy Lieberman became the first female head coach of a men's team under the NBA umbrella, when she coached the development league team the Texas Legends in 2010. She is currently the assistant general manager of the Legends.[44] No other men's professional sports have had a female coach.

Few women have reached the level of president/CEO of a professional sports team, and none in MLS. In the 2011–2012 season, two women held the role of president for NBA franchises.[45] By comparison, as seen in figure 11.18, more women have held vice president roles. Women hold 18 percent of sport presidencies and vice presidencies in the NBA, 17 percent in MLB, 16 percent in the NFL, and 6 percent in MLS, a slight decrease from 2009 for MLS and MLB.[46]

COMPENSATION

At the collegiate level, female athletes are less likely than male athletes to receive recruiting dollars and scholarships. At NCAA member colleges, women athletes receive $136 million less than male athletes. Women in Division I colleges are over 50 percent of the student body, yet they receive only 32 percent of the athletic recruiting dollars and only 37 percent of the total money spent on athletics.[47]

Salaries for NCAA head coaches depend largely on the division and the gender of the team, as shown in figure 11.19. In 2009–2010, the median salary for Division I coaches for men's teams was $916,400 compared to $244,100 for Division III coaches. Not surprisingly, a coach's salary for women's teams is lower than that of men's teams. Division I coaches of female teams earned a median salary of $646,200, while Division III coaches earned $196,800.[48] The pay gap in college sports based on the gender of the team is one of the largest of any industry examined in this 2013 study, with the coaches of women's Division I teams earning approximately 68 percent of what the coaches of male teams earned ($646,200 versus $916,400).

To gain perspective on earnings in professional sports, researchers of this study have focused more on men and women in golf and tennis.

Figure 11.19   Collegiate Head Coach's Salary by Division

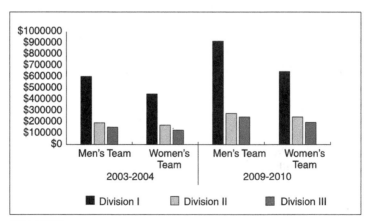

Source: NCAA 2012.

Professional basketball would not be accurate, because too many extenuating variables exist between the men's and women's leagues. For instance, men have played professional basketball in the United States for 63 years, and women have played for 13 years. In addition, the men have 30 teams and play 82 games over a seven-month season, whereas women have 13 teams and play 34 games over a four-month season. As a result, women have had far less time to establish the popularity of women's basketball with the public and reap the licensing and sponsorship rewards that follow. However, it is still important to note that the largest salary within the WNBA was $89,000, compared to the salary of $15.355 million for an NBA player.[49]

In the 2012 *Forbes* list of the highest-paid athletes in all sports, men comprised the entire list. Tennis is the one sport where women come closest to men in overall earning power (table 11.11). In addition to higher prize money, the sport's global appeal has increased endorsement and sponsorship opportunities for women. In fact, 5 of the top 10 highest-paid tennis stars are women—a hard-won achievement not seen in any other sport. The Grand Slam tournaments offer a promising story for women. These four premium tournaments (Wimbledon Tennis Championships, the French Open, the Australian Open, and the U.S. Open) are among the high-profile, internationally televised tournaments in which women and men play in the same place, at the same time. The Grand Slams are also the only tournaments in which the prize money for men and women is equal. Tennis legends Billie Jean King and Venus Williams campaigned to achieve pay equity.[50]

Table 11.11   Top 10 Highest-Paid Tennis Players 2011[51]

Rank	Athlete	Total Pay (in millions)	Gender
1	Roger Federer	$47	M
2	Rafael Nadal	$31	M
3	Maria Sharapova	$25	F
4	Novak Djokovic	$18	M
5	Andy Murray	$13.5	M
6	Andy Roddick	$13	M
7	Caroline Wozniacki	$12.5	F
8	Venus Williams	$11.5	F
9	Kim Clijsters	$11	F
10	Serena Williams	$10.5	F

Source: Forbes 2011b.

For professional tennis players and golfers, the gender pay gap can also be dramatic. The pay difference is especially noticeable when the pay of top 10 athletes is compared to the top 10 highest-paid female athletes. Shown in table 11.12, Maria Sharapova, who is the highest-paid female athlete (tennis) at $25 million, made substantially less than Haloti Ngata, who is ranked as the 10th highest-paid male athlete (football) overall at $37.3 million. A similar trend emerges in golf, where the top 10 highest-paid golfers are also all men (table 11.13). The total prize money for the PGA tour is $256 million, which is over five times more than the total prize money for the women's LPGA tour.[52]

Table 11.12   Top 10 Highest-Paid Professional Female Athletes, 2012[53]

Rank	Athlete	Total Pay (in millions)
1	Maria Sharapova	$25
2	Caroline Wozniacki	$12.5
3	Danica Patrick	$12
4	Venus Williams	$11.5
5	Kim Clijsters	$11
6	Serena Williams	$10.5
7	Kim Yu-Na	$10
8	Li Na	$8
9	Ana Ivanovic	$6
10	Paula Creamer	$5.5

Source: Forbes 2011a.

Table 11.13   Top 10 Highest-Paid Golfers, 2012[54]

Rank	Athlete	Total Pay (in millions)
1	Tiger Woods	$61.2
2	Phil Mickelson	$46.7
3	Ernie Els	$22.3
4	Luke Donald	$20
5	Rory Mcilroy	$16.4
6	Sergio Garcia	$16.2
7	Bill Haas	$16.1
8	Lee Westwood	$12.8
9	Matt Kuchar	$12.5
10	Adam Scott	$11.9

Source: Forbes 2012b.

CONCLUSIONS

The sports industry's disparate salaries and opportunities for women to participate, coach, or lead sends a clear message to women that they lack value and are disposable. But the post-Title IX explosion of girls' and women's athletic participation injected new energy and growth into the sports sector. To ensure that newfound passion for sports moves beyond the locker room and into leadership positions for women, the sports industry will need to make some changes.

As with the other sectors studied, we urge the industry to work toward creating a critical mass of women in top leadership positions. There is a dearth of women directors in college athletics, on IOC commissions, on IPC committees, and in USOC governing body leadership. There are also comparatively few women in professional sports leadership as head coaches, owners, and commissioners. We have impressive numbers of women athletes, but the United States lacks similar representation within the leadership of this sector.

- Enforce the provisions under Title IX that govern resource allocations for students, coaches, and administrators. Again, more can be done to comply with pay-equity legislation (i.e., Lilly Ledbetter Fair Pay Act of 2009, Equity Pay Act, and Title VII) as it pertains to ensuring workplace equity and opportunities for leadership.
- Encourage and enforce compliance with existing policies throughout the amateur athletic community. The provisions that are outlined by the Equal Employment Opportunity Commission, Amateur Sports Act, Title IX of the Education Amendments Act, and the USOC and IOC are not consistently implemented.
- Protect women and men from retaliation or job loss when they report inequities. Coaches, administrators, parents, and other interested persons in high schools and colleges must feel safe to inform authorities of inequities.
- Professional sports organizations should make expanding leadership opportunities for women a top priority. Commissioners and leagues should revisit hiring criteria and procedures with the goal of at least one-third participation by women, including women of color.
- Business organizations across the sports sector should adopt policies that expand high-level employment opportunities for women, using accountability measures that are made public to assess progress. As girls' and women's participation in sports has increased from playing power to buying power, it is good business, for sports marketing,

media entertainment, equipment, and apparel industries, to employ a critical mass of women at high levels to help shape the future of this industry.

• Allow greater opportunity for women to be represented in the ESPY Awards and other sports-related awards. Although there are some female-specific categories the "gender-neutral" categories are almost exclusively and repeatedly won by men.

NOTES

1. Weaver, M. (March 8, 2010). "Kathryn Bigelow Makes History as First Woman to Win Best Director." *The Guardian.* Accessed June 29, 2012, at http://www.guardian.co.uk/film/2010/mar/08/kathryn-bigelow-oscars-best-director.

2. Jacobs, S. (Jan. 31, 2012). First Black Woman Wins Best Director at Sundance. Accessed June 29, 2012, at http://africasacountry.com/first-black-woman-wins-best-director-at-sundance/.

3. Internet Movie Database. (2012). Accessed June 2012 at:
   http://www.imdb.com/title/tt1201607/combined
   http://www.imdb.com/title/tt1399103/
   http://www.imdb.com/title/tt1324999/
   http://www.imdb.com/title/tt1411697/fullcredits#cast
   http://www.imdb.com/title/tt1298650/
   http://www.imdb.com/title/tt1596343/fullcredits#cast
   http://www.imdb.com/title/tt1229238/fullcredits#writers
   http://www.imdb.com/title/tt1515091/
   http://www.imdb.com/title/tt0800369/fullcredits#directors
   http://www.imdb.com/title/tt1318514/fullcredits#writers.

4. Lauzen, M. (2009a). The Celluloid Ceiling: Behind-the-Scenes Employment of Women on the Top 250 Films of 2008. *Center for the Study of Women in Television & Film.* Accessed June 2012 at http://womenintvfilm.sdsu.edu/files/2008_celluloid_ceiling.pdf.

5. Box Office Mojo. (2011). *2011 Domestic Grosses.* Accessed June 2012 at http://www.boxofficemojo.com/yearly/chart/?yr=2011&p=.htm.

6. Ms. Dorothy Pomerantz calculated earnings based on acting performances and not endorsements or sponsorships. Pomerantz, D. (2011a). "Hollywood's Highest-Earning Actors." *Forbes.* Accessed June 2012 at http://www.forbes.com/sites/dorothypomerantz/2011/08/01/hollywoods-highest-earning-actors/.

Pomerantz, D. (2011b). "Hollywood's Highest Paid Actresses." *Forbes.* Accessed June 2012 at http://www.forbes.com/sites/dorothypomerantz/2011/07/05/hollywoods-highest-paid-actresses/.

Pomerantz, D. (2011c). "Hollywood's Highest-Paid TV Actors." *Forbes.* AccessedJune2012athttp://www.forbes.com/sites/dorothypomerantz/2011/10/11/hollywoods-highest-paid-tv-actors/.

Pomerantz, D. (2011d). "Hollywood's Highest-Paid TV Actresses." *Forbes.* Accessed June 2012 at http://www.forbes.com/sites/dorothypomerantz/2011/09/27/hollywoods-highest-paid-tv-actresses/.

Pomerantz, D. (2011e). "TV's Top Earning Hosts." *Forbes.* Accessed June 2012 at http://www.forbes.com/sites/dorothypomerantz/2011/07/25/tvs-top-earning-hosts/.

7. Lauzen, M. (2009b). Boxed In: Women on Screen and Behind the Scenes in the 2008–2009 Prime-time Season. *Center for the Study of Women in Television & Film.* Accessed June 2012 at http://www.wif.org/images/repository/pdf/other/2009-10_boxed_in_sum_2.pdf.

Lauzen, M. (2012a). The Celluloid Ceiling: Behind-the-Scenes Employment of Women on the Top 250 Films of 2011. *Center for the Study of Women in Television & Film.* Accessed June 2012 at http://womenintvfilm.sdsu.edu/files/2011_Celluloid_Ceiling_Exec_Summ.pdf.

Lauzen, M. (2012b). Boxed In: Employment of Behind-the-Scenes Women in the 2010–11 Prime-time Television Season. *Center for the Study of Women in Television & Film.* Accessed June 2012 at http://womenintvfilm.sdsu.edu/files/2010-2011_Boxed_In_Exec_Summ.pdf.

8. Lauzen, M. (2009b). Boxed In: Women on Screen and Behind the Scenes in the 2008–2009 Prime-time Season. *Center for the Study of Women in Television & Film.* Accessed June 2012 at http://www.wif.org/images/repository/pdf/other/2009-10_boxed_in_sum_2.pdf.

Lauzen, M. (2012a). The Celluloid Ceiling: Behind-the-Scenes Employment of Women on the Top 250 Films of 2011. *Center for the Study of Women in Television & Film.* Accessed June 2012 at http://womenintvfilm.sdsu.edu/files/2011_Celluloid_Ceiling_Exec_Summ.pdf;

Lauzen, M. (2012b). Boxed In: Employment of Behind-the-Scenes Women in the 2010–11 Prime-time Television Season. *Center for the Study of Women in Television & Film.* Accessed June 2012 at http://womenintvfilm.sdsu.edu/files/2010-2011_Boxed_In_Exec_Summ.pdf.

9. Nielsen. (2012). Media and Entertainment. Accessed at http://www.nielsen.com/us/en/newswire/2012/nielsen-tops-of-2012-television.html.

10. Billboard. (2012). Billboard Reveals the 2012 Power 100. Accessed June 27, 2012, at http://www.billboard.biz/bbbiz/industry/record-labels/billboard-reveals-the-2012-power-100-1005969352.story.

11. Billboard. (2011). Year End Charts. Accessed at http://www.billboard.com/articles/news/42340/the-best-of-2011-the-year-in-music.

12. Caulifield, K. (Jan. 4, 2012). Adele Rules 2011 with Top Selling Album & Song. Accessed June 27, 2012, at http://www.billboard.com/news/adele-rules-2011-with-top-selling-album-1005784152.story#/news/adele-rules-2011-with-top-selling-album-1005784152.story.

13. O'Malley Greenburg, Z. (June 15, 2011). "World's Highest-Paid Musicians." *Forbes.* Accessed June 27, 2012, at http://www.forbes.com/sites/zackomalleygreenburg/2011/06/15/the-worlds-highest-paid-musicians/;

Caulifield, K. (Jan. 4, 2012). Adele Rules 2011 with Top Selling Album & Song. Accessed June 27, 2012, at http://www.billboard.com/news/adele-rules-2011-with-top-selling-album-1005784152.story#/news/adele-rules-2011-with-top-selling-album-1005784152.story.

14. Publishers Weekly. (June 2012). "The Global 50: The World's Largest Book Publishers, 2012." *Publishers Weekly*. Accessed July 1, 2012 at http://www.publishersweekly.com/pw/by-topic/industry-news/financial-reporting/article/52677-the-world-s-54-largest-book-publishers-2012.html.

15. Bercovici, J. (Aug. 17, 2011). "The World's Highest-Paid Authors." *Forbes*. Accessed June 2012 at http://www.forbes.com/sites/jeffbercovici/2011/08/17/the-worlds-highest-paid-authors/.

16. DeBarros, A., M. Cadden, and C. Schnaars. (Jan. 11, 2012). "100 Best-Selling Books of 2011, At the Top Down." *USA Today*. Accessed June 27, 2012, at http://www.usatoday.com/life/books/news/story/2012-01-11/100-best-selling-books-of-2011/52504752/1.

17. National Endowment for the Arts. (2012a). Grants Awards: Literary Prose. Accessed September 29, 2012, at http://apps.nea.gov/GrantSearch/.

National Endowment for the Arts. (2012b). National Medal of Arts. Accessed September 29, 2012, at http://arts.gov/honors/medals.

18. National Endowment for the Arts. (2012a). Grants Awards: Literary Prose. Accessed September 29, 2012, at http://apps.nea.gov/GrantSearch/.

National Endowment for the Arts. (2012b). National Medal of Arts. Accessed September 29, 2012, at http://arts.gov/honors/medals.

19. Hambrecht, W. (2012). The U.S. Professional Sports Market and Franchise Report 2012. Accessed at http://www.wrhambrecht.com/wp-content/uploads/2013/09/SportsMarketReport_2012.pdf.

20. Sebo, D. and P. Veliz. (2008). Go Out and Play: Youth Sports in America. Women's Sports Foundation. East Meadow, NY.

21. U.S. Census. (2012). Participation in NCAA Sports by Sex: 2009 to 2010. Accessed at http://www.census.gov/compendia/statab/2012/tables/12s1247.pdf.

22. Sebo, D. (2009). The Gender Gap in Youth Sports: Too Many Urban Girls Are Being Left Behind. *Journal of Physical Education, Recreation & Dance*. 80(8): 36.

23. Sebo, D. (2009). The Gender Gap in Youth Sports: Too Many Urban Girls Are Being Left Behind. *Journal of Physical Education, Recreation & Dance*. 80(8): 37.

24. Acosta, R. and L. Carpenter. (2012). Women in Intercollegiate Sport: A Longitudinal, National Study Thirty-Five Year Update. Accessed at http://acosta-carpenter.org/AcostaCarpenter2012.pdf.

25. National Collegiate Athletic Association (NCAA). (Feb. 2011). Race and Gender Demographics: 2009–2010. *NCAA*. Accessed at http://www.ncaapublications.com/productdownloads/2010RaceGenderMember.pdf.

26. Acosta, R. and L. Carpenter. (2012). Women in Intercollegiate Sport: A Longitudinal, National Study Thirty-Five Year Update. Accessed at http://acosta-carpenter.org/AcostaCarpenter2012.pdf.

27. Bowling Green University (BGU). (2009). Title IX: Implications for Women in Sport and Education. Accessed at http://wbgu.org/programming/titleIX/titleix.pdf.

28. Acosta, R. and L. Carpenter. (2012). Women in Intercollegiate Sport: A Longitudinal, National Study Thirty-Five Year Update. Accessed at http://acosta-carpenter.org/AcostaCarpenter2012.pdf.

29. NCAA. (January 2012). NCAA Gender-Equity Report: 2004–2010. *NCAA.* Accessed at http://www.ncaapublications.com/productdownloads/GEQS10.pdf.

30. NCAA. (January 2012). NCAA Gender-Equity Report: 2004–2010. *NCAA.* Accessed at http://www.ncaapublications.com/productdownloads/GEQS10.pdf.

31. Ibid.

32. Acosta, R. and L. Carpenter. (2012). Women in Intercollegiate Sport: A Longitudinal, National Study Thirty-Five Year Update. Accessed at http://acosta-carpenter.org/AcostaCarpenter2012.pdf.

33. NCAA. (January 2012). NCAA Gender-Equity Report: 2004–2010. *NCAA.* Accessed at http://www.ncaapublications.com/productdownloads/GEQS10.pdf.

34. United States Olympic Committee (USOC). (2012). Key Leadership. Accessed at http://www.teamusa.org/About-the-USOC/Inside-the-USOC/Leadership.

35. Chappell, B. (2012). "Year of the Women at the London Games For Americans? It's True." *National Public Radio.* Accessed at http://www.npr.org/blogs/thetorch/2012/08/10/158570021/year-of-the-woman-at-the-london-games-for-americans-its-true.

36. NCAA. (January 2012). NCAA Gender-Equity Report: 2004–2010. *NCAA.* Accessed at http://www.ncaapublications.com/productdownloads/GEQS10.pdf.

37. USOC. (2012). Key Leadership. Accessed at http://www.teamusa.org/About-the-USOC/Inside-the-USOC/Leadership.

38. Smith M., and Wrynn, A. (2009). Fulfilling the Promise of Equity: Women in the 2000, 2004 and 2008 Olympic and Paralympic Games, *Congress of the International Society for the History of Physical Education and Sport.* Stirling, Scotland.

39. International Paralympic Committee (IPC). (2012). About the International Paralympic Committee. Accessed at www.paralympic.org/TheIPC.

40. Lapchick, R. (2011a). The 2011 Racial and Gender Report Card: Major League Soccer. Accessed at http://www.tidesport.org/RGRC/2011/MLS_RGRC_FINAL.pdf.

Lapchick, R. (2011b). The 2011 Racial and Gender Report Card: National Football League. Accessed at http://www.tidesport.org/RGRC/2011/RGRC_NFL_2011_FINAL.pdf.

41. Lapchick, R. (2012a), p. 2. The 2012 Racial and Gender Report Card: National Basketball Association. Accessed at http://www.tidesport.org/RGRC/2012/2012_NBA_RGRC[1].pdf.

42. Sipple, G. (2012). Shannon Eastin Makes History. *USA Today.* Accessed at www.usatoday.com/sports/football/nfl/story/2012-09-09/shannon-eastin-lions-rams/57717274/1.

43. WNBA. (2012). Front Office. Accessed at http://www.wnba.com/dream/frontoffice/about_the_owners.html.

44. Stein, M. (2011). Nancy Lieberman named assistant GM. *ESPN*. Accessed at http://espn.go.com/dallas/nba/story/_/id/6778575/nancy-lieberman-named-assistant-gm-d-league-legends.

45. Lapchick, R. (2012a), p. 2. The 2012 Racial and Gender Report Card: National Basketball Association. Accessed at http://www.tidesport.org/RGRC/2012/2012_NBA_RGRC[1].pdf.

46. Ibid. Lapchick, R. (2011b). The 2011 Racial and Gender Report Card: National Football League. Accessed at http://www.tidesport.org/RGRC/2011/RGRC_NFL_2011_FINAL.pdf.

47. Acosta, R. and L. Carpenter. (2012). Women in Intercollegiate Sport: A Longitudinal, National Study Thirty-Five Year Update. Accessed at http://acosta-carpenter.org/AcostaCarpenter2012.pdf.

48. NCAA. (January 2012). NCAA Gender-Equity Report: 2004–2010. *NCAA*. Accessed at http://www.ncaapublications.com/productdownloads/GEQS10.pdf.

49. Women Sports Foundation. (2011). Equity Issues: Pay Inequity in Athletics. Accessed at http://www.womenssportsfoundation.org/home/research/articles-and-reports/equity-issues/pay-inequity.

50. The Raw Story. (2007). Female Stars Hail Wimbledon Equal Pay. *Raw Story*. Accessed August 5, 2009, at http://newsinfo.inquirer.net/breakingnews/world/view/20070222-51066/Female_stars_hail_Wimbledon_equal_pay_deal_.

51. Forbes. (2011b). The World's Highest-Paid Tennis Players. Accessed at http://www.forbes.com/sites/kurtbadenhausen/2011/08/25/the-worlds-highest-paid-tennis-players/.

52. Women Sports Foundation. (2011). Equity Issues: Pay Inequity in Athletics. Accessed at http://www.womenssportsfoundation.org/home/research/articles-and-reports/equity-issues/pay-inequity.

53. Forbes. (2012a). The World's Highest Paid Athletes. Accessed at http://www.forbes.com/athletes/.

54. Forbes. (2012b). Highest Paid Golfers. Accessed at http://www.forbes.com/sites/kurtbadenhausen/2012/08/01/tiger-woods-tops-list-of-the-worlds-highest-paid-golfers/.

12

Best Practices and Strategies for Employing Excellence

If the axiom, often erroneously attributed to Albert Einstein, "not everything that counts can be counted, and that not everything that can be counted counts" is a testament to performance and climate, then let us surrender to measuring that which matters.[1] Yet, there are ways to measure what matters, as long as we are willing to determine what it is that matters. It may seem redundant but it is not, and here is why. Objective metrics refer to the subjective criteria deemed most important to an organization. It is objective because it measures the criteria uniformly across the entire organization, regardless of gender or race. It is objective because employees should know when success is measured. Subjective criteria refer to illusive or ambiguous metrics that may or may not apply uniformly. A sticking point for critics is that companies cannot measure whether an inclusive climate exists, or if companies can measure climate they can only do so crudely. If one cannot demonstrate when employees are not engaging in biases, then they cannot show when an employee engages in behavioral and attitudinal biases, which is deeply problematic. Perhaps algebraic in nature, this logic seeks to improve the notion of performance and climate to ensure the best and brightest rise. The results of the national study contained in the pages of this book strongly suggest that when an organization focuses on performance and climate, women rise in the leadership ranks and receive more equitable compensation. Developmental programs and training should support an inclusive climate and performance management, but alone, employee development will have little positive effect. Will some find it difficult to *really* measure performance? Yes, for a variety of technically nuanced and visceral reasons.

Case studies were conducted to identify human resource policies and standards for hiring practices and performance management to determine how standardized hiring practices affect executive leadership positions for women. The research question presented included what conditions exist or do not exist within an organization related to talent management (hiring/promotional) policies and practices that help or hinder the ability of women to obtain executive level leadership positions? The hypothesis, which formed the basis of the research question, centered on a theory that companies who have fewer women in leadership positions are more likely to have nonuniform talent management practices that do not align with the documented values and policies of the organization. Such companies would have more subjective rather than objective practices, making room for favoritism and other behaviors that can block access for women into high-level positions.

Data collection included anonymous interviews with senior leaders and staff, an analysis of government surveys, public business records, human resource policies, organizational practices, and pending and resolved lawsuits. The entities chosen were:

- Google
- U.S. Department of Treasury
- Social Security Administration
- TIAA-CREF
- Walmart
- Xerox

The research team grouped common themes to determine the policies and practices for hiring and promotion within each entity. After combing through thousands of pages of data, we assigned numeric values and calculated percentages for each theme. Several subsets under each theme were created to allow for a deeper level of analysis. The overall themes were:

- Selection—hiring and recruitment practices
- Retention—efforts made to retain current employees
- Development—efforts made toward growth and development

- Motivation/Rewards—motivation to succeed and rewards for success for employees
- Gatekeeping—formal structures that advance or inhibit hiring and promotion, and applied consistently to employees

Because my team and I found gatekeeping present throughout each theme, we sought to distinguish between informal and formal gatekeeping. Informal gatekeeping refers to practices inconsistently applied and "policy" adaptation that achieves an intended result for some select persons or employees. Informal gatekeeping tends to have the most detrimental consequences on employee performance and climate, and adversely affects opportunities for women's advancement. Formal gatekeeping may have positive results, although as it relates to hiring, it could create inefficiencies, and/or fail to achieve its intended purpose.

The strategies and best practices emerged from the companies' practices and policies as they relate to climate and performance. It is important to note that gaining extensive access to Xerox and Walmart proved difficult. High-level employees were unwilling to speak in great detail about hiring and promotional practices, and they promptly cut off interview access due to nondisclosure clauses in their employment contracts.

Two primary lessons gleaned from the case studies convey precisely that senior leadership must invest in an inclusive, performance-based climate. This conclusion holds much truth for the hiring and promotion of women leaders. The first lesson: the members of the executive leadership team matter greatly in setting the tone and practices of the organization. It is insufficient to have stellar policies if the leadership does not embrace them, and fails to employ them when hiring executive team members. The second lesson indicated that staff and leadership development programs will prove beneficial only when an entity has a strong grasp on the current practices, both informal and formal, and the areas of needed improvement. In other words, development programs should target those policies and practices that require corrections and/or enhancements.

Some of the entities are models to emulate, and others suggest what not to do. It is fair to summarize that all of the entities we examined seek to improve their leadership demography. In interviewing human resources and diversity officers and managers and positional leaders of some of the most influential and successful businesses in the United States, we identified the formulaic strategies and best practices that encourage a high-performance and inclusive culture. A focus on performance and an inclusive climate allows greater opportunities for all women, as well as men of color. Some of the entities had a higher than average percentage of women leaders, some fell significantly below average, while other exceeded the industry percentages.

UNDERSTAND WHAT IS BROKEN BEFORE ATTEMPTING TO FIX IT

In his article *Talent management: Aligning your organisation with best practices in strategic and tactical talent management,* Dr. William J. Rothwell[2] discusses the importance of employee development, as well as rewards and retention as best practices in talent management. Dr. Rothwell's discussion supports the data in this national study, particularly regarding the investment of resources for employee development, employee retention, and motivation and rewards. While his premise aligns well with best practices for employing excellence contained herein, an important qualification became evident. Focusing on developmental activities, trainings, and so on for employees will ensure an inclusive, highly successful culture, *if* the existing climate and performance management system aligns with and supports the developmental activities (see figure 12.1). Additionally, development programs should specifically reinforce that which the company does well and focus on areas of needed improvement.

The alignment of climate, development, and performance became the cornerstone of success for many of the selected companies and organizations, and the failure of such an alignment caused continued problems. Focusing on development programs that sought to reduce racial biases, for example, when the problem area was that an insufficient performance-based climate existed will not render positive results for a company. When specific performance-based criteria and metrics lack in practice or transparency, staff developmental programs will prove fruitless.

Figure 12.1   The Relationship between Climate and Performance, and the Effective Role of Development

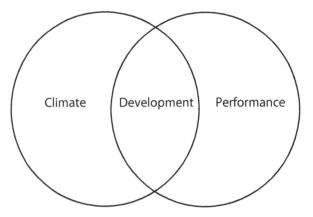

Climate   Development   Performance

Many of the selected companies and organizations have invested a great deal to realize a more equitable system and improve leadership demography. However, not all financial and staff investments have improved leadership demography ultimately. The primary reason for the lack of improvement, despite the plethora of resources contributed, was due to poor alignment of climate, performance, and development programs. Google, on the other hand, reflects a very different conundrum, a similar conundrum that the federal government has corrected in recent years: gatekeeping. The Venn diagram above demonstrates the role of staff and leadership development. The needs of an organization will determine where it should place the emphasis. As you will see from the Venn diagrams below, capturing the foci of the entities reveal that the emphasis is not always placed correctly.

CLIMATE AND THE UNINTENDED-INTENDED CONSEQUENCES

Walmart: Executive Leadership Largely Informs Climate

The first Walmart store, with a focus on one-stop shopping, opened in 1962. The company grew from 190 stores in the 1970s to 800 stores in 1985, and the company strategically opened in small towns rather than big cities.[3] Revenue totaled $469.162 billion in 2012. Walmart is the largest employer in the United States, employing almost five times as many people as IBM, which is the second largest employer in the United States. Women comprise approximately 57 percent of Walmart's U.S. workforce, compared to 48.3 percent in the retail industry, and 46.9 percent in the U.S. labor force.[4]

One of the most powerful lessons from Walmart is to remain unafraid to have difficult conversations regarding leadership demography and performance. Walmart has invested a great deal in developmental activities and trainings for employees, yet the predominate climate and performance culture have remained intact, obstructing a major climate shift. Walmart is conflicted between the personal values of its CEOs and the legacy of the founding family, company policy, and substantive societal pressure. Since the first Walmart store opened, the company has had just four CEOs, creating consistency in culture and climate that does not always serve a company. On the one hand, Walmart states that it has expanded its antidiscrimination policy, protecting gay and lesbian employees,[5] and announced their new definition of "family" that includes same-sex partners.[6] On the other hand, Walmart's Michael Terry (Duke), president and CEO, signed a petition in 2008 that put Act 1 on the ballot in Arkansas, Duke's home state. The controversial initiative, which passed by 57 percent of the voters, states that only married couples may become adoptive or foster parents in Arkansas, closing the door for same-sex couples. This is just one example suggesting that mounting litigation and criticism from the public and its employees have pressured Walmart to address its lack of diversity, yet inclusivity has not become a cornerstone value of its leadership.

The message from Walmart is that the company is prepared to invest in employees and is willing to hire and promote diverse candidates, particularly in middle management. Walmart has consistently delivered this message in response to specific criticisms, and the public has perceived Walmart as reactive and defensive rather than offensive. Walmart receives more than its share of public criticisms, deserved or not, likely because it is one of the largest employers. Yet, the company has invested and spent millions in improving diversity, which is more than many other companies can report. The unfortunate aspect is that the company's has spent a great deal of focus on improving the climate surrounding middle management, with some limited success:

After a thorough analysis and several interviews, the company appears to lack focus in ensuring a performance-based, inclusive climate for senior hires and promotions, in particular. Generally speaking women are represented in middle management across sectors. The gap remains in the top positional leadership roles. When a company focuses on middle management to near singularly, rather than on executive leadership as well, it demonstrates that the company does not really understand how biases and/or perception infuse and infiltrate actual practices and policies.

Walmart is average compared to its peer companies in terms of hiring and promoting female senior leaders, hovering around 26 percent, yet women are still underrepresented. Walmart's strategy included a heavy emphasis on development, without fully understanding where it is most vulnerable: executive leadership. When it comes to hiring and promoting executive leaders there is a lack of development, and performance metrics are not applied consistently, adversely affecting the company's overall climate.

With nearly 2.2 million employees worldwide, Walmart has faced many lawsuits and issues regarding its workforce. Issues have included low wages, poor working conditions, inadequate health care, and the company's strong antiunion policies. I concede that some pending and dismissed lawsuits add little value in understanding the policies and practices of a company; however, resolved and fully vetted suits with extensive discovery processes disclose a great deal about practices and policies. To this end, we identified and analyzed fully vetted suits that specifically detailed hiring and promotion practices and policies.

Critics point to Walmart's high employee turnover rate of 70 percent, although its turnover rate is only slightly higher than the retail industry as a whole (67 percent[7]). Like other retail companies, the majority of employees leave within the first year.[8] Despite the turnover rate, the company has a significant impact on reducing unemployment rates. A study, conducted by Oklahoma State University, indicates that "Walmart is found to have substantially lowered the relative unemployment rates of *blacks* in those counties where it is present, but to have had only a limited impact on relative incomes after the influences of other socio-economic variables were taken into account."[9]

Among the dozen lawsuits or more during the past 10 years, plaintiffs, many of whom included the U.S. Equal Employment Opportunity Commission (EEOC), claimed that Walmart discriminated based on gender, race, and disability. The gender discrimination claims follow. In 2001, six former female employees filed a lawsuit in federal court claiming that Walmart systematically denied promotions and equal pay to its female employees. To counter mounting criticisms and lawsuits, former Walmart CEO Lee Scott pledged that his company would become a leader in employment practices. To this end, Scott created the Office of Diversity in 2004 to focus on programs that develop pools of qualified, diverse candidates. Scott and his human resource team adopted a new job classification system to determine pay and promotions, specifically focused on women.

In the same year, as the new diversity initiatives began, 1.6 million past and present female employees joined a class action lawsuit, noted as the largest discrimination lawsuit in American history. The class action suit detailed how two-thirds of all hourly wage employees at Walmart are female, women account for only one-third of managers, and only 15 percent of senior managers. Walmart appealed the class action status. In 2011, the United States Supreme Court ruled in favor of Walmart stating that the plaintiffs did not have enough in common to constitute a class. The court ruled, in a five to four decision, that because of the variability of the plaintiffs' circumstances, the class action could not proceed as any kind of class action suit.[10]

Spokeswoman Mona Williams made a public statement that, "Walmart continually evaluates employment practices."[11] Walmart has invested a great deal in staff development, programming, and training with a particular focus on building a pipeline of qualified women and men of color. To this end, and as part of its performance metrics, Walmart includes mentoring as a criterion. Managers that serve as mentors receive higher "marks" on their performance evaluations. Walmart, in the last five years, has made significant strides in hiring female middle managers. Like many of the

Fortune 1000 companies, there exists a proportional representation of females in middle management. In Fortune 1000 companies as the influence of the position increases, the percentage of women decreases. This same trend exists with Walmart. In short, Walmart compares similarly to most of the Fortune companies, although it receives a great deal more pressure, likely due to the vast number of employees.

Yet, despite their best efforts since 2004, legal challenges for Walmart continue. In 2010, Walmart paid more than $11.7 million to settle an EEOC sex discrimination suit.[12] Again, in 2013, the EEOC sued Walmart for sexual harassment, retaliation, and disability discrimination. Walmart settled the EEOC lawsuit for $50,000.[13] In 2011, Walmart posted the following progress on its Web site:[14]

- 38 percent of our executive vice president promotions were women.
- 34 percent of officer promotions were women; 22 percent were people of color.
- 27 percent of our corporate officers were women; 20 percent were people of color.
- 54 percent of hourly associates promoted in our stores and clubs were women.
- 77 percent of our store and club operations management started as hourly associates.
- Nearly 42 percent of our Walmart U.S. first- and mid-level officials/managers are women.
- Walmart is one of the most diverse employers in the United States [with] 813,000 female [employees]. [The statement followed a chart comparing Walmart and EEOC standards.]
- 27 percent of Walmart's U.S. officers are women, compared to 17.9 percent in the retail industry and 14.3 percent in U.S. business.[15]

Using the same criteria employed for other companies, our analysis revealed the following. With 38 people in the top level executive positions, 10 were female, or 26 percent, and 28 are male, or 74 percent. Eight of the 10 women identify as white, one of the females is Latina, and another is African American, or 16 percent identifying as women of color. Of the 10 female executives, only one is among the top 12 executives (8 percent), Rosalind G. Brewer, president and CEO of Sam's Club. Brewer identifies as African American. Of the 11 male executives, 8 are white, and one is African American. The number of women serving on Walmart's board of directors has not changed since 2011, and the number of women officers has also remained stagnant.

Among the themes analyzed, more than 50 percent of Walmart's focus resided in employee development, and 20 percent focuses on performance metrics, including promotion criteria, and only 1 percent on gatekeeping. Overall, the analysis demonstrates that Walmart has a relatively healthy approach for its staff and middle management. The outlook changes drastically when examining the practices and policies of their executive team. Such practices and policies lack transparency and are prone to high levels of subjectivity, and have little emphasis on a performance-based management system. There exists virtually no emphasis on climate as it pertains to the behaviors and attitudes of senior leaders. Had Walmart focused with the same vigor on development for its executive leadership team to improve climate, a positive result would have occurred. Consider figures 12.2 and 12.3 to understand where and how Walmart expends its resources.

Walmart, like most companies, would have benefited greatly from its employee development programs had the company focused on creating an inclusive climate where its employees, including its leaders, seek to overcome inherent biases. Creating an "office of diversity" could have a very

Figure 12.2   Hiring and Promotion: A Depiction of Walmart's Approach for Staff, 2012–2013

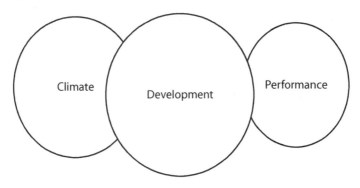

Figure 12.3   Hiring and Promotion: A Depiction of Walmart's Approach for Executive Leadership, 2012–2013

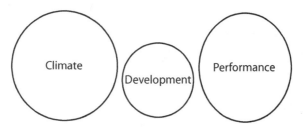

positive impact on corporate culture and performance, when other elements align. In other words, development programs have value, but they are only part of the equation. Women, and men of color, will rise in leadership roles when an inclusive, performance-based climate is the focus, along with a balanced approach utilizing developmental programs to improve weak aspects.

In explaining Walmart's diversity goals, an interviewee described the ways in which Walmart measures success. "Walmart monitors indicators, such as workforce demographics, our associate opinion survey, associate feedback through our intranet site and Town Hall meetings, and through hiring and retention rates."[16] According to the interviewee, "Walmart is expanding these measurement tools to include an inclusion survey and interactive learning programs to help associates develop a greater understanding of the value of diverse perspectives and to increase cultural competencies across every level of our organization."[17] To this end, Walmart holds more than 55,000 managers across the United States accountable for meeting diversity goals, yet it appears that Walmart fails to hold senior executives as accountable as its middle management.

One of the more important contributions Walmart offered this study is that a corporation should ask, before it embarks on measuring diversity, what it seeks to achieve in ensuring a diverse workforce. An important question essential before determining what kind of measurement tools will work. Another contribution learned from the Walmart case study is that if a climate does not work to allow women leaders to rise, then it will also not work for other non-hegemonic groups. Finally, it is insufficient to ensure a performance-based management system and an inclusive climate for middle management and lower, if such a system and climate does not exist at the executive level.

Google: Gatekeeping to What End?

Google, an innovative, successful company, has something in common with the federal government. Both institutions have a 50 percent focus on formal gatekeeping through employee selection. While the federal government is reducing its focus on selection, Google sits solidly at 50 percent; it also appears the company views its selection process as a point of pride, believing the focus is key to maintaining a highly competitive entree. While efficacy is often a criticism with formal gatekeeping, the more troubling aspect with Google is its informal gatekeeping practices. Informal gatekeeping has a profound impact on climate. Google's selection process for executive positions is incredibly limiting for those outside the exclusive circle of potential and existing positional leaders.

The U.S. Department of Justice sued six companies engaged in anti-poaching agreements, including Google, for entering into non-recruitment contracts, keeping the companies from "poaching" each other's employees. While the lawsuit for the antipoaching agreements settled in 2010, Google and others faced a similar accusation again in 2013.

While public documents and interviewees indicated that Google is a performance-driven organization, analytic results indicated a mere 5–10 percent focus on performance-based motivation and rewards. Concededly, the minimal focus on performance may have been the result of the company's determination that satisfactory practices and policies already exist. Interviewees reported that Google consistently employs promotional and hiring practices and policies for entry and middle management. Additionally, recruiters spend a good deal of effort ensuring that candidates have degree credentials and are a "good cultural fit" for the organization.[18] Whereas entry and middle management had a transparent performance-based process and system, promoting and hiring for senior leadership did not. For senior and executive leadership little consistency or transparency in performance-based practices or policies are evident.

An interviewee disclosed that Google employs and relies heavily on a metrics system in combination with peer-to-peer review among its entry and mid-level employees. Employees also have an opportunity to self-describe extenuating circumstances that may have impacted their performance. According to the interviewee, Google primarily employed the metrics tool to measure performance and determine promotions, and indicated uniformity and consistency in its application.[19] The interviewee identified three skill areas of promotional consideration: critical thinking, problem solving, and consistency in performance. The interviewee expressed some skepticism of the metrics system. All employees receive a "ticket," much like information technology staff, to determine effectiveness of service and project completion, and this ticket system plays a large role in the metrics system.

Another interviewee offered that Google has a robust and positive informal practice of cross-training within the organization. The interviewee indicated that if an employee is willing to learn a new area of the business, Google encourages the employee to do so. Promotion opportunities within middle management are robust; however, the interviewee was quick to note that practices within middle management differ from practices in senior leadership. Gatekeeping at senior levels become much more inconsistent and veiled, which may explain why in 2012, Google had zero women in executive leadership roles, as did Apple, one of the other antipoaching collaborators. Interestingly and doubtfully coincidental, Yahoo recruited Marissa Mayer, now CEO, from Google. Yahoo was *not* one of the antipoaching collaborators identified in the Department of Justice lawsuit.

When examining all six case studies as a whole, general conclusions found that some aspects of climate had a greater impact than other aspects. Illustrated in table 12.1, subthemes that had subjective elements created greater risks in adversely affecting employee, and therefore, company performance. While organizations cannot remove all subjectivity, nor should they, organizations should ensure that they apply subjectivity consistently, or under consistent circumstances. Consider the analogy to creating one's personal or professional brand. Often, there are two brands. One brand is the one that the professional intends to create. The other brand is the one that the professional acquires from her/his actions and attitudes, which are unintended. The unintended brand often prevails more often than the intended brand. Organizational climate operates similarly. The actions and attitudes of leadership directly influence the climate and employee performance. Let me remind you that climate and performance have everything to do with who sits at the leadership table.

Table 12.1   Understanding Climate and Its Impact on Performance

Climate	Examples	Impact on Performance*
Selection Criteria in Hiring/Promotion	Education, Recruitment, Testing, Experience/Skills	3
Gatekeeping	Communication Strategies, Probation, Recruitment, Temporary Appointments	5
Benefits	Retirement Match, Health Care Options, Education	3
Compensation	Monetary, Stock Options, Training	3
Peer/Supervisor Relationships	Evaluation processes, Competitive or Cooperative	5
Formal Policies	Mandatory Mentoring, Employee Leave, Flex Time	3
Informal Policies	Different enforcement or uncertain application of practices	5

*Impact Scale.

1	2	3	4	5
none	little	moderate	high	very high

Performance Levels the Playing Field

Nearly every manager or human resource professional believe they hire and promote based on performance. Such denial or mistaken accounts of how to measure performance reminds me of counting caloric intake. Since this is a book about women's leadership and there has been no mention of age, beauty, family, children, caretaking or weight thus far, using an analogy about calorie counting may fulfill someone's expectations, feignly stated. To proceed with the analogy, (American?) people tend to believe they consume far fewer calories than they do; in fact, many times they are simply unaware of the caloric difference in a bagel versus a doughnut, a peanut butter and jelly versus a grilled cheese sandwich. The average caloric ignoramus, blissfully or not, has a perception or belief that overrides reality. The same figment is often true for performance. As the adage suggests, because we (want to) believe something to be true, does not make it so.

How do evaluators overcome the performance quagmire? Truly measuring performance, particularly for leadership roles, is difficult. Measuring the performance of a restaurant server, for example, is easier. There are tangible, direct results. Those results include: order accuracy, cleaniness, timliness of delivery once meal is prepared, appropriateness of appearance for the style of the restaurant, balancing attentiveness to customers without appearing intrusive, amount of tips received, and the frequency with which non-familial customers return and/or request a certain server. These elements, if a restauranteur sought to create an inclusive climate, would apply to all servers.

There were a number of commonalities among the case studies pertaining to performance. These commonalities, shown in table 12.2, also follow the impact on climate. As I have attempted to demonstrate, performance and climate are deeply intertwined. The Social Security Administration and the Department of the Treasury case studies illuminate the interrelation between climate and performance.

U.S. Social Security Administration: Failing to Fix What's Broken

On August 23, 2011, President Obama issued an executive order requiring the implementation of a *Government Wide Diversity and Inclusion Initiative and Strategic Plan* through the U.S. Office of Personnel Management (OPM). This order required an overall federal government implementation of a human capital plan, as well as agency level implementations. Requiring human capital management sought to create unwanted

Table 12.2   Understanding Performance and Its Impact on Climate

Performance Management System	Examples	Impact on Climate*
Criteria	Position Outcomes/Expectations	5
Metrics	Formula for Rewarding	3
Evaluations	Supervisor and Peer	3
Motivations	Time, Value in Work/Colleagues, Monetary, Title/Promotion	3
Rewards	Promotions, Merit and COL Increases	4
Formal Policies	Position qualifications, Cross Training	3
Informal Policies	Gatekeeping, temporary appointments	5

*Impact Scale.

1	2	3	4	5
none	little	moderate	high	very high

gatekeeping that may stymie performance and climate. The challenge any organization faces is that creating an office or officer position to address workplace issues often fails to transcend the climate and culture on a whole.

OPM's policy directly affected agency focus on selection of employee hiring and promotion, which are formal gatekeeping processes. Formal gatekeeping, in an intentional effort to improve efficacy, fell to 29.7 percent from nearly 50 percent. OPM's focus on development, particularly to improve climate, increased from 28 percent to 45.7 percent, and performance foci increased modestly from 9.4 percent to 16.2 percent. Clearly, OPM sought to improve both climate and performance, but placed a greater emphasis on climate.

Upon OPM's policy implementation, each agency created and implemented strategic initiatives to address leadership demography. Two agencies were the primary focus of this book, the Department of the Treasury and the Social Security Administration (SSA). Recall from the chapter on politics and government, having a female or a male of color leading the agency had a positive effect on the overall percentage of female leaders. We discovered this observation in all agencies except for the SSA and Treasury. The Treasury has one the highest percentages of female senior leaders, although a female or male of color had never led the agency. The SSA has among the lowest percentages of female leaders of any federal agency, despite its large percentages of females in the workforce, and having had several non-hegemonic heads.

Figure 12.5   Hiring and Promotion: Treasury's Approach

Department of the Treasury 2012–2013 (post OPM development plan)

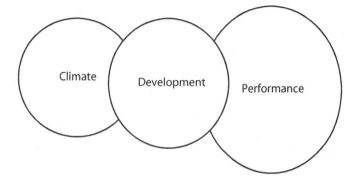

Human Capital Strategic Plan, which began in 2008. This plan, shown in figure 12.5, ensured a strong focus on development to improve climate, at 49.6 percent. The remaining aspects of the plan focused on the continuous improvement of performance-based rewards and motivations. The Treasury had no designs on gatekeeping, formal or informal. Its recent efforts in bolstering development to improve its climate have proved successful for the agency. Note that the Treasury's notable focus on development to improve climate, pursuant to its strategic plan, is deeply appropriate based on the pre-2008 analysis of its areas of needed improvement.

From the Treasury and other organizations, we also gleaned performance management strategies and criteria that, if adapted, would prove highly useful across sectors. The Treasury was particularly successful in employing the strategies with precision. Those strategies include:

- Work closely with human resource teams, and invest time to ensure processes and practices fulfill purposes
- Ensure candidate selection and assessment practices align with skills and competencies required to do the job well. When the position is new or different, outside experts can assist in determining requisite skills for "doing the job well"
- Require structured interviews, evidence of work products or results, and opportunities to evaluate the candidate's situational judgment
- Be specific in the criteria. For illustrative purposes, is obtainment of a master's degree the real criteria? Is it something else such as a certain meritorious research or project award? How much value should a criterion receive?

- Ask, what does the job look like when done well? How do you know?
- Employ a "double blind" candidate evaluation process, where evaluators "know" the applicant by her qualifications and skills but not by demographic information including name, gender, ethnicity, or race. This is a useful strategy for educating existing leaders or when there is gross underrepresentation in leadership.
- Ensure that evaluators have an opportunity to review candidates anonymously particularly when power differentials exist among the evaluators
- Be certain that the evaluators adequately reflect the climate of the organization, otherwise an organization will receive more of the same
- Track descriptive data, and use data as an assessment tool of not only the positional leader but of the organization as well. The inventory assessment mentioned earlier would be one approach.
- Ensure quantifiable benchmarks and outcomes using qualitative and quantitative data, and have multiple evaluators including peers and supervisors. Determine the weight and emphasis of each type of evaluator in advance.
- Avoid the temptation to employ all of the above as a mere formality, or avoid it entirely to "appoint" an internal candidate. When appointments of internal candidates do occur, consistency in practice and process should exist for all candidates
- Avoid artificial processes to give an appearance of uniformity and consistency, even when "time is of the essence"
- Obtain meaningful input from all constituencies within or connected to the entity. Determine the definition of meaningful as appropriate to the organization.

USING DEVELOPMENT FOR CONTINUOUS IMPROVEMENT

Xerox: Continuous Improvement Includes Development for Executive Leadership

Xerox is one of the top 10 businesses in the technology sector and has one of the highest percentage of women in leadership, with 33 percent in senior and executive positions in 2012 and 32 percent in 2013. In examining the practices and policies of Xerox, we learned that the company seeks to continuously improve its performance system and climate using development opportunities strategically, and with great alignment. Leaders, middle managers, and staff embrace the three elements with consistency and uniformity. It is important to note that Xerox has been working to improve and align its practices and policies for approximately a decade; therefore, this more or less evenly distributed, continuous improvement approach makes a good deal of sense for where the company is in its maturation.

Claiming that diversity is its core, Xerox ensures that all phases of its business, including its suppliers, value the demography of the United States.[23] The employees of Xerox appear to have voice and impact within the company. Several committees and groups exist within Xerox, creating effective voices that influence the company. For example, the Xerox Women's Alliance and the Xerox Innovation Group Women's Council were started by the women. The Xerox Women's Alliance provides women with mentorship and other developmental opportunities, encourages participation from men to increase awareness, and expands the group's mission and effectiveness to various aspects of the business. The Executive Diversity Council consists of senior leaders from across Xerox. Select council members may also be involved in other diversity initiatives like the Corporate Champion Program, where senior executives are matched with employee caucus groups. The "champions" educate senior management on their groups' unique environmental perspective and community initiatives.

The council meets at selected times throughout the year to discuss matters such as:

- Workforce representation
- Work environment
- Diverse customer markets
- Organizational efforts to address the needs of a multicultural workforce.

Independent caucus groups appear to play an important role in Xerox's diversity. These caucuses are instrumental in advocating openness, opportunity, and inclusion for the entire Xerox community. They work with management to achieve common business objectives, self-advocacy, and to create an environment of inclusion. Six caucus groups currently exist to address the concerns and meet the needs of employees who are African American, Hispanic, Asian, women, African American women, and/or gay, bisexual, lesbian, and transgender. These groups convene and directly affect corporate culture and policy. It will be interesting to see how such groups will continue to affect practices and policies. A current analysis suggests that it has had, to date, a very positive effect.

Consistently, and for numerous years, Xerox Corporation has been recognized as a positive work environment for minorities. A list of 2011 accomplishments follows:

- Named one of the "50 Best Companies for Latinas" to work by *Latina Style*.
- Named one of the 2011 "Top 40 Companies for Diversity" by *Black Enterprise*.
- Won the Human Rights Campaign list of "Best Companies to Work" Award for GBLT employees, scoring 100% on the index.
- Named one of the "Top 50 Companies for Diverse Managers to Work" by *Diversity MBA Magazine*.
- Recognized by Deans of the Accreditation Board of historically Black Colleges and Universities (HBCUs) for Engineering and Technology, specifically Advancing Minorities' Interest in Engineering (AMIE).
- Recognized by *Careers & the Disabled Magazine* as one of the top employers over the past 20 years.

It is important to note that Xerox went from an accounting scandal, which landed a $10 million fine and almost bankrupted the company, to a leader in less than 10 years. In 2003, the Securities and Exchange Commission charged six former senior executives of Xerox Corporation including long-time CEO, Paul A. Allaire, and former CFOs G. Richard Thoman and Barry D. Romeril. Anne Mulcahy followed Allaire as CEO, and she took a nearly bankrupt and scandal-laden Xerox to a fiscally healthier and stronger company. CEO Ursula Burns, a female African American, earned her bachelors and masters in engineering and began her career in Xerox as a mechanical engineer intern in 1980. In 2007, Xerox Corporation named her president and in 2009 named her CEO. In 2010, Burns became chairperson.

Xerox has still had its share of gender and race discrimination lawsuits, including the following:

- In 2002, the EEOC found racial discrimination at Xerox's Cincinnati office with five male African Americans. In 2003, *Carol Frank, et al. v. Xerox* claimed discrimination due to race, which may have contributed to the company's decision to donate $1 million to the National Underground Railroad Freedom Center later that year.
- In 2008, Xerox settled a class action suit for $12 million regarding discrimination.
- In 2010, a long-time employee of 22 years, Kimberly Smith, sued for discrimination of sex and age.
- In 2011, Julie Angelone filed suit against Xerox in NY for gender discrimination in the workplace.

TIAA-CREF: Enhancing Climate to Drive Performance

In 1918, the Carnegie Foundation first created the Teachers Insurance and Annuity Association (TIAA), which was supplemented in 1952 by the College Retirement Equities Fund (CREF). For 90 years, TIAA-CREF has provided financial services to college professors and staff members. Congress eliminated TIAA-CREF's tax-exempt status in 1998, but the company still perceives itself as a mission-driven organization committed to providing high quality services, like a nonprofit would, and its board of directors provide oversight of the company.[24] TIAA-CREF boasts a position among the Fortune 100, manages $481 billion in assets, and is the largest institutional landowner in the United States.[25] The organization's unique holding in the United States prompted a further curiosity. TIAA-CREF's senior executive leaders reflect 36 percent women and 64 percent men, one of the highest of any of the researched institutions. Perhaps more importantly, TIAA-CREF's asset manager is female, highly unusual in the financial services industry. The company devotes approximately 31 percent to performance, and 60 percent to employee development to improve organizational climate. TIAA CREF's gatekeeping is virtually non-existent. The foci appear to be very appropriate based on the needs and opportunities for growth. Its performance management system is exceptionally strong and the company continues to find ways to improve it, such as with recent additions of cross-training and peer reviews.

It is important to emphasize that TIAA-CREF's CEO, Roger Ferguson, Jr., who joined the company in 2008, identifies as an African American male. This study has uncovered a positive correlation between a man of color as chief and the percentage of women in leadership, as well as the emphasis on diversity and corresponding leadership demography, similar to that of when a female of any race heads an organization. In government and business, to illustrate, the highest percentage of female executives existed among agencies and companies with a female head or CEO.

Executive interviews revealed that corporate climate is among the most important factors in ensuring a performance-driven and inclusive culture. Such a climate extends to customers, clients, vendors, and investment businesses. In particular, a customer-centered climate ensures that the clientele's best interests, needs, and wants are foremost. This helps to translate to a climate where employees are also valued. When asked about the most important attributes for leaders, one interviewee revealed that someone interested in a senior position must demonstrate she or he is collaborative and emotionally intelligent in employing listening skills, adaptability, and willingness to learn. Development for senior leadership has become an embedded institutional aspect of TIAA-CREF's climate. Leaders must walk the walk inside and outside the company to convey that TIAA-CREF leaders, managers, and staff reflect the brand. Such focus may explain the relatively large percentage of female leaders.

Further research conducted explains that the advancement from management to senior leadership roles usually includes informal *sponsorships* from other senior leaders. In speaking with several organizational leaders, a few formal and informal strategies emerged. To begin, employees with aspirational leadership goals combined with effective sponsors are believed to be most successful in attaining promotions. Distinguishing between mentors and sponsors should be noted. While the role of a mentor consists of guiding and advising a mentee, a sponsor privately and publically supports and advocates for a sponsee. During the interviews, executives placed great emphasis on the quality and depth of the interaction.

To stimulate mentor-mentee relationships, TIAA-CREF provides networking, mentorship, formal/informal training, and support groups. TIAA-CREF sponsored associations and external groups include: Financial Women's Association (FWA), Women's Leadership Institute (WLI), Higher Education Resource Services (HERS), and American Council on Education (ACE) Women's Network. Internal organizations include: Woman to Woman Financial Empowerment Series, a four-part interactive workshop series, and Women's Employee Resource Group (WERG). One interviewee stressed the importance of internal groups and/or programs that support employees, particularly women, with young children.

Another important strategy is cross-training within the organization and across departments and areas of specialty. Cross-training includes both formal and informal opportunities. Cross-training opportunities are essential to skill-development, individual and company performance, and climate for it fosters an inclusive, collaborative environment. Cross-training also encourages opportunities to learn from colleagues, for peer review, and assists in developing a strong internal candidate pool. Additionally, members of the executive team ensure that the office of human resources aligns with and helps to realize the climate of inclusivity and performance including cross-training.

To realize a climate of performance and inclusivity, TIAA-CREF does not rely on financial services recruitment pools because such typical recruitment strategies do not yield a diverse pool of candidates. Without a diverse pool of candidates, the company believes it will lack diverse ideas and strategies needed to remain on the cutting edge of the industry. Moreover, a successful team must be well balanced in terms of skills, attributes, and perspectives. For illustrative purposes, Google employs a high level of selection and gatekeeping in its recruitment practices, recruits from industry-specific pools, and as a result, has poor diversity among its senior leaders.

TIAA-CREF, like Xerox, has achieved several noteworthy accomplishments. For example:

- Named one of the "40 Best Companies for Diversity" by Black Enterprise (recent award years: 2007, 2008, 2009, 2010, 2011, 2012).
- Named "Top 10 Companies for Executive Women" by the National Association of Female Executives in 2012.
- Named one of the "Best Companies for Latinas" by Latina Style Magazine (recent award years: 2011, 2012).
- Earned a 100 percent rating for support of LGBT employees from the Human Rights Campaign Foundation (recent award years: 2010, 2011, 2012).
- Named one of the "100 Best Companies for Working Mothers" (recent award years: 2003, 2011, 2012).
- Won the Silver Language and Cultural Diversity Award for TIAA-CREF's U.S. Hispanic/Latino initiative and partnership with Rice University from the Profit Sharing/401(k) Council of America in 2010.
- Won the Diversity Trailblazer Award from The Diversity Forum in 2009.[26]

Despite TIAA-CREF success, the company has had its share of employment discrimination lawsuits. To illustrate:

- In 2013, in reaction to CREF's shareholders resolution to divest business interests from companies substantially contributing to human rights abuses globally, including the occupation of Palestinian territory, Israel Law Center threatened suit.[27]
- In 2012 *(Audrey) Scott v. TIAA-CREF*, plaintiffs filed a civil rights claim. During the same year, (Jill) Kane sued TIAA-CREF Investment Management for employment discrimination.
- In 2011, *(Susan) Ogle v. TIAA-CREF Individual and Institutional Services LLC* detailed a discrimination claim based on age.
- In 2010, plaintiff (Kay) Stanney sued TIAA-CREF Individual and Institutional Services, LLC in a retirement class action suit.
- In 2009, TIAA-CREF defended three lawsuits based on civil rights and employment discrimination.[28]

One TIAA-CREF interviewee offered advice for candidates seeking employment at any level, the paraphrasing of that advice follows: As a candidate, you must interview the company and be certain it is a good fit with your values and goals. While you evaluate the company to which you are applying to, you should consider whether the company and industry have opportunities for growth to determine whether you will have opportunities to grow as a leader.[29] Other advice was to investigate and research the senior leadership team to determine whether members of the team conduct themselves in alignment with stated diversity goals to determine whether the company's actual brand is true to its stated brand. Seek opportunities for cross-training and sponsorships, and listen, learn, employ an inclusive, collaborative attitude, and be of service to your community and organization. Finally, whatever the assumed or given tasks, be certain to complete such tasks to your utmost ability.

CONCLUSIONS AND NEXT STEPS

This book has focused on a descriptive analysis conveying one aspect of women's leadership including an examination of the top echelon in each industry. In particular, the focus highlighted the persistent gap in salary and positional influence despite a sufficient pipeline, qualifications, and performance of women. Another aspect of this book explains why the gender gap persists, and offers strategies and practices to close the gap. The proffered strategies do more than remediate the problem, they will assist in company growth, profitability, and success. Moreover, inclusivity must include all marginalized or non-hegemonic groups. Otherwise, inclusivity does not really exist.

It is important to note that the strategies and practices identified require a balanced approach depending on the needs of a company and opportunities for growth. A comprehensive inventory assessment will uncover strengths and weaknesses in each of the thematic areas. Most importantly, a company must align all three thematic areas. For example, Walmart, heavy on some aspects of employee development, must invest in performance and climate for its executive leadership, including the CEO, for he must "walk" the company "talk" inside *and* outside his "office." TIAA-CREF has aligned and struck a balanced approach in all three thematic areas, and is focusing on improving climate and enhancing employee development. The Department of the Treasury had focused heavily on performance, until recent years where a shift encouraged greater developmental opportunities for employees to improve climate. SSA needs development programs to assist the agency in improving its performance management system and application. In other words, where a company should begin in adopting best strategies and practices depends on its areas of weakness and/or vulnerability. The company should also be clear about its short- and long-term goals and values before it completes an internal assessment. I refer to an internal assessment to explain that a company must undergo a formal and comprehensive inventory to uncover areas prohibiting growth.

Most of the strategies and practices identified above can either serve or hinder an organization. Gatekeeping, for example, may serve an organization if it seeks to exclude unethical employees, and some form of it can exist in other thematic areas as well. Some gatekeeping is formal and applies to all applicants, while other gatekeeping is informal. Informal gatekeeping, which is sometimes inadvertent, includes a poorly executed or nonexistent internal communication plan among senior leadership and staff, or temporary appointments and promotions. With temporary appointments and probation, an organization should assess its purpose and intent, and whether probation and/or temporary roles fulfill intended purposes, and applied equally to employees. Google's gatekeeping ensures that most employees possess an Ivy League degree, for instance. This type of gatekeeping will serve Google if it aligns with the company's intended climate, and whether an Ivy League degree ensures a particular employee or company outcome, beyond mere internal and external perception.

If an organization measures demography of occupants holding such positions, the descriptive narration will speak volumes about its values and climate. The challenge for the organization will be to avoid justifications and qualifications about why the narration tells the story it does. Consider the facts: 19–20 percent of leaders happen to be women, and they earn 80 to 82 cents on the $1.00 for the same work and in the same industry roles. Many fallacious accounts offer justifications and qualifications for these persistent facts. Consider also that black men are three times more likely to go to prison than white men are, and that black men comprise 50 percent of the prison population. Could someone legitimately claim that black men are more prone to criminal activity and delinquent behavior? Most would not accept this justification without conceding that larger, systemic, and structural issues fuel and perpetuate the societal problem. American society must not justify or qualify why women are not running more companies, organizations, and agencies. Instead, society should demand that American values and global influence depend on a set of systems that work for most people, more often than not. It is an issue of integrity, ethics, and competition. As a peoples, wherever we may lead from and whatever our gender, race or ethnicity may be, our livelihood depends on ingenuity and hard work, we cannot afford to exclude any talent.

APPENDIX III

Hiring Practice Protocol[30]

1. **Apply**   Once you find a job opportunity that complements your background and skills, you can immediately apply for it. Our talent acquisition team reviews each application and then contacts those applicants who best fit the skills and experiences needed for a particular position.

2. **Interview**   This is your opportunity to tell us more about your skills and for us to share more about the position, career opportunities and our company. We'll call to arrange a date, time and location for the meeting. As many teams are geographically dispersed, your meeting may be conducted over the phone. Depending on the position, your interview could include discussions with a recruiter, a member of our leadership team, a peer within the department and other professionals. As we get closer to a decision, you may be invited for another round of interviews.

3. **Offer**   If your skills, experiences and commitment are the right fit for the position, we'll extend a formal offer. It will include compensation, bonus opportunities, medical, dental and work/life benefits, your office location and a start date.

4. **Pre-Employment Screening**   Your formal offer will be contingent upon passing a thorough pre-employment screening. This may include, but is not limited to, verifying your work and education history, a criminal background investigation and a drug screening.

5. **Hire**   Once you have successfully completed the hiring process your next step is to report to work. Although this is the last step in the hiring process, we expect it will be your first step toward a fulfilling career with TIAA-CREF.

In voluntary compliance with federal and state requirements, TIAA utilizes the E-Verify tool to confirm work eligibility for new hires. E-verify is an internet-based system that enables businesses to confirm a job candidate's eligibility to work lawfully in the United States. The E-verify system confirms eligibility through the Social Security Administration (SSA) and the Department of Homeland Security (DHS). The federal government views E-verify as an essential workforce tool for employers.

NOTES

1. Cameron, William B. (1957). "The Elements of Statistical Confusion Or: What Does the Mean Mean?" *AAUP*.

2. Roswell, William J. (February 2012). "Talent Management: Aligning Your Organisation with Best Practices in Strategic and Tactical Talent Management." *Training Development* 39:1.

3. "Sam Walton." Encyclopedia Britannica Online.

4. Catalyst. (2013). Catalyst Pyramid: Women in U.S. Retail Trade.

5. Kershaw, Sarah. (July 2, 2003). "Wal-Mart Sets a New Policy That Protects Gay Workers." *New York Times*.

6. "Corporate Equality Index." (2006). *Human Rights Campaign*.

7. Hay Group (May 7, 2012). "Ecommerce growth and demand for part-time workers fueling employee turnover." Accessed at http://www.haygroup.com/ww/press/details.aspx?id=33790.

8. Peled, Micha (2001). "Store Wars: When Walmart Comes to Town." *PBS*. Accessed at http://www.pbs.org/itvs/storewars/story.html.

9. Keil, Stanley R., and Lee C. Spector. (Winter 2005). "The Impact of Walmart on Income and Unemployment Differentials in Alabama." *Review of Regional Studies* 35(3): 336–355.

10. *Wal-Mart Stores, Inc., Petitioner v. Betty Dukes et al.* (June 20, 2011). United States Supreme Court.

11. Frontline (2003). "Is Wal-Mart a Bargain for its Workers?" *PBS*. Accessed at http://www.pbs.org/wgbh/pages/frontline/shows/walmart/transform/employment.html.

12. EEOC (March 1, 2010). "Walmart to Pay More Than $11.7 Million to Settle EEOC Sex Discrimination Suit." EEOC. Accessed at http://www.eeoc.gov/eeoc/newsroom/release/3-1-10.cfm.

13. EEOC (April 10, 2013). "EEOC Sues Walmart for Sex Discrimination, Retaliation and Disability Discrimination." Accessed at http://www1.eeoc.gov/eeoc/newsroom/release/4-10-13.cfm.

14. Walmart. Diversity and Inclusion Statement. Accessed at http://corporate.walmart.com/global-responsibility/diversity-inclusion.

15. Catalyst. (2013). Catalyst Pyramid: U.S. Women in Business.

16. Anonymous Interviewee of Walmart.

17. Ibid.

18. Anonymous Interviewee of Google.

19. Ibid.

20. Anonymous Interviewee of the Social Security Administration.

21. Ibid.

22. Ibid.

23. Xerox Web site. Accessed at http://www.xerox.com/about-xerox/citizenship/supplier-diversity/enus.html and http://www.xerox.com/assets/pdf/Xerox_Diversity_Brochure.pdf.

24. TIAA CREF Web site. Accessed at https://www.tiaa-cref.org/public/pdf/pubs/pdf/governance_policy.pdf.

25. TIAA CREF Web site. Accessed at https://www.tiaa-cref.org/public/pdf/Farmland-Sustainability-Report.pdf.

26. TIAA CREF Web site. Accessed at https://www.tiaa-cref.org/public/about-us/employee-diversity-inclusion.

27. Skeens, Deborah (May 10, 2013). Letter from SEC. Accessed at http://www.sec.gov/divisions/investment/noaction/2013/steve-tamari-shareholder-letter-cref-050113-14a8.pdf; Israeli Law Center (April 10, 2013). "Israel-based civil rights groups informs Fortune 100 pension giant against divestment proposal." Accessed at http://www.israellawcenter.org/page.asp?id=341&show=photo&pn=1333&ref=report.

28. *Brenda Collins v. TIAA-CREF*. Filed: October 22, 2009 as 09-2209; *(Jose) MARTINEZ v. TIAA-CREF ENTERPRISES, INC.* Filed: July 7, 2009 as 1:2009cv01258; *(Gwen) Herndon v. TIAA-CREF Individual & Institutional Services, LLC.* Has Decisions Filed: March 25, 2009 as 3:2009cv00120.

29. Anonymous Interviewee of TIAA CREF.

30. TIAA CREF Web site. Accessed at http://www1.tiaa-cref.org/public/about/careers/recruiting_applying/index.html.

A Concluding Synopsis and Areas of Future Research

Gender bias, both subtle and culturally embedded, remains the primary reason why women have stagnated in salaries and senior leadership positions since the 1980s. Gender biases exist among males and females alike, and such biases exist most in the "visible" leadership of a company. Strategy is essential in recognizing women leaders and curing inequities. There are a great many strategies to overcome gender discrimination embedded in our culture. To illustrate, some have suggested that flextime, telecommuting, parental rather than maternal leave, and the Equal Pay Act will cure systemic biases. Perhaps over time, these strategies will cure biases. However, I do not believe that society should wait another 30 years to see if these strategies have worked. After all, the pay gap and percent of positional leadership have made only modest gains, and in some cases remained virtually the same, since the 1980s across most sectors.

The purpose of this book is to highlight the gender disparity, recognize the contributions of female leaders, identify strategies and practices that will ensure greater female representation, and reward high performance. More than 100 years since the women's suffrage movement, this benchmark study on women's positional leadership in the United States demonstrates that:

- Generally, women outperform men in most sectors but do not earn comparable salaries or obtain comparable positions that reflect their high performance. For example, when comparing the nation's top businesses and organizations to their industry as a whole, there exist more women among the industry's top performers, than in the industry as a whole.

- Moreover, women have been acquiring the necessary education to compete, and recently, the fact that women earn more degrees has been a topic of concern for many, which is unfortunate. Because women are earning more college degrees, much of American society has grown concern about the negative consequences for men. Rather than being concerned with how many women are earning degrees, society should focus on who are not earning degrees—men of color.

- Women perform exceptionally well because they need to in order for businesses and organizations to recognize and consider them for hiring and promotion. Based on these points, I posit women-to a large extent-are "leaning in," and yet, little change has occurred in 30 years, and much of the discourse has remained the same.

- The purpose of this book is not to suggest that women make better leaders, or are smarter than men, nor do I believe that women are less susceptible to biases.

- Women are not lacking in leadership roles because they prefer less demanding or time-consuming positions that accommodate their families or lifestyle. This hetero-normative, socioeconomic privileged perspective highlights the lack of comprehensive discourse that permeates the media. It would behoove society to engage in meaningful conversations about how to ensure a globally competitive marketplace. What women earn, or fail to earn, affects the marketplace, families, and the global economy.

- When women leaders are present, revenue is greater, sales increase, impact and reach are more expansive, and industry distinctions are more prolific.

- The lack of women leaders in the United States is not a female problem. It is a societal problem.

- Without strategies to address promotion and advancement of women, U.S. corporations and organizations will continue to fall behind their competition.

- Gender disparities, if unaddressed, will become fodder for legal and/or policy action.

- As stakeholders become aware of the potential for greater profits with women also in leadership roles, they will likely act and apply pressure to change business practices accordingly.

  The most important recommendation that emerged throughout all sectors was implementation of objective performance measurements and performance-based promotion practices. Employee development will serve an organization only as far as it supports a performance culture and inclusive climate. Employee development, particularly as it pertains to creating an inclusive climate, should include senior executives and leaders, and not just staff and middle management.

AREAS OF FUTURE RESEARCH

In creating a multi-year snapshot of female leaders, the intent was to uncover trends across sectors, determine which organizations and businesses are doing better than most, and finally, investigate the commonalities among those entities. In addition to the case studies, we relied on descriptive data available publically. As we reviewed publically available data, we discovered that most sectors resisted transparency. Those with the least transparency also had the lowest percentages of women and men of color in leadership. To this end, additional research would aid in shifting the discourse regarding women's leadership.

Academia

In most sectors, public institutions claimed more diverse representation than private ones. Additionally, when men of color are better represented, typically so are white women and women of color. In academia, however, the public institutions and entities have better representation among white men and men of color but poorer representation among white women and women of color. All women are better represented in private institutions.

- Industry distinctions should be more closely monitored and assessed when determining performance and overall leadership. Distinctions specific to each sector allow one to measure leadership outside of positional leadership alone.
- Because women outperform men in the number of national awards and grants obtained, the review committees of each of the award-granting institutions should be reviewed and demographically assessed. Similarly, the male and female percentages on review committee for tenured and tenure track positions should also be evaluated. This data may help explain the discrepancy between female professor's performance and their low percentage among tenured faculty ranks.

Arts and Entertainment

In measuring achievement, the Oscar, Emmy, and Grammy awards, for example, have attempted to identify top performers in film, television, and music. There are various awards, and they are too numerous to contain herein. Relying on some, but not all, industry awards creates limitations, and specifically fails to include all members of the industry, particularly those who have been historically excluded. To illustrate, the Grammy and Oscar awards often fail to recognize the same artists and entertainers as other national awarders, such as the Latin Grammy Awards, NAACP Image Awards, and the Sundance Film Festival. An analysis of the various national awarders and their processes for determining recognition would inform the perspective on gender and race. It should also be noted who among the awarders has a history of inclusion and exclusion.

Education (K–12)

A comparison between the hiring and promotion practices of small and large districts should be conducted to better understand the differences, if any, and to determine explanations for why fewer female leaders exist in small districts.

Entrepreneurship

- To begin, more research needs to be conducted to determine the relationship, if any, among the gender of capital investors and the types of businesses they support. Preconceived notions about women have driven investors to conclude that female enterprises are small, lifestyle businesses with little regard for economic growth. Research can play an important role in overcoming this erroneous conclusion. Different characteristics may better define business success with greater precision, by adopting, for example, measures of performance for new enterprises.

- While financial indicators, such as volume, profit, and size, help to define successful entrepreneurship, they do not explain the value and impact of the business on society. The desire for economic rewards comprised only one part of an owner-operator's set of motivations, goals, and aspirations. The need for better measurement tools to evaluate success is not exclusive to entrepreneurship and includes most sectors, such as arts and entertainment, journalism, media, and business. It has been argued that economic measures alone might not be appropriate in assessing the success of owner-operated small- and medium-sized enterprises (SMEs). The suggested measurements for SMEs should be adapted and adopted for all entrepreneurial businesses, regardless of size, to define success with greater precision. A more holistic set of measurements are offered below and derived from the SME model to better understand the value of entrepreneurship and the impact of entrepreneurial leaders.

An Alternative Way to Measure Entrepreneurial Success

- Extrinsic rewards
  - Increasing personal income
  - Contributing to the economic development of the community
  - Building personal and community wealth
  - Achieving financial security for self and employees
  - Increasing income and professional opportunities for self and employees
- Time flexibility and family
  - Having flexibility for nonbusiness activities
  - Providing development opportunities for your family
- Staff relations
  - Providing economic security of employment for staff
  - Having loyal and highly satisfied staff
  - Having a highly competent and professional staff
  - Encouraging staff growth, including promotions and competitive salary scales
  - Ensuring globally competitive skill development
- Quality and customer relations
  - Providing high quality products and services
  - Having a reputation for quality
  - Contributing intellectually and productively to the United States
- Independence
  - Defining your own corporate culture
  - Making business decisions and taking selected risks
- Intrinsic rewards
  - Developing a greater sense of self and community
  - Believing you are making a difference in your own life and in the lives of others

The challenges in measuring such objectives include cost and time in data compilations. It is much easier and more time efficient for researchers to compile data on financial growth and size, which can be obtained in census data as opposed to conducting implicit bias tests,[1] interviews and/or surveying entrepreneurs. Despite these challenges, a more comprehensive survey instrument, which incorporates the characteristics above while minimizing participant bias, will inform business practices and models of success.

Business, Finance, and Commercial Banking

- A comprehensive study should be conducted to determine women's performance in business and banking, besides revenue and profitability only.
- An exploration of characteristics of hedge fund management, such as access to capital, succession planning, and performance measures, should be undertaken to better understand why more hedge funds are not managed by women despite their continued success in the industry.
- Mid-cap companies, where there exists the greatest pay equity between men and women, should be assessed to determine the merit and compensation process and procedure for senior executives.

Technology

It would behoove the technology sector for future researchers to:

- Understand the factors that influence young women's degree choices to generate more interest for science and engineering degrees. Ensuring more young women consider technology and science degrees may help to change the demographics of the workforce.
- Understand the reasons why women leave the technology workforce and make a concerted effort to create a more inclusive environment for women.
- Study women's patent activity, particularly how it corresponds to future entrepreneurial activity.

Law

- Researchers should continue to track and monitor the demographic composition of equity and managing partners. The representation among women in these more economically lucrative and structurally powerful positions has declined since 2008.
- Qualitative data on the merit and promotional practices of law firms would inform new retention and recruitment practices. Law firms need effective merit and promotional practices, as well as other sectors.

- Data tracking for women of color continues to lack in all sectors, and in particular, law. It is essential for women to self-report demographic information. Researchers should not presume a race based on name, skin color, or other seemingly apparent, yet flawed, attributes.
- A case study analysis should be conducted on Bingham McCutchen, LLP, and on small- and medium-sized firms with the highest percent of female partners to learn from their promotional and hiring practices.

Medicine

More comprehensive data is needed among the nation's top hospitals. Several studies have been conducted regionally, but there lacks a comprehensive knowledge of executive compensation.

Military

- A case study should be conducted on the Department of Homeland Security, Veterans Affairs, and the Air Force to better understand the disproportionate percentage of women leaders. From this analysis there may emerge a better understanding of equitable practices that promote women at the same pace as men.

Nonprofit Organizations and Foundations

- A research study should be conducted to compare organizations with budgets in excess of $25 million to those with small budgets. Of particular interest are the promotion and compensation processes and practices to determine the relationship between gender disparity in compensation and leadership and the size of the nonprofit.

Politics and Government

- A qualitative study exploring motivations and decision-making in campaign funding would help to uncover why female candidates are unsupported proportionately to men.
- External campaign funding should continue to be tracked and monitored on behalf of female candidates.

- Because agency appointments are such an integral part of U.S. domestic policy and enforcement, research should further explore high-performing agencies with high representations of women.

Arts and Entertainment Including Sports

- The gender disparity in this sector is apparent, and reflects much of the existing societal attitudes about that which is feminine. To help stem inequities, the industry must provide more transparent hiring and compensation practices. This industry should be closely monitored, and the public must employ discretion in viewing and supporting particular genres and programming, which devalue and/or dismiss women and girls.
- Universities should exemplify the inclusive climate, which most claim to embody. All universities with NCAA athletes should examine and remedy the percentage of recruiting dollars given to female and male athletes. The NCAA should work with and require universities to disseminate recruiting dollars with parity.

NOTE

1. Harvard University (2011). Implicit Bias Test. *Project Implicit.* Accessed at https://implicit.harvard.edu/implicit/

Select Bibliography

Ackerman, Ruthie. "Clients from Venus." *Wall Street Journal Online.* (April 30, 2012). Accessed from http://online.wsj.com/article/SB1000142405297020 4190504577040402069714264.html.

American University's Women & Politics Institute (WPI). "Sunday Morning Monitor." *American University.* (2012). Accessed June 2012, from http://www.american.edu/spa/wpi/sunday-morning-monitor.cfm

Ashcraft, Catherine, and Anthony Breitzman. "Who Invents IT?" *National Center for Women and Information Technology.* (2012). Accessed from http://www.ncwit.org/sites/default/files/resources/2012whoinventsit_web_0.pdf

Association of American Colleges and Universities (AACU). "Circuitous Routes: AAUW Study Examines Women's Paths to College." *Diversity Digest.* (1999). Accessed from http://www.diversityweb.org/digest/sm99/study.html

Aylmer, Philippa. "50 Leading Women in Hedge Funds" *The Hedge Fund Journal.* (2010). Accessed from http://www.thehedgefundjournal.com/magazine/201002/research/thfj-50-women-in-hedge-funds.pdf

Beede, David, Tiffany Julian, David Langdon, George McKittrick, Beethika Khan, and Mark Doms. "Women in STEM: A Gender Gap to Innovation." *Economics and Statistics Administration. U.S. Department of Commerce.* (August 2011). Accessed from http://www.esa.doc.gov/Reports/women-stem-gender-gap-innovation.

Bhide, Amar. "The Questions Every Entrepreneur Must Answer." *Harvard Business Review.* (November 1996). Accessed from http://hbr.org/1996/11/the-questions-every-entrepreneur-must-answer/ar/1.

Bureau of Labor Statistics (BLS). "Highlights of Women's Earnings in 2010." *U.S. Department of Labor. BLS.* (2011a). Accessed from http://www.bls.gov/cps/cpswom2010.pdf.

Bureau of Labor Statistics (BLS). "Household Data Annual Averages." *U.S. Department of Labor. BLS.* (2012). Accessed from http://bls.gov/opub/ee/2012/cps/annavg37_2011.pdf.

Bureau of Labor Statistics (BLS). "Median Weekly Earnings of Full-time Wage and Salary Workers by Detailed Occupation and Sex." *U.S. Department of Labor. BLS.* (2011b). Accessed from http://www.bls.gov/cps/cpsaat39.pdf.

Bureau of Labor Statistics (BLS). "National Industry-Specific Occupational Employment and Wage Estimates." *BLS.* (May 2011). Accessed from http://www.bls.gov/oes/current/naics3_334000.htm#15-0000.

Bureau of Labor Statistics (BLS). "Table 5–4. Bachelor's Degrees Awarded to Women by Field, Citizenship, and Race/Ethnicity: 2001–2009. *BLS.* (2009). Accessed from http://www.bls.gov/cps/cpswom2009.pdf.

Byerly, Carolyn M. "Global Report on the Status of Women in the News Media." *International Women's Media Foundation.* (2011). Accessed from http://www.iwmf.org/wp-content/uploads/2013/09/IWMF-Global-Report-Summary.pdf.

Carter, Nancy M., Colette Henry, Barra O. Cinneide, and Kate Johnston, eds. *Female Entrepreneurship: Implications for Education, Training and Policy.* New York, NY: Routledge, 2007.

Casserly, Meghan. "The Five Most Powerful Female Venture Capitalists." *Forbes.* (May 2, 2012). Accessed from http://www.forbes.com/sites/meghancasserly/2012/05/02/midas-list-five-most-powerful-female-venture-capitalists/

Catalyst. "2011 Catalyst Census: Fortune 500 Women Board Directors." *Catalyst Knowledge Center.* (2011c). Accessed from http://www.catalyst.org/file/533/2011_fortune_500_census_wbd.pdf.

Catalyst. "African-American Women in the United States." *Catalyst Knowledge Center.* (2012e). Accessed from http://www.catalyst.org/publication/222/african-american-women.

Catalyst. "Buying Power." *Catalyst Knowledge Center.* (2012d). Accessed from http://www.catalyst.org/publication/256/buying-power.

Catalyst. "Statistical Overview of Women in the Workplace." *Catalyst Knowledge Center.* (2012a). Accessed from http://www.catalyst.org/publication/219/statistical-overview-of-women-in-the-workplace.

Catalyst. "U.S. Labor Force, Population, and Education." *Catalyst Knowledge Center.* (2012h). Accessed from http://www.catalyst.org/knowledge/people-color-us.

Catalyst. "U.S. Women in Business." *Catalyst Knowledge Center.* (2012b). Accessed from http://www.catalyst.org/publication/132/us-women-in-business.

Catalyst. "Women CEOs of the Fortune 1000." *Catalyst Knowledge Center.* (2012c). Accessed from http://catalyst.org/publication/271/women-ceos-of-the-fortune-1000.

Catalyst. "Women in Financial Services." *Catalyst Knowledge Center.* (2012i). Accessed from http://www.catalyst.org/file/700/qt_women_in_financial_services.pdf.

Catalyst. "Women in High Tech." *Catalyst Knowledge Center.* (August 2012). Accessed from http://www.catalyst.org/knowledge/women-and-men-employed-select-high-tech-occupations-us-2012.

Catalyst. "Women in Media." *Catalyst Knowledge Center.* (March 2012).

Catalyst. "Women in U.S. Management." *Catalyst Knowledge Center.* (2012g). Accessed from http://www.catalyst.org/publication/206/women-in-us-management.

Catalyst. "Women MBAs." *Catalyst Knowledge Center.* (2012f). Accessed from http://www.catalyst.org/knowledge/women-mbas.

Catalyst. "Women's Representation by NAICS Industry." *Catalyst Knowledge Center.* (2011a). Accessed from http://www.catalyst.org/etc/Census_app/11US/2011_Fortune_500_Census_Appendix_7.pdf.

Catalyst. "Women's Representation by Region." *Catalyst Knowledge Center.* (2011b). Accessed from http://www.catalyst.org/etc/Census_app/11US/2011_Fortune_500_Census_Appendix_6.pdf.

Center for Women's Business Research (CWBR). "The Economic Impact of Women-Owned Businesses in the United States." *CWBR.* (October 2009). Accessed from http://www.nwbc.gov/sites/default/files/economicimpactstu.pdf

Center for Women's Business Research (CWBR). "Key Facts about Women-Owned Businesses." *CWBR.* (2012). Accessed from http://www.womensbusinessresearchcenter.org/research/keyfacts/

CNNMoney. "Fortune 500: Women CEOs 2011." *CNNMoney.* (2011). Accessed from http://money.cnn.com/magazines/fortune/fortune500/2011/womenceos/.

Committee for Economic Development (CED). "Fulfilling the Promise: How More Women on Corporate Boards Would Make America and American Companies More Competitive." *Committee for Economic Development Washington, D.C.* (2012). Accessed from http://www.fwa.org/pdf/CED_WomenAdvancementonCorporateBoards.pdf.

Coy, Peter, and Elizabeth Dwoskin. "Shortchanged: Why Women Get Paid Less Than Men." *Business Week.* (June 21, 2012). Accessed from http://www.businessweek.com/articles/2012-06-21/equal-pay-plaintiffs-burden-of-proof.

Credit Suisse. "Gender Diversity and Corporate Performance." *Credit Suisse Research Institute.* (August 2012). Accessed from https://www.credit-suisse.com/newsletter/doc/gender_diversity.pdf.

Daily Beast, The. "Newsweek's Power 50: The List." *The Daily Beast. Newsweek.* (November 1, 2010). Accessed June 2012, from http://www.thedailybeast.com/newsweek/2010/11/01/power-list.html.

Deckelman, Selena. "To Sir, with Love: How to Get More Women Involved in Open Source." *O'Reilly Community. Women in Technology.* (September 2007). Accessed from http://www.oreillynet.com/pub/a/womenintech/2007/09/28/to-sir-with-love-how-to-get-more-women-involved-in-open-source.html.

Decker, Susan. "Women Inventors Double Their Share of Patents." *Businessweek.* (March 2012). Accessed from http://www.businessweek.com/articles/2012-03-01/women-inventors-double-their-share-of-patents.

Department of Labor (DOL). "Quick Stats on Women Workers." *U.S. Department of Labor.* (2010). Accessed from http://www.dol.gov/wb/factsheets/QS-womenwork2010.htm.

Eagly, Alice, and Linda Carli. Navigating the Labyrinth. *School Administrator.* (September 2009) 66(8): 10–16.

Easy Media Lists. "Top 100 U.S. Newspaper Opinion Editors." *Easy Media Lists.* (2012). Accessed June 2012, from http://www.easymedialist.com/usa/top100opinion.html.

Entreprenuer.com. "Top 100 Venture Capital Firms for Early Stage Companies." *Entrepreneur.com.* (2007). Accessed from http://www.entrepreneur.com/vc100/stage/early.html.

Ernst, H. Olmand. "Patent Information for Strategic Technology Management." *World Patent Information.* (2003). *25:233–242.* Accessed from http://aspheramedia.com/v2/wp-content/uploads/2011/02/Patent-information-for-strategic-technology-management.pdf.

"Expanding Opportunities for Women Entrepreneurs: The Future of Women's Small Business Programs." *Hearing before the Democratic Policy Committee* (DPC). (2007). 110th Congress.

Fairlie, Robert W. "Kauffman Index of Entrepreneurial Activity." *Kauffman Foundation.* (2009). Accessed from http://www.kauffman.org/what-we-do/research/kauffman-index-of-entrepreneurial-activity.

Fisher, Anne. "Leaping the Venture-Capital Gender Gap." *Crain's New York Business.com.* (June 22, 2012). Accessed from http://mycrains.crainsnewyork.com/blogs/executive-inbox/2012/06/leaping-the-venture-capital-gender-gap/.

Forbes. "400 Richest Americans: Larry Page." *Forbes.* (September 2012). Accessed from http://www.forbes.com/profile/larry-page/.

Forbes. "America's Largest Private Companies." *Forbes.* (2011). Accessed from http://www.forbes.com/lists/2011/21/private-companies-11_rank.html.

Forbes. "The Midas List." *Forbes.* (January 25, 2007). Accessed from http://www.forbes.com/lists/2007/99/biz_07midas_The-Midas-List_Rank.html.

Forbes. "The Midas List." *Forbes.* (January 24, 2008). Accessed from http://www.forbes.com/lists/2008/99/biz_08midas_The-Midas-List_Rank.html.

Forbes. "The Midas List." *Forbes.* (May 2, 2012). Accessed from http://www.forbes.com/lists/midas/2012/midas-list-top-tech-investors.html.

Galbraith, Sasha. "Financial Services: The Industry Women Love to Hate." *Forbes.* (March 18, 2011). Accessed from http://www.forbes.com/sites/sashagalbraith/2011/03/18/financial-services-the-industry-women-love-to-hate/.

Goudreau, Jenna. "Forbes Woman of the Year: Women in Tech." *Forbes.* (February, 2011). Accessed from http://www.forbes.com/sites/jennagoudreau/2011/12/26/forbes-woman-of-the-year-women-in-tech/.

Hadary, Sharon G. "Why Are Women-Owned Firms Smaller Than Men-Owned Ones?" *Wall Street Journal.* (May 17, 2010). Accessed from http://online.wsj.com/article/SB10001424052748704688604575125543191609632.html.

Heavey, Susan. "In Heart of Corporate America, Women Struggle to Break into Top Jobs." *Reuters*. (March 21, 2012). Accessed from http://www.reuters.com/article/2012/03/21/uk-usa-women-business-idUSLNE82K01720120321.

Holmes, Robert. "10 Best-Performing IPOs of 2011." *The Street*. (2011). Accessed from http://www.thestreet.com/story/11170093/1/10-best-performing-ipos-of-2011.html.

Inc. Magazine. "30 under 30." *Inc Magazine*. (2011). Accessed from http://www.inc.com/30under30/.

InterOrganization Network (ION). "Gender Imbalance in the Boardroom: Opportunities to Change Course." *InterOrganization Network*. (2011). Accessed from http://www.ionwomen.org/wp-content/uploads/2011/12/ION_Status-Report_2011.pdf.

Kantor, Susan. "The Top 25 U.S. Consumer Magazines from June 2011 FAS-FAX." (June 2011). Accessed June 2012, from http://accessabc.wordpress.com/2011/08/09/the-top-25-consumer-magazines-from-june-2011-fas-fax/.

Lahart, Justin, and Mark Whitehouse. "Few Businesses Sprout with Even Fewer Jobs." *Wall Street Journal*. (November 18, 2010). Accessed from http://online.wsj.com/article/SB10001424052748704648604575621061892216250.html.

Lulofs, Neal. "The Top U.S. Newspapers for March 2012." *Audit Bureau of Circulations*. (2012). Accessed June 2012, from http://accessabc.wordpress.com/2012/05/01/the-top-u-s-newspapers-for-march-2012/.

Managed Funds Association (MFA). "Hedge Fund Pulse: Affirmative Investing: Women and Minority Owned Hedge Funds." *Barclays Capital*. (2011). Accessed from http://www.managedfunds.org/wp-content/uploads/2011/08/HF-Pulse-Affirmative-Investing-June-2011-Letter.pdf.

Marketing Charts. "Top 10 Current Events and News Online Destinations March 2010." *Marketing Charts*. (April 26, 2010). Accessed June 2012, from http://www.marketingcharts.com/interactive/top-10-current-events-news-online-destinations-march-2010-12691/.

Marketing Charts. "Top 10 Print Media Websites—April 2012." *Marketing Charts*. (May 9, 2012). Accessed June 2012, from http://www.marketingcharts.com/interactive/top-10-print-media-websites-april-2012-22024/.

Mondo Times. "American Media Companies." *Mondo Times*. (2012). Accessed June 2012, from http://www.mondotimes.com/company/.

National Committee of Pay Equity (NCPE). "Pay Equity Information." *NCPE*. (2012). Accessed from http://www.pay-equity.org/info.html.

National Council for Research on Women (NCRW). "Women in Fund Management: A Road Map for Achieving Critical Mass—And Why It Matters." *NCRW*. (2009). Accessed from http://www.ncrw.org/reports-publications/women-fund-management-road-map-achieving-critical-mass-%E2%80%94-and-why-it-matters.

National Information Center (NIC). "Top 50 Bank Holding Companies." *NIC*. (2012). Accessed from http://www.ffiec.gov/nicpubweb/nicweb/Top-50Form.aspx.

National Women's Business Council (NWBC). "Intellectual Property and Women Entrepreneurs: Quantitative Analysis." *NWBC*. (February 2012). Accessed from http://nwbc.gov/sites/default/files/IP%20&%20Women%20 Entrepreneurs.pdf.

National Women's Law Center (NWLC). "Analysis of New 2010 Census Poverty Data." *NWLC*. (2011). Accessed from http://www.nwlc.org/ analysis-new-2010-census-poverty-data-—september-2011.

National Women's Law Center (NWLC). "Closing the Wage Gap Is Especially Important for Women of Color in Difficult Times." *NWLC*. (2012). Accessed from http://www.nwlc.org/sites/default/files/pdfs/womenofcolorfactsheet.pdf.

Nevedomski Berdan, Stacie, and Anna Catalano. "Why Corporate Boards Should Be Looking for a Few Good Women" *Huffington Post*. (August 9, 2012). Accessed from http://www.huffingtonpost.com/stacie-nevadomski-berdan/ why-corporate-boards-shou_b_1751320.html).

Organisation for Economic Co-operation and Development (OECD). "Enterprising Women: Local Initiatives for Job Creation." *OECD Publishing*. (1990).

Papper, Bob. "RTDNA/Hofstra Survey Finds Mixed News for Women & Minorities in TV, Radio News." *RTDNA*. (2011). Accessed June 2012, from http:// www.rtdna.org/media/RTDNA_Hofstra_v8.pdf.

Pew Research Center. "Ideological News Sources: Who Watches and Why: Americans Spending More Time Following the News." *Pew Research Center*. (September 12, 2010). Accessed June 2012, from http://www.people-press. org/files/legacy-pdf/652.pdf.

Pew Research Center. "State of the Media: Top Circulated Magazines." *Pew Research Center*. (2011). Accessed June 2012, from http://stateofthemedia. org/2011/magazines-essay/data-page-4/

Pine, Karen. "Sheconomics: Why More Women on Boards Boosts Company Performance." *Significance*. (2011). 8: 80–81.

The Pulitzer Prizes. "Search: Winner, 2011." *Pulitzer*. (Jan. 25, 2012). Accessed June 2012, from http://www.pulitzer.org/faceted_search/results/ taxonomy-2-158.

Renaissance Capital. "IPO History by Industry." *Renaissance Capital Greenwich, CT*. (September 2012). Accessed from http://www.renaissancecapital.com/ IPOHome/Press/IPOIndustry.aspx.

Schonfeld, Erick. "The Top 10 VC Firms, According to InvestorRank." *Tech Crunch*. (2011). Accessed from http://techcrunch.com/2011/05/25/ top-10-vc-firms-investorrank/.

Shaughnessy, Haydn. "Who Are the Top 50 Social Media Power Influencers?" *Forbes*. (January 25, 2012). Accessed June 2012, from http://www. forbes.com/sites/haydnshaughnessy/2012/01/25/who-are-the-top-50- social-media-power-influencers/.

Simard, Caroline. "Obstacles and Solutions for Underrepresented Minorities in Technology." *Anita Borg Institute for Women and Technology*. (2009). Accessed from http://www.cssia.org/pdf/20000280-ObstaclesandSolutions forUnderrepresentedMinoritiesinTechnology.pdf.

Simmons Marketing. "Experian Simmons Multi-Media Engagement Study." *Experian.* (2009). Accessed June 2012, from http://www.experian.com/assets/simmons-research/white-papers/multi-media-engagement-study.pdf.

Smith-Hunter, Andrea. *Women Entrepreneurs across Racial Lines.* Northampton, MA: Edward Elgar Publishing, 2006.

Stock, Kyle. "Women Unplug from the Tech Industry." *Fins Technology.* (April 2011). Accessed from http://it-jobs.fins.com/Articles/SB13008024644 3096737/Women-Unplug-From-the-Tech-Industry.

Talkers. "The Top Talk Radio Audiences." *Talkers.* (2011). Accessed June 2012, from http://www.talkers.com/top-talk-radio-audiences/.

Twitaholic. "The Twitaholic.com Top 100 Twitterholics based on Follower." *Twitaholic* (2012). Accessed June 25, 2012, from http://twitaholic.com/top100/followers/.

Tyndall Report. "Year in Review 2011." *Tyndall Report.* (2011). Accessed June 2012, from http://tyndallreport.com/yearinreview2011/.

U.S. Census. "SCORE: Survey of Business Owners." *U.S. Census Bureau.* (2002). Accessed from http://www.census.gov/econ/sbo/historical.html.

U.S. Census. "Statistics for All U.S. Firms by Industry, Gender, Ethnicity, and Race for the U.S., States, Metro Areas, Counties, and Places: 2007." *2007 Survey of Business Owners, U.S. Census.* (2007). Accessed from http://fact-finder2.census.gov/faces/tableservices/jsf/pages/productview.xhtml?pid=S BO_2007_00CSA01&prodType=table.

Zieminski, Nick. "Fewer Women in Top U.S. Tech Jobs since 2010 Survey." *Reuters.* (May 2012). Accessed from http://www.reuters.com/article/2012/05/14/harveynash-women-technology-idUSL1E8G93KX20120514.

Index

About the Author

Tiffani Lennon, JD, LL.M, chairs the Law and Society and Community-Based Research departments at Colorado Women's College of the University of Denver. She is also the managing partner of Tiffani Lennon, LLC, a consulting practice dedicated to strategic and research-based practices and policies.

Her research areas include systems of inequity, governmental and organizational strategies for successful development, and policy impact on unrepresented communities. Lennon received her LL.M from the University of London. Her dissertation explored political economics and development in southern Africa.

Professor Lennon began her legal career as a constitutional law and civil rights attorney; she worked on numerous federal appeals, criminal, and immigration law issues. Lennon was a fellow in Washington, D.C., where she helped to frame strategic litigation to systematically address voting and education rights violations. She authored several policy and research reports with national implications.